Postcard History Series

Elizabeth

On the Front Cover: This card, printed by the Tichnor Brothers between 1930 and 1945, shows a bustling section of Broad Street in Elizabeth. As the country attempted to rise out of the Great Depression, capitalism and consumerism played an important, if overstated role, even as Franklin Delano Roosevelt's "New Deal" brought social progress to the welfare state. In the foreground, one can see Charles Michael's Clothing and Jewelry store, as well as several taxi buses. On the right, if one looks closely, a faint Coca-Cola marquee can be viewed. (Courtesy of the Boston Public Library Digital Commonwealth.)

On the Back Cover: The lake in Warinanco is one of the most popular locations within the park. Back then, the lake was used for small recreational purposes like toy-boat sailing, as this postcard shows. Today, the lake still serves a similar purpose but also installed paddleboats. It is a medium-sized lake with a lovely trail that people strolling the park can easily circumvent in order to observe all the various vantage points that the lake offers. (Authors' collections.)

POSTCARD HISTORY SERIES

Elizabeth

Nayeli L. Riano and M. Earl Smith

ARCADIA PUBLISHING

ISBN 978-1-4671-0336-7

Published by Arcadia Publishing
Charleston, South Carolina

Printed in the United States of America

Library of Congress Control Number: 2018964794

For all general information contact Arcadia Publishing at:
Telephone 843-853-2070
Fax 843-853-0044
E-mail sales@arcadiapublishing.com
For customer service and orders:
Toll-Free 1-888-313-2665

Visit us on the Internet at www.arcadiapublishing.com

To the citizens of Elizabeth, young and old:
may the history of your home be a guiding light in its future

Contents

Acknowledgments

This was a big project, about a big town with a big personality and a big heart. Thus, this work required the gargantuan efforts of a host of people. We would like to thank, as always, Erin Vosgien, Caroline Anderson, Erin Owens, and the staff at Arcadia, who work ceaselessly to bring out the best in the product we present. Much thanks must be given to each member of the Elizabeth community that assisted us in the crafting of this work: Mayor Christian J. Bollwange; Gordon F. Haas, the head of the Greater Elizabeth Chamber; Frank J. Cuesta of Elizabeth Public Schools; Bill Schroh of the Liberty Hall Museum; the kind and helpful staff at Boxwood Hall; and the Elizabeth Public Library.

M. Earl would personally like to thank his other coauthors: Jade Huguenin, Maggie Rymsza, and Gustavo Ferres. He would also like to thank Savannah Swearingen, Breanna Himschoot, Juliet Stein, Melissa Jensen, Laura Williams McCaffrey, Renee Watson, David Yoo, Nicole Flibbert, Henrique Laurino, and Kate Sydnes. Finally, he would like to thank his children: Lydia, Nicholas, and Leah.

Nayeli extends her gratitude to all those who taught her during her years in Elizabeth and made her years there a memorable experience, especially teachers Louis Sobo, Rebecca Aiello, Paul Gruber, Nicholas Perretti, Marilyn D'Antoni, Lynn Rubin, Phyllis Taub, principal Michael Cummings, and the Elizabeth High School Marching Band. She would also like to thank her parents, Maurizio Riano and Ruth Romer—it is them who she most sincerely thanks for their boundless support in everything.

All images appear courtesy of the authors' collections unless otherwise noted.

Introduction

Elizabeth, New Jersey, is a city today that is home to many immigrants from all parts of the world. It is truly a place that can epitomize the meaning of a "melting pot," where waves of immigrant communities from different generations interact and integrate into school settings, commercial settings, and leisure settings. Such was my experience when I first moved to the city in 2001 from Colombia. I often like to say that I consider myself a product of my upbringing, a large part of which was shaped by my time as a student who went through the entirety of the Elizabeth Public Schools system, from kindergarten all the way to 12th grade. During those years, I was able to explore my city for all of its raw and industrial beauty as well as its colorful and lively atmosphere; this is all thanks to the city's hardworking and vibrant residents.

What I never realized during my years in Elizabeth was the rich history that the city boasts and the immense contribution that Elizabeth made to American independence and US history at large. It is natural, with the passing of years and the coming and going of people, that certain places—cities are a great example of this—become forgotten; what a place once was is no longer what it is today, and how can we expect new residents or younger generations to know this? The answer is simple: we keep the history alive and teach them about it. Herein lies the mission of this book. When my colleague and friend M. Earl Smith and I decided to undergo this project roughly a year ago, we were sitting at the Rare Book and Manuscripts Library at the University of Pennsylvania, where we were both students at the time. As a historian, M. Earl Smith had already written several books to highlight city histories through the important medium of images. I realized there was so much history about my adopted hometown that I never knew because I had never cared to explore it. We decided to change that.

In manuscript studies, we often talk about palimpsests; a manuscript page that has been used and reused over the years but still bears visible traces of its earlier form. When looking at a palimpsest, one can see the old text that was scrapped, loosely erased, or washed off to make room for the new text written over it, yet traces of the original text always remain, if one looks closely enough. I can speak for M. Earl Smith and myself when I say that after completing this project, we have come to view Elizabeth as a living palimpsest. The history we uncovered, and rediscovered, granted us moments of excitement, from learning about the city's origins when it was part of claims from Dutch and Swedish settlers in the early 1600s, to Elizabeth's formal founding in 1664 and the role it played in the American Revolutionary War, to its modern-day significance as one of New Jersey's most populated cities. The history in these pages is so rich that we are honored to be able to share it and tell it through the city's postcard images. What better testament to Elizabeth's enduring spirit over the ages than postcards from and about Elizabeth that have withstood the test of time?

—Nayeli L. Riano
BA, The University of Pennsylvania; MLitt, University of St Andrews

One

Workin' Man's PhD
Business in Elizabeth

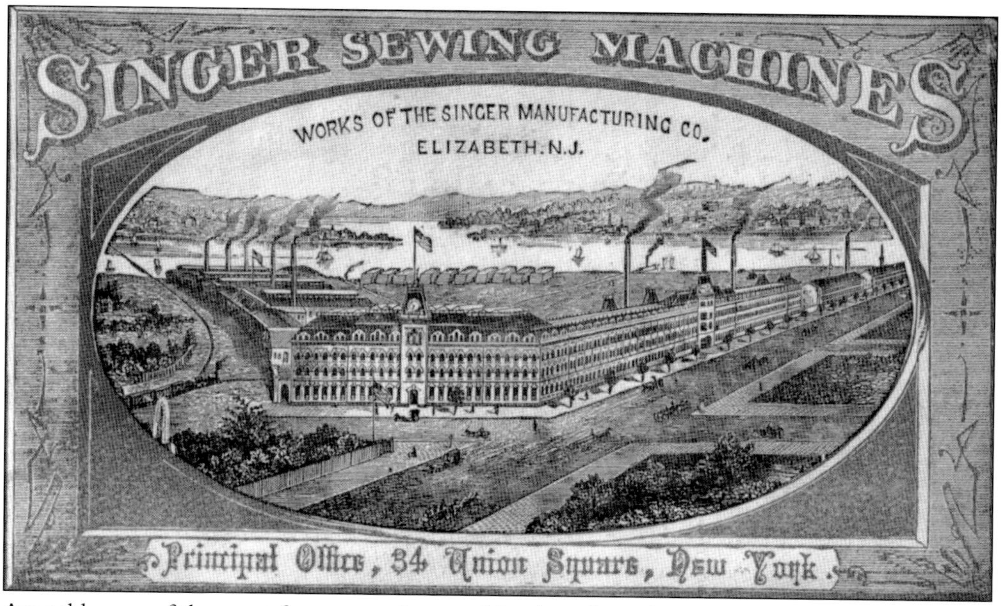

Arguably one of the most famous sewing machine brands in the United States, Singer had one of its largest plants in the city of Elizabeth, with another plant in Clydebank, Scotland. The Elizabeth factory was a perfect location since it was adjacent to the Central Railroad of the New Jersey Mainline. This postcard shows a detailed sketch of the original factory as it stood in the city. For many years, the factory was a large and famous reference point for locals given the vast size of the building. Originally spanning 32 acres of land and covering almost a half-mile in length, the factory has been torn down since then.

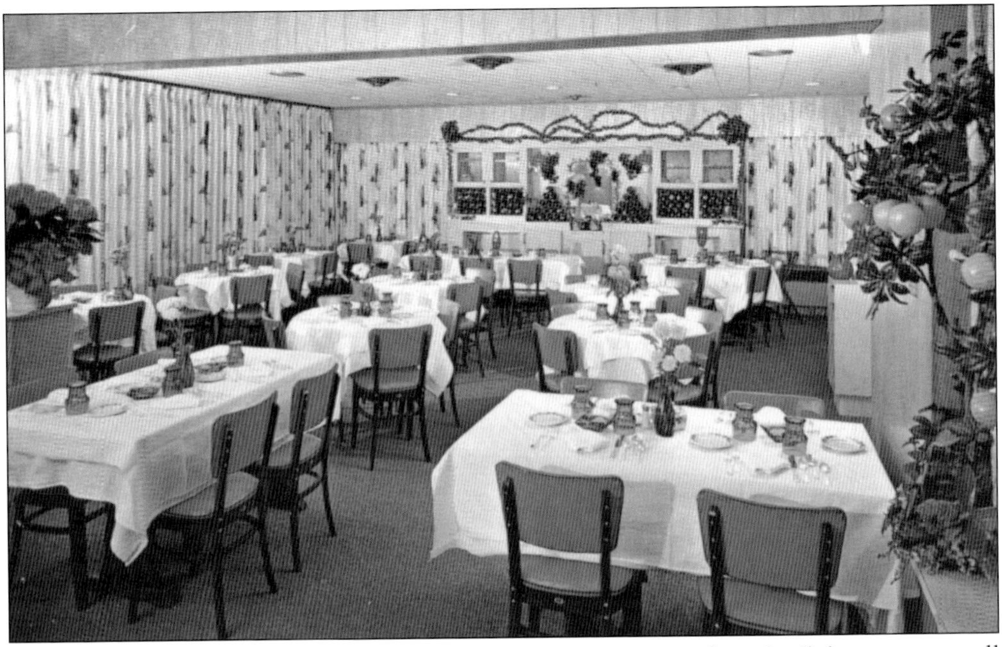

Shown here is the interior of the former Lynn restaurant and cocktail lounge, a small establishment at 624 Westfield Avenue in Elizabeth. The back of the card states, "Wonderfully intimate, and comfortable, the LYNN features two beautiful dining rooms in which to have dinner by candlelight. The Lounge is highlighted by Parisian murals. There is entertainment nightly at the Hammond organ. Air Conditioned—Banquet Facilities. For Reservations Call: Elizabeth 2-1654." The restaurant and the building it was in no longer exist, giving way to the Grand luxury apartment development.

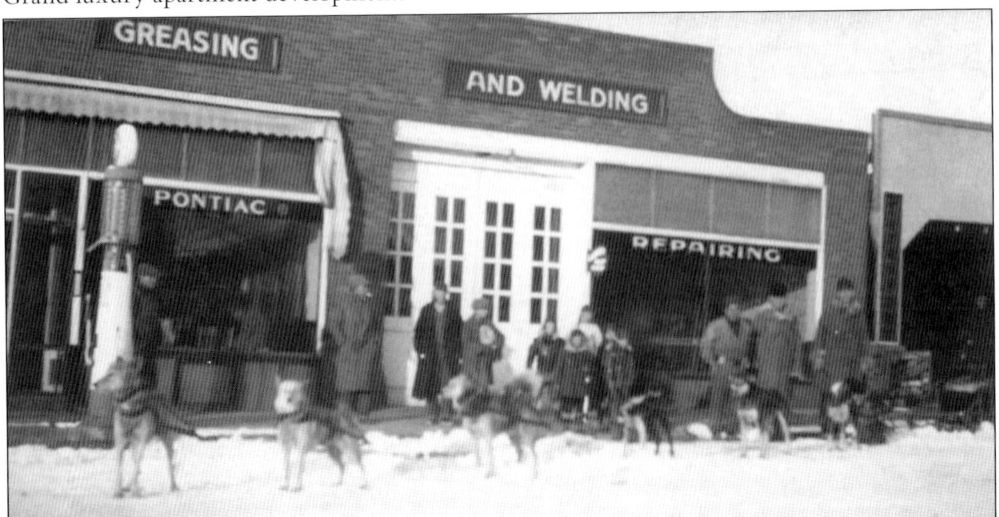

The irony of a group of sled dogs in front of Elizabeth's early Pontiac dealership should not be lost on the reader of this text. Pontiac was a car brand founded in 1926 by General Motors (GM) to serve as a companion brand to its more expensive luxury brand Oakland, which it would supplant in 1933. GM would later market the brand as a performance brand, strengthened by both the popularity of the sporty GTO and the performance of Pontiac drivers such as Richard and Kyle Petty. The brand was discontinued in 2010 as a part of GM's Chapter 11 bankruptcy.

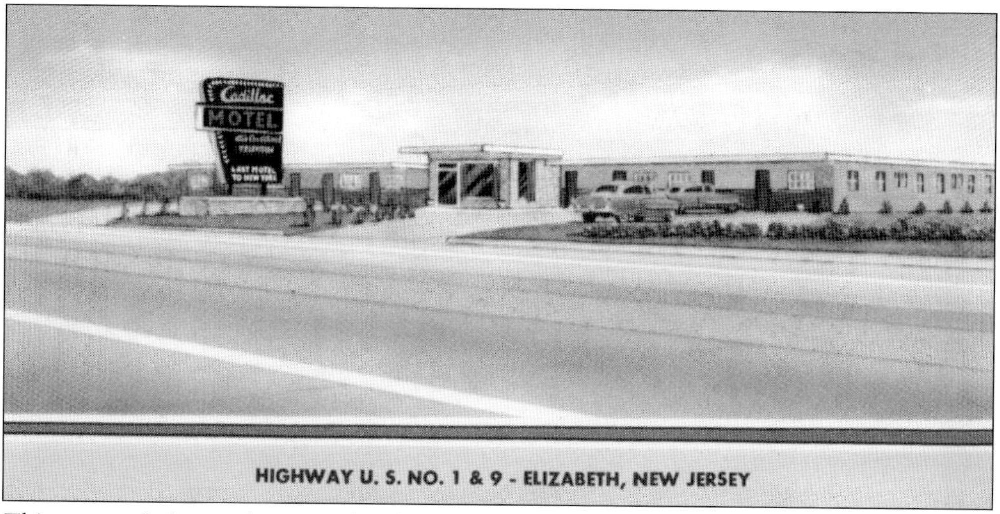

This postcard shows the now-closed Cadillac Motel, at what was then the corner of US Highways 1 and 9 and is now 853 Spring Street in Elizabeth. The back of the card reads, "Cadillac Motel. 62 Units–Fireproof–Open All Year. On Hwy. U.S. 1 & 9, Elizabeth, New Jersey. Telephones: Elizabeth 4-4239 & EL 4-7737. Air-Conditioned–Cross Ventilation. Hot Water Heat—Television. Simmons Beauty Rest Mattresses. Last Motel to N.Y.–9 Miles from N.Y.C." The hotel has since been torn down.

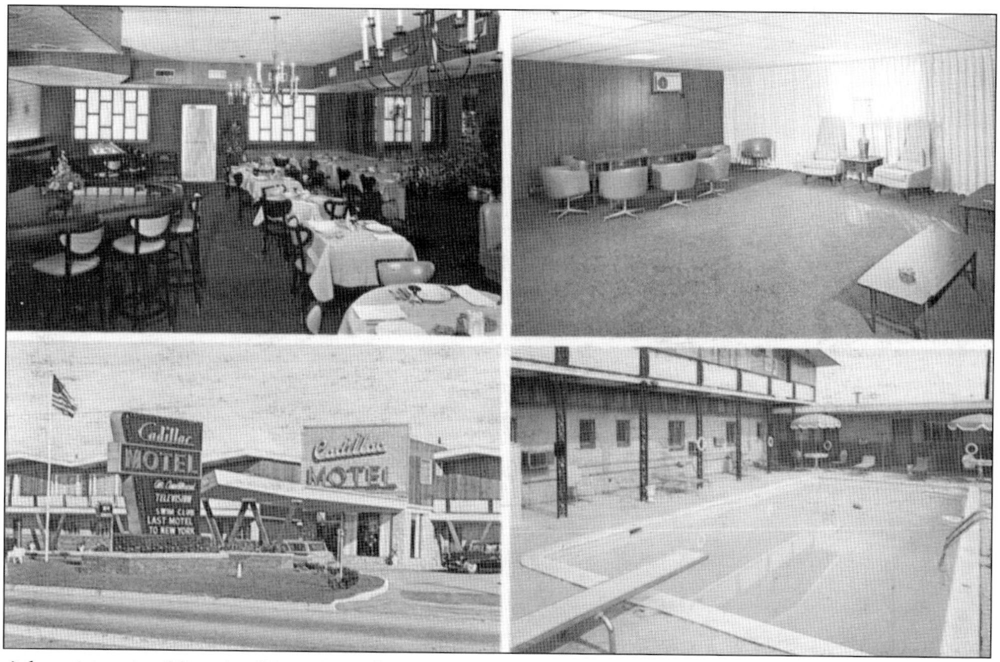

Advertising itself as the "Last Motel To New York" worked well for the Cadillac Motel, until the popularity of the young New Jersey Turnpike (Interstate 95) saw others spring up beyond it. The back of this card reads, "Cadillac Motel. 125 Modern Units–Open All Year. On Hwy. U.S. 1 & 9, Elizabeth, New Jersey. Telephone: 354-3840. Air-Conditioned–Swimming Pool–Restaurant–Cock-tail Lounge–Television–Conference Rooms–Execu-tive Suites. Between Exits 13 & 14, N.J. Turnpike. 2 Miles to Newark Airport. Last Motel to N.Y.–9 Miles from N.Y.C. All Major Credit Cards Honored."

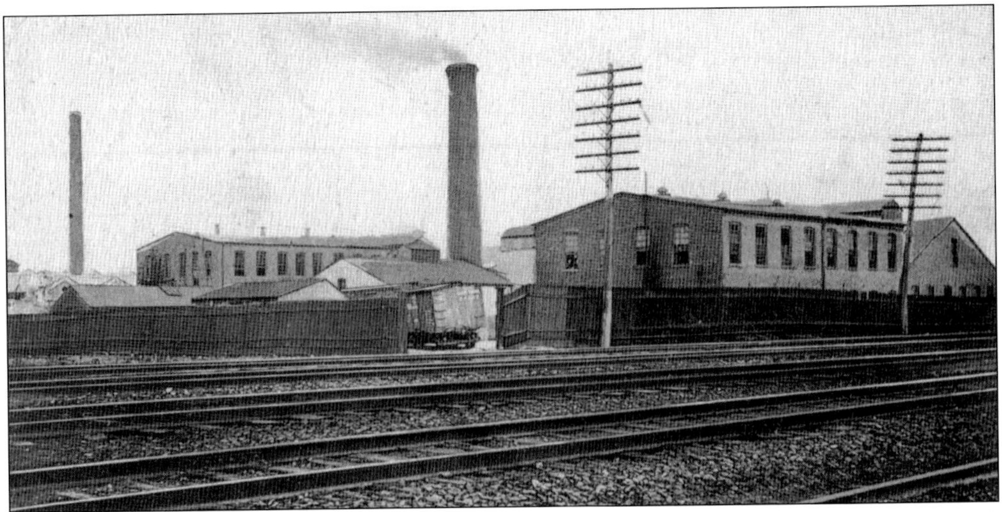

This card shows the Jenkins Rubber Company and the Bronze Powder Works factories, which faced each other on the corners of Magnolia and Division Streets. The Jenkins Rubber Company was established in 1894 and made rubber discs, packing, and gaskets for the parent company Jenkins Valves of New York. Destroyed by a fire in 1908, the building would be replaced with a more modern building in 1918. Today, the building is occupied by, among others, Francisco Welding and Redline Performance.

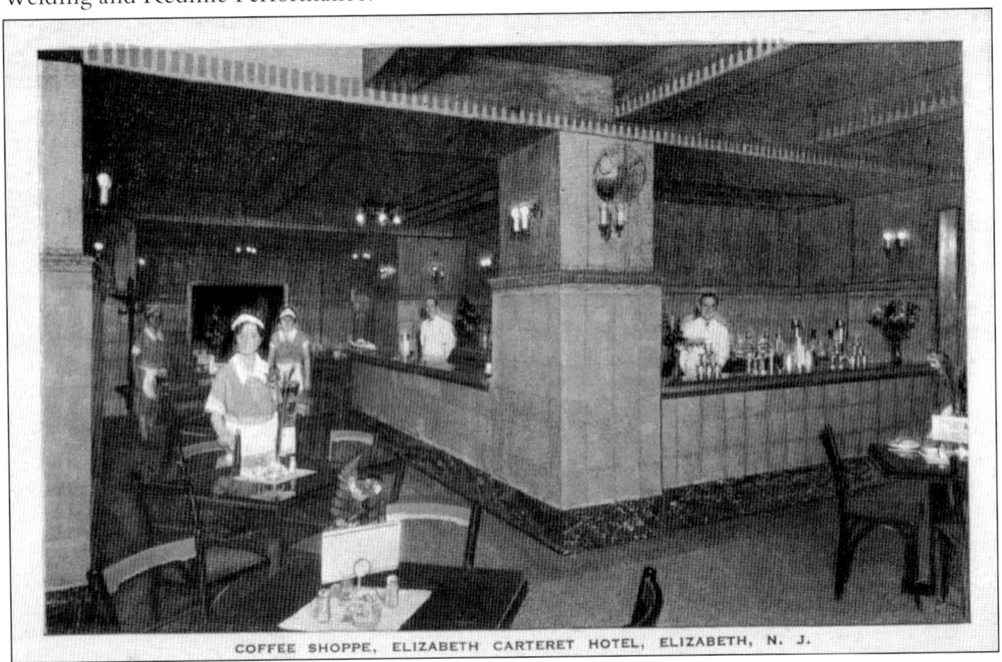

This postcard shows an inner view of the coffee shop in the former Elizabeth Carteret hotel. The advertisement on the back, in part, reads, "You will enjoy a cocktail or two most before dinner . . . a chat with friends you are bound to meet here. The strain of a busy day will ease off . . . care-free cheer will take its place. Certainly the right mood in which to approach your dinner . . . an evening of amusement or in the quiet of your library or den reading the news or an unfinished book. A past master of the mixing art is ready to serve you. Tidbits served. Do drop in."

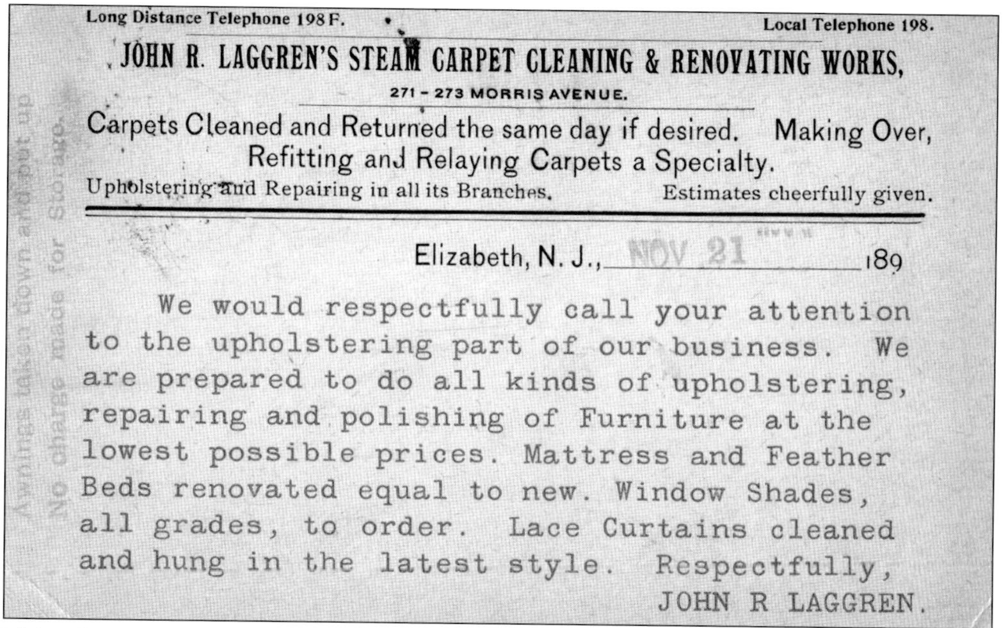

Long Distance Telephone 198 F. Local Telephone 198.

JOHN R. LAGGREN'S STEAM CARPET CLEANING & RENOVATING WORKS,

271 - 273 MORRIS AVENUE.

Carpets Cleaned and Returned the same day if desired. Making Over, Refitting and Relaying Carpets a Specialty.

Upholstering and Repairing in all its Branches. Estimates cheerfully given.

Awnings taken down and put up

No charge made for Storage.

Elizabeth, N. J., NOV 21 189

We would respectfully call your attention to the upholstering part of our business. We are prepared to do all kinds of upholstering, repairing and polishing of Furniture at the lowest possible prices. Mattress and Feather Beds renovated equal to new. Window Shades, all grades, to order. Lace Curtains cleaned and hung in the latest style. Respectfully,

JOHN R LAGGREN.

This advertising card was sent to Mrs. N.A. Adams at 457 Grier Avenue, a single-family residence that still stands today. It was sent by a John R. Laggren, whose business served as a general contractor of sorts. He offers assistance in things such as steam cleaning, carpet repair, upholstering, furniture polishing, mattress refurbishing, window shades, curtain cleaning, and even the installation, storage, and removal of awnings. Standing at his address of 271-273 Morris Avenue is part of a parking lot and a single-family home that was built in 2006.

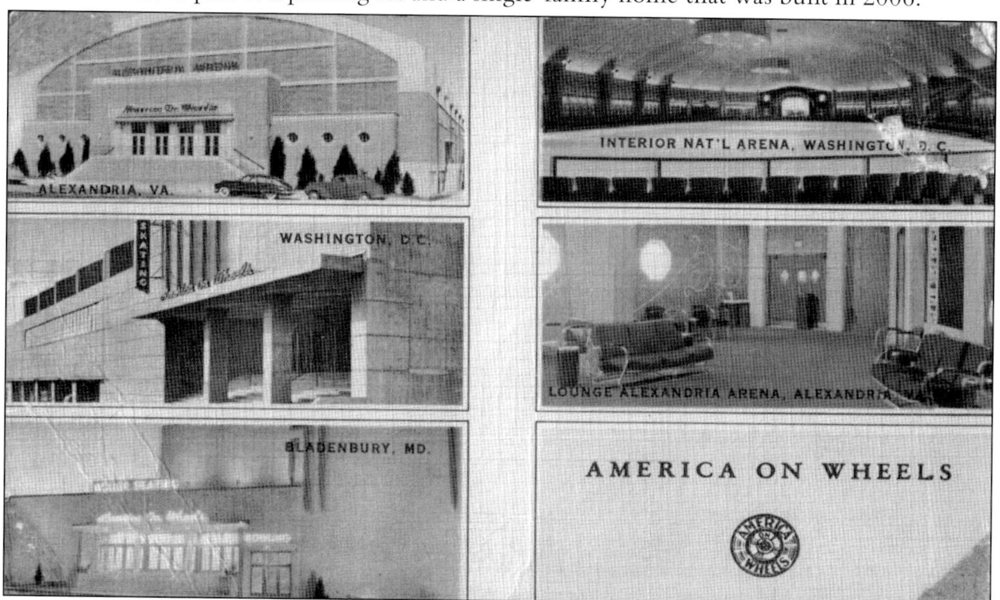

Although the building now houses the Twin City Supermarket, it, at one point, hosted America on Wheels, the largest chain of roller rinks in America. The front of the card shows three of those roller rinks: interior and exterior shots of the Alexandria Arena in Alexandria, Virginia; interior and exterior shots the National Arena in Washington, DC; and the exterior of the arena in Bladenbury, Maryland.

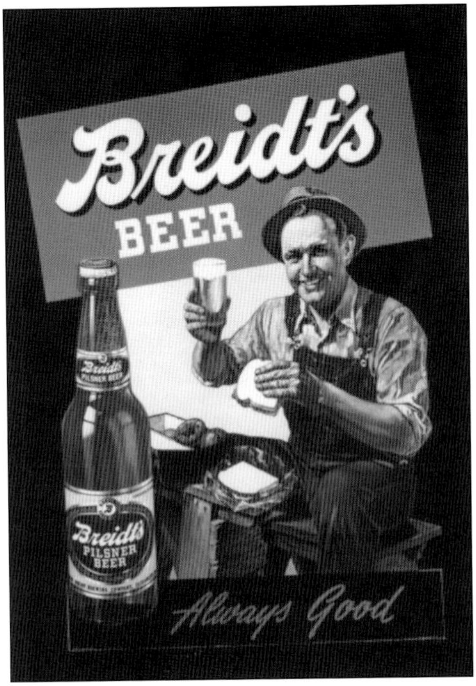

This postcard, used as a mailing advertisement, shows Breidt's Beer, brewed initially by German immigrant Peter Breidt, who learned his craft at several Newark breweries before opening his own on Pearl Street in 1882. During Prohibition in the 1920s, the company was forced to brew "near beer," which had an alcohol content of less than one half of one percent. The company switched back to regular beer in 1933 and brewed until 1951. Elizabeth High School is now standing where the brewery once was.

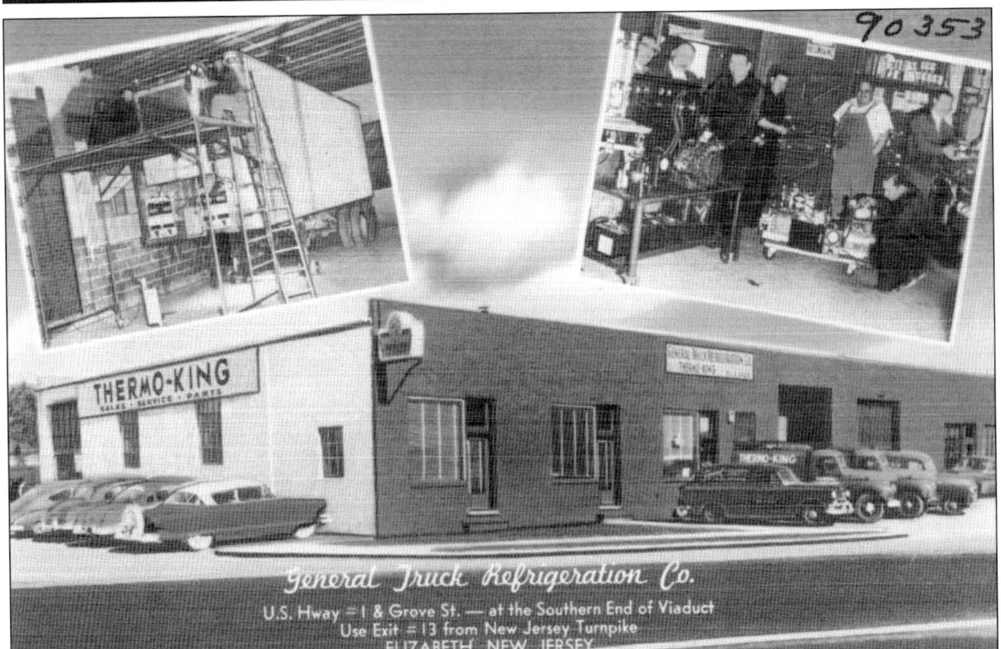

This card, printed around 1930–1945, shows General Truck Refrigeration Company, located formerly at the intersection of US 1 and Grove Street in Elizabeth. Truck refrigeration became popular in 1925 due to the desire to move ice cream long distances. Seeing how such technology would allow different parts of the country to experience several different kinds of food, the technology grew widely in use. As of 2010, there were over 4 million refrigerated trucks in use worldwide. The address today plays home to the Portuguese Instructive Social Club. (Courtesy of the Boston Public Library Digital Commonwealth.)

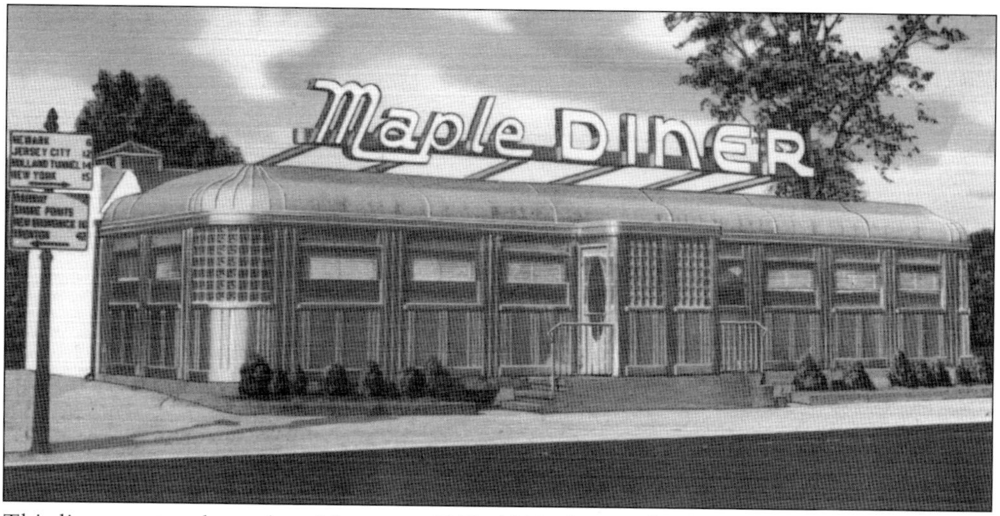

This linen postcard, produced between 1930–1945, shows Elizabeth's classic take on the old American diner, Maple Diner. The diner was located at 460 Maple Avenue in Elizabeth and, in its trailer-style construction, featured glass blocks, a popular accent during the era. An eatery still occupies the site, as Elizabeth is now served by Urban Griddle, which abandoned the old-style diner decor and rebuilt in hipster fashion, with repurposed barn wood that dates back 150 years and a corrugated tin roof. The new diner also offers craft beers, cocktails, and high-end coffee. (Courtesy of the Boston Public Library Digital Commonwealth.)

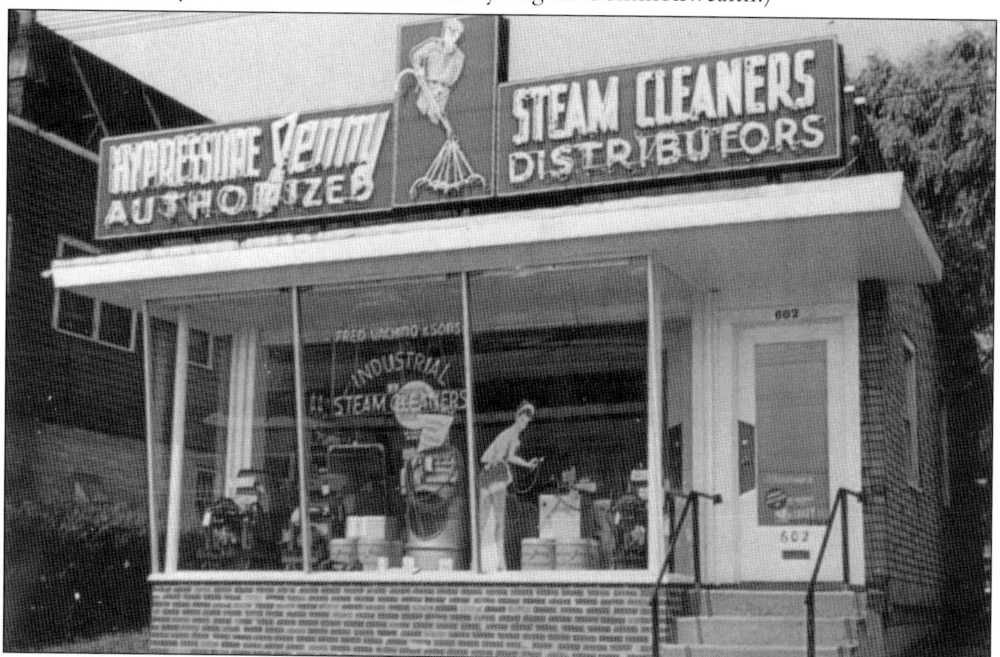

This card, published sometime in the early 1960s, shows Fred Vachino & Sons, Inc, a business dedicated to services such as steam cleaners, steam generators, hot water heaters, and pressure washers. Located at 602 Spring Street (a part of US Highway 1), the business is still in operation today and has expanded, according to their website, to offer services such as portable generators, water recycling, and space heaters. They are open Monday through Friday from 9:00 a.m. to 5:00 p.m. and can be reached at 908-355-4433.

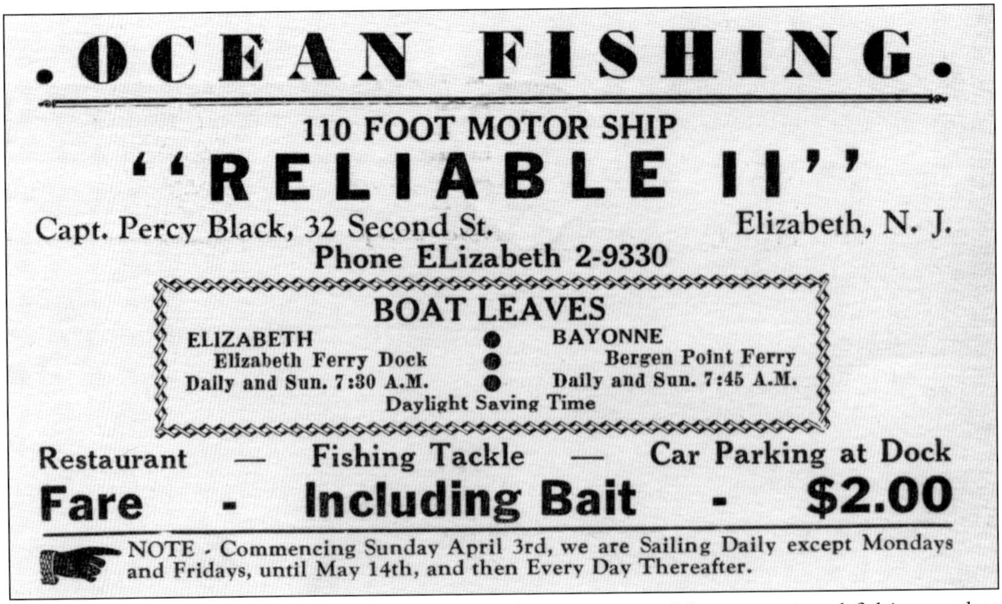

This postcard, mailed from Elizabeth in 1938, advertises one of the recreational fishing outlets headed up by Capt. Percy Black and his 110-foot ship, the *Reliable II.* The ship, constructed in 1918, was originally built as a sub chaser by the United States for France to use during World War I. She never saw combat action, however, and was sold at the end of the war under the civilian name *Modesty.*

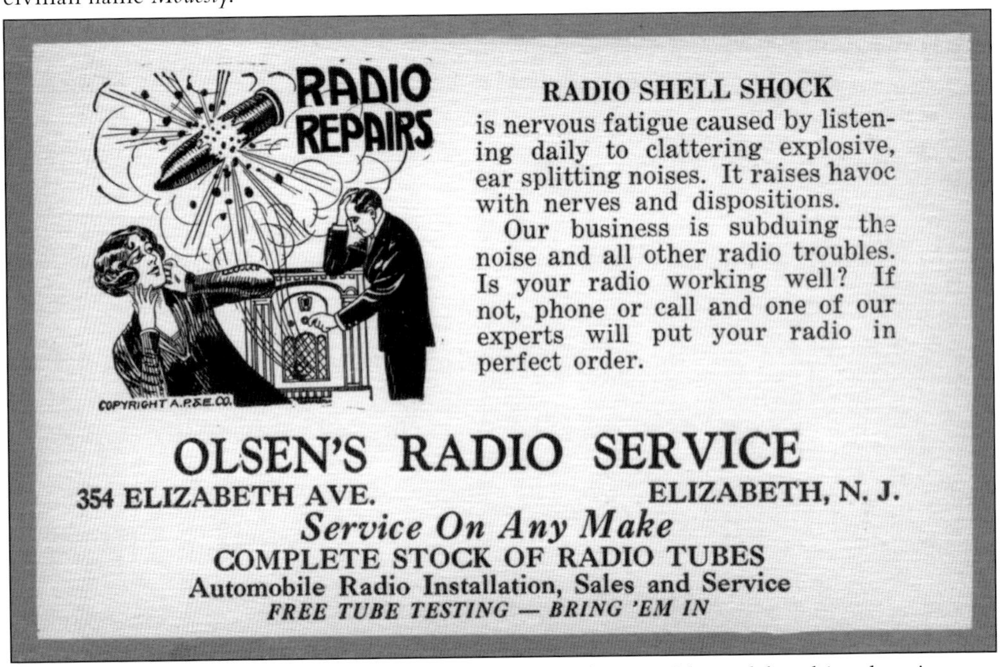

Radio technology was extremely popular in Elizabeth, as evidenced by this advertisement mailed by Olsen Radio Service in Elizabeth. Printed during the height of the Cold War, this card is almost egregious in its claim of helping one deal with what was termed "radio shell shock" by its authors. Their goal, it seems, was to convince their customers that unless their machine was in fine working order, they were subject to adverse health effects.

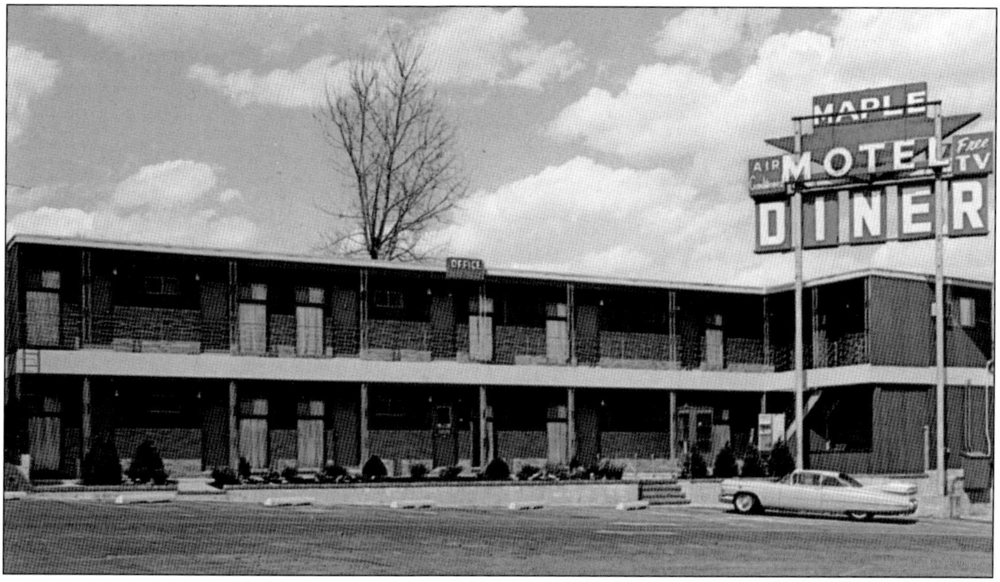

Still standing today, the Maple Motel is a popular layover stop both for those flying into the Newark International Airport and those traveling by car into New York City. The back of this card reads, "Maple Motel & Maple Diner. U.S. Route P, #1–17 miles from New York. Elizabeth, New Jersey. 'Air Conditioned.' –Free T. V. Motel & Diner Open 24 Hours. Phone FL 1-3434. Color Photo by: Jim E. Hess." Today, the Maple Motel is a solid, economical choice for those traveling to and from the Elizabeth area.

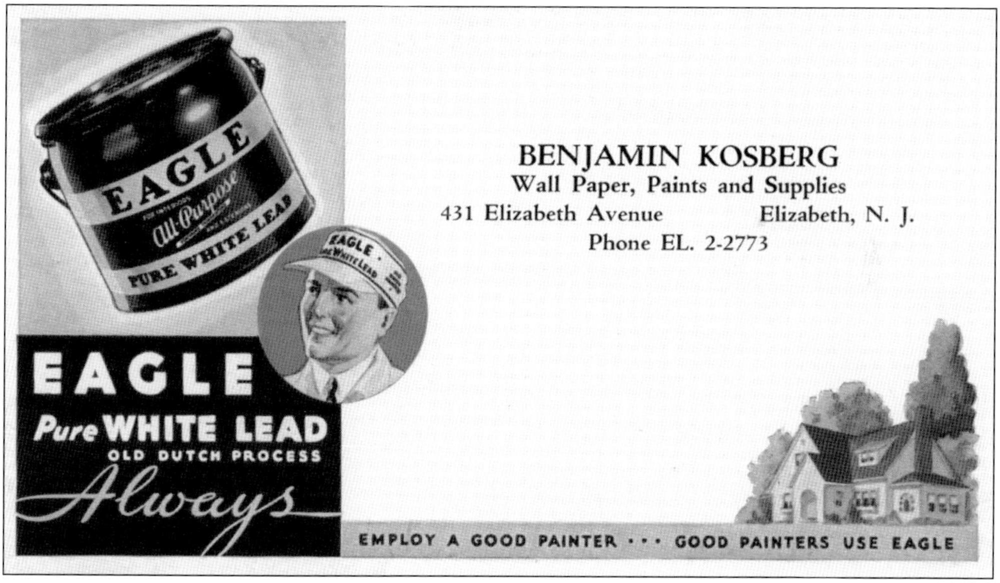

Given the state of what is known about the deadly effects of lead paint today, its use would seem foolhardy, but back in the 1950s, it was all the rage. The lead was purported to both last longer and give a better appearance, although later research and technological improvements have rendered such claims obsolete. This card was sent by Benjamin Kosberh Wallpaper, Paints and Supplies, formerly of 431 Elizabeth Avenue. Today, the building at this address houses Salermo Insurance Agency, who, according to the Facebook page, mainly focuses on automobile insurance.

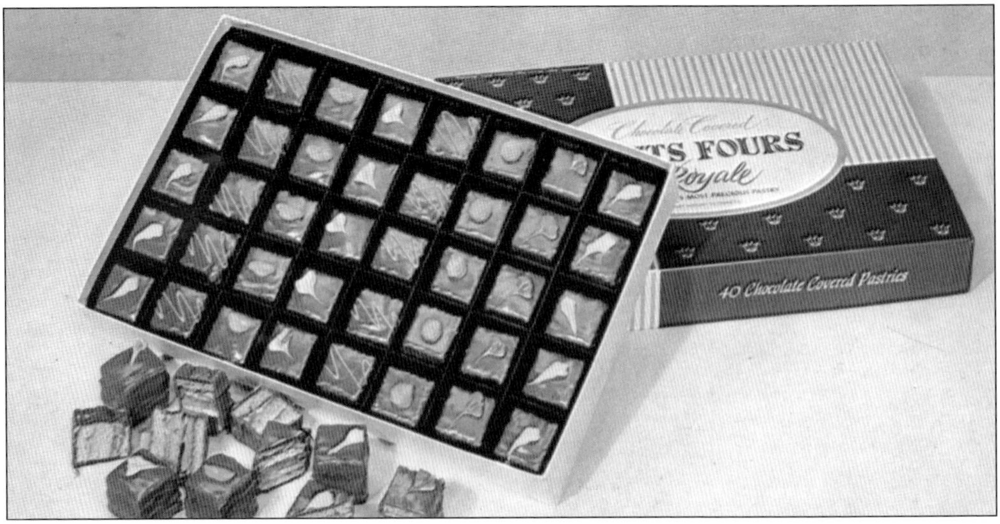

This card is a mail-order advertisement for "Petits Fours Royale," a pastry delicacy offered by the Damar Products Company, a mail-order company that operated in Elizabeth. The back of the card offers platitudes expected of a mail-order company, such as, "It would take a poet to describe the taste of these incomparable real chocolate covered candy-cakes made from a recipe know to very few!" It goes on to claim that Louis XIV of France was fond of the pastries and that one could order a single box for $3 or six boxes for $15.

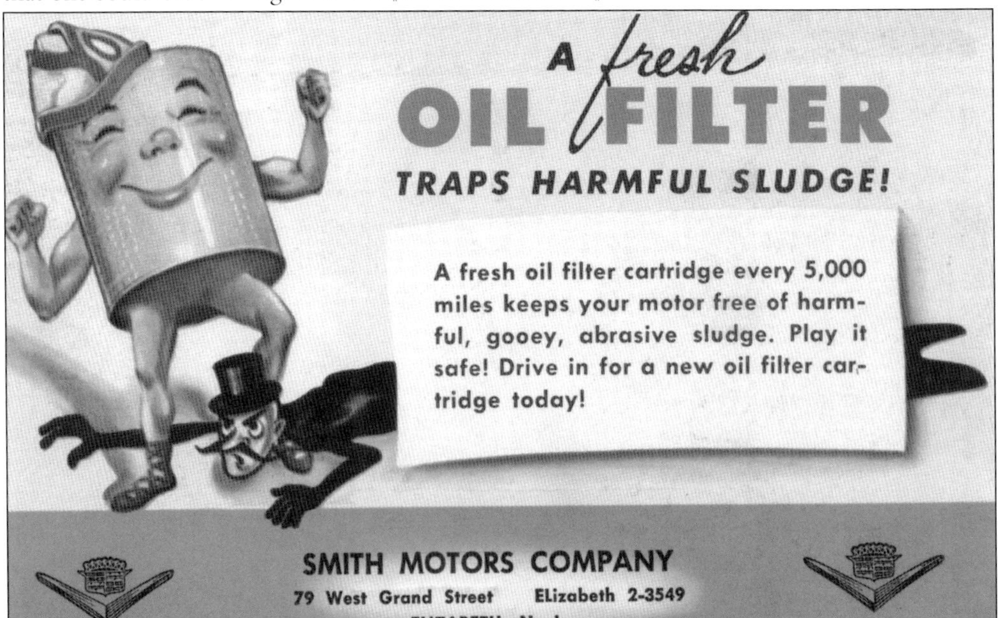

The timeframe for when an oil change is needed for one's car seems to change at the whims of auto manufacturers, but the fact remains that if you are going to own a car, you must change the oil. This card was sent as a reminder to S.S Weinstein by Smith Motors Company at 79 Grand Street in Elizabeth on December 10, 1953. By this point, the luxury car brand had been in business in America for over half a century. Today, on the lot at 79 Grand Street, the Union County government has a garage to host the maintenance facilities for the county's fleet of vehicles.

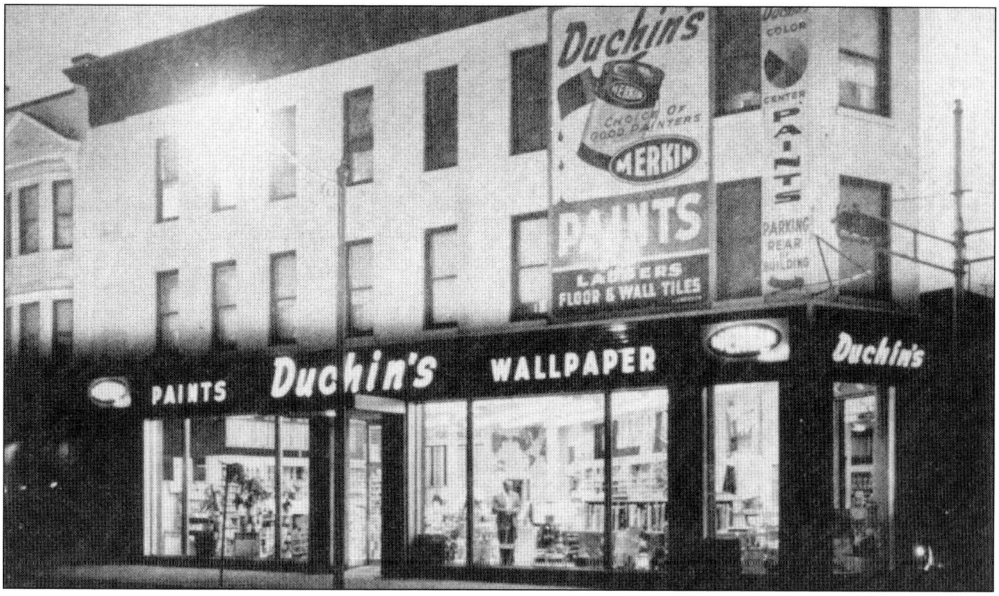

This postcard was sent by the Duchin's Paint and Wallpaper store. The back of the card reads, "Here at Duchin's modern showroom you will find one of New Jersey's largest selections of Nationally Advertised Brands of wallpaper, paints, floor and wall tiles, custom window shades and blinds, plus the 'know-how' of a well trained staff of employees. Duchin's Paints-Wallpapers. Morris at Westfield Aves., Elizabeth. Parking Rear of Bldg."

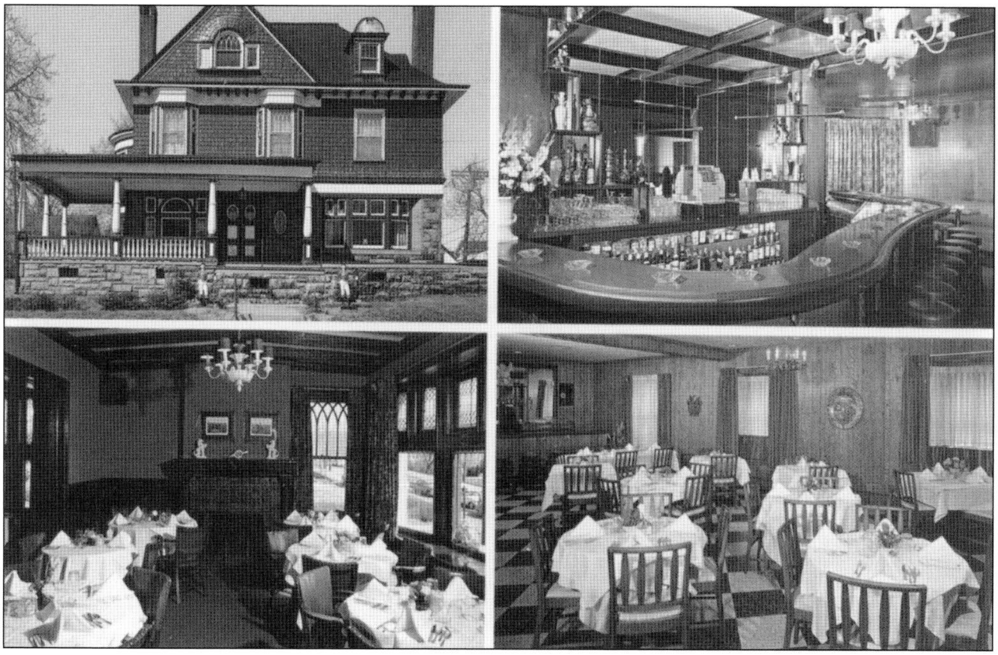

This card shows the popular Brass Horn restaurant and cocktail lounge, formerly located at the corner of Cherry and West Grand Streets in Elizabeth. The restaurant was formerly owned by Johnny Murphy and was situated across the street from Smith Cadillac. The establishment had a reputation for being a date hotspot and opened in 1954. The establishment was torn down in 1987 to make room for Joelle Manor Condominiums, which stands on the location to this day.

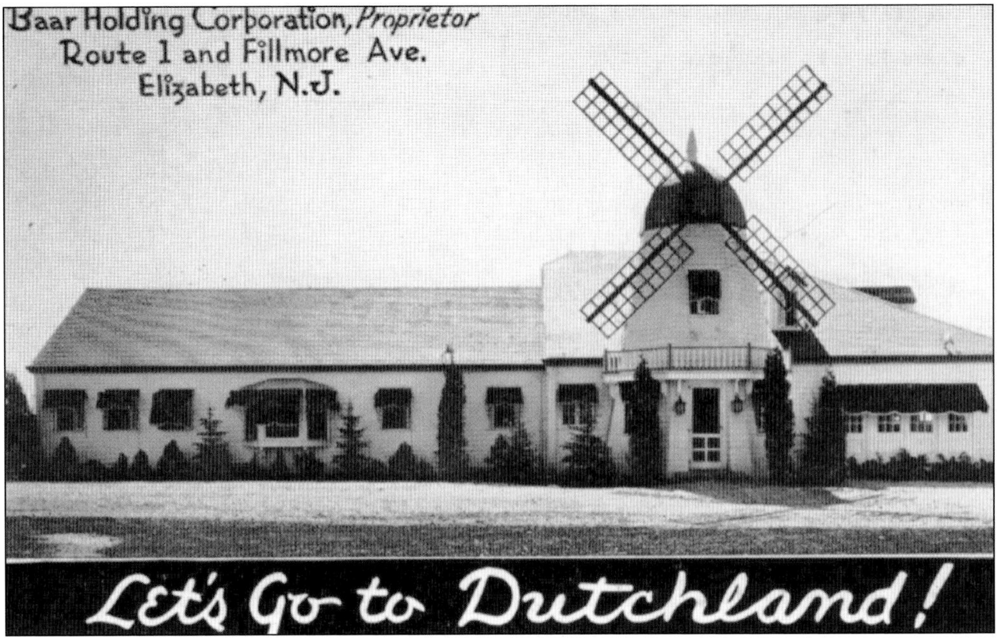

Shown here, with its iconic "Let's Go to Dutchland" logo and aesthetic windmill, is the Dutchland Farms convenience store that once stood on the corner of US 1 and Fillmore Avenue in Elizabeth, a quick on and off for travelers headed to New York City. Started in 1897, Dutchland Farms had as many as 50 locations in Massachusetts, Rhode Island, New Hampshire, Connecticut, and New Jersey. As with many businesses, the advent of larger retail stores, with stronger and quicker supply chains, brought on the end of Dutchland Farms. The last store closed in 1951.

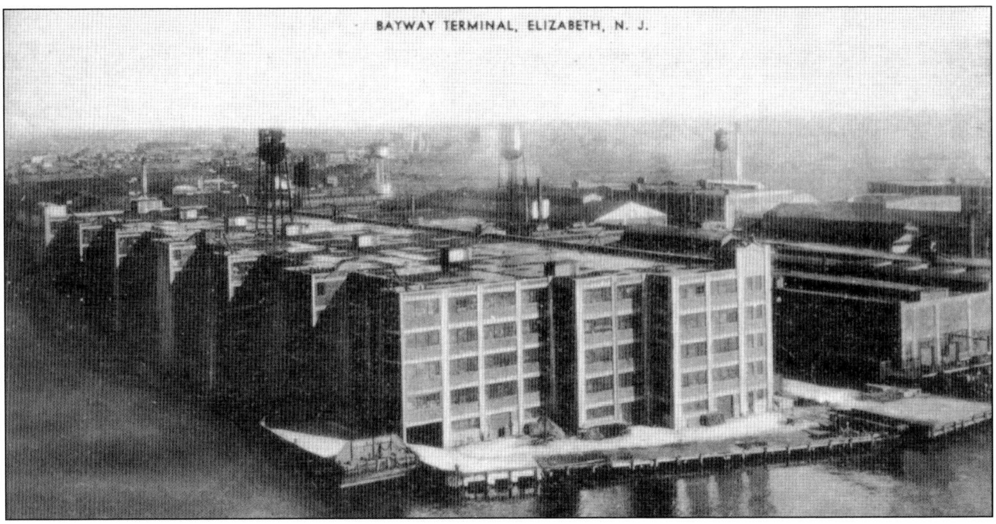

Shown here is Bayway Terminal, which borders Elizabeth and Linden. It was constructed as a refinery site for John D. Rockefeller's Standard Oil Company in 1907. The site, now owned by Phillips 66, has a standard output of 238,000 barrels of oil a day. The site is not without its issues, however, as the State of New Jersey and the Environmental Protection Agency have labeled it a repeat offender of environmental codes. In 2015, site partner ExxonMobil was forced into a $225 million cleanup settlement with the State of New Jersey.

The Elizabeth Carteret Hotel was constructed in 1927, at the height of the Roaring 20s. The building was massive, supporting 200 rooms for guest use. Its name comes from the Carteret family, whose roots run deep in the founding of the area and the state as a whole. Formerly at this site was the Chetwood House, which was one of the earliest examples of Greek Revival homes in the area. The hotel was converted in 2004 to senior housing. Known as Amber Court, this facility provides both assisted living and independent living options. (Courtesy of the Boston Public Library Digital Collections.)

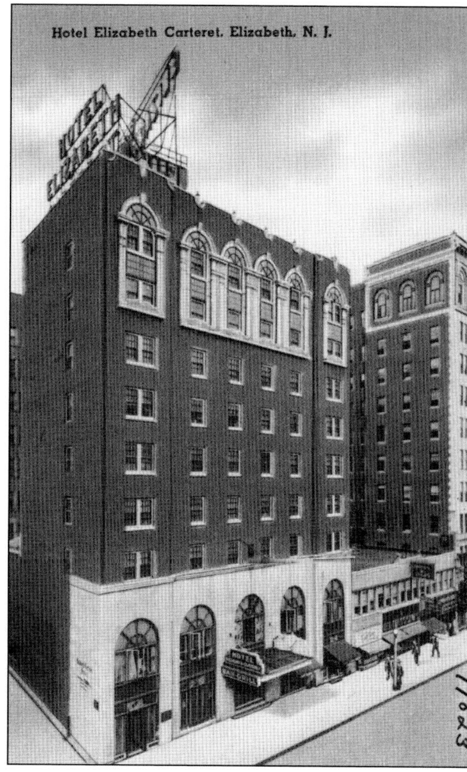

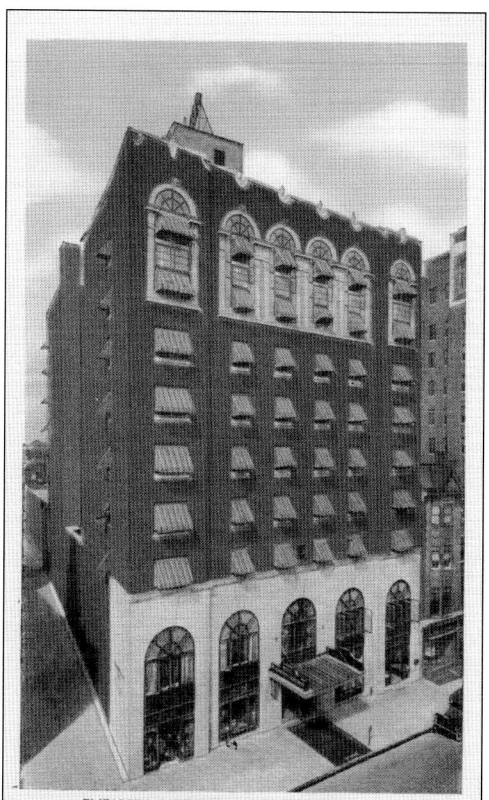

The Elizabeth Carteret hotel was located on East Jersey Street, built in 1927. The original building had 200 rooms with baths as well as banquet facilities and a bar. In 2004, the hotel was turned into an assisted living residence for senior citizens under the name of Amber Court, which is still operating today. The portrait format of this postcard captures the hotel's grandeur as one of the taller buildings near the city center at the time.

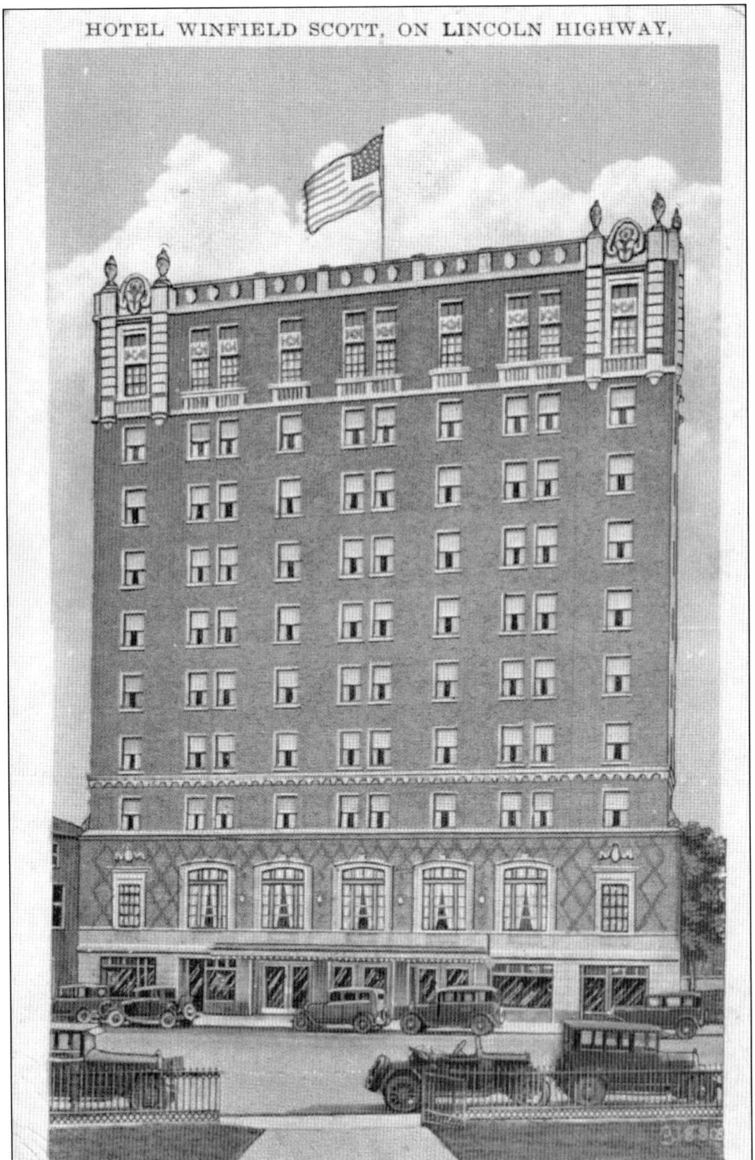

This postcard shows an image of the Hotel Winfield Scott on Lincoln Highway. The hotel was named after Gen. Winfield Scott, who fought in the Mexican War (1846–1848). Winfield Scott once lived at the corner of Madison Avenue, in 1105 East Jersey Street. The hotel, however, was also inhabited by another famous Elizabeth resident—the location of the hotel was on North Broad Street, once the residence of Frederick H. Levey, the president of the printing and lithographic ink company, the Frederick H. Levey Company. Levey was also a director of the Elizabethtown Water Company. Because Elizabeth used to be a place where wealthy merchants, bankers, financiers, industrialists, and lawyers would make their homes, many of their estates used to be located on main streets like North Broad Street. By the 1920s, however, the street was becoming more commercial, and the Scott Hotel replaced the Levey home. The 10-story-tall hotel was built in 1928. The building has been converted into a residence home called the Winfield Scott Senior Towers.

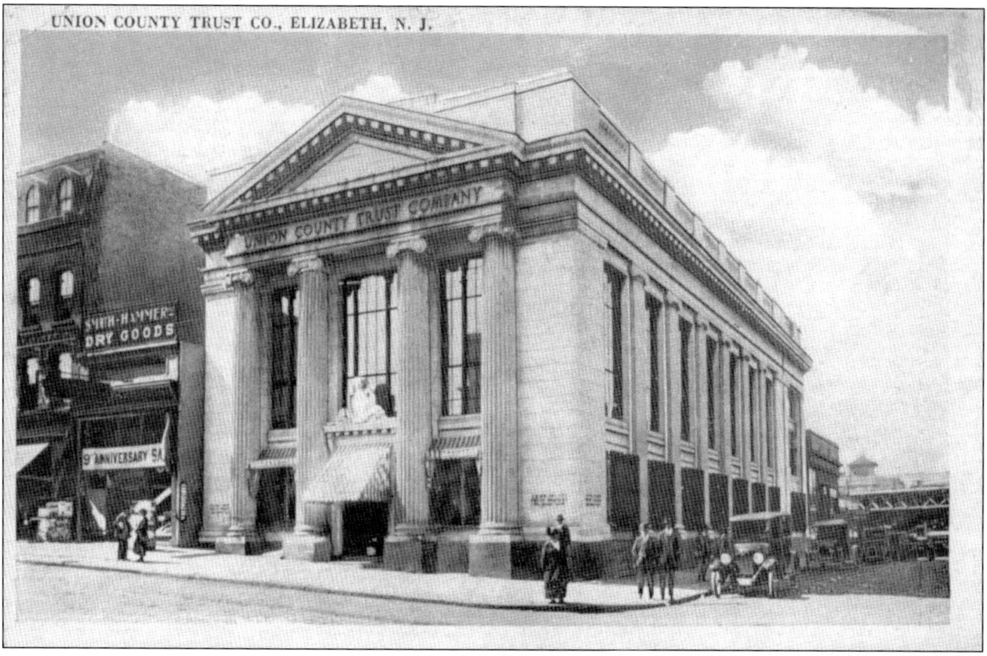

The Union County Trust Company is located on Broad Street, near the Elizabeth train station. Today, the building is called the Garden State Community Bank. The Union County Trust Company was headed for several years by a man called Louis F. Hersh, an immigrant from Austria who was born in 1857. Hersh was vice president of the Union County Trust Company, apart from also owning a wholesale grocery business and an automobile dealership. Hersh eventually erected the 14-story Hersh tower on the corner of East Grand and Broad Streets in 1931.

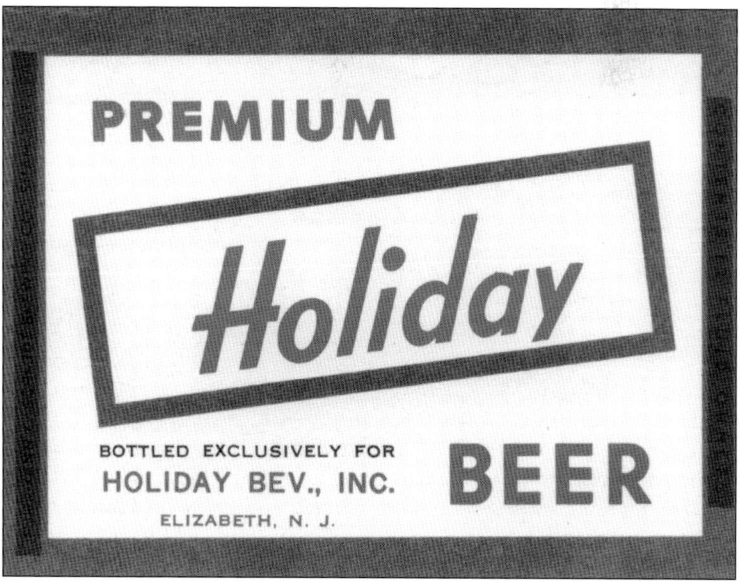

A company known as Holiday Beverage Inc. was once located in Elizabeth. This advertisement for their "Holiday" beer was bottled exclusively for the company in Elizabeth, which demonstrates that the target audience for this drink would have been New Jersey residents that would recognize Elizabeth as a local location.

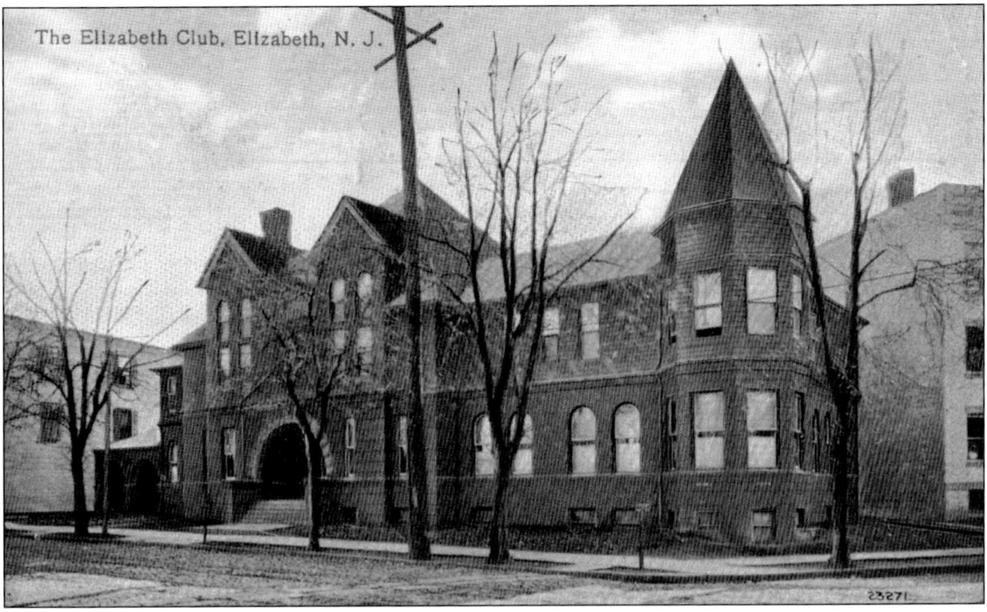

The Elizabeth Club is located on East Grand Street and is visible from the corner of Jefferson Avenue. The club's president in the early 1900s was a man called Franklin Brooks, who was an executive of the mica mining industry. This Elizabeth Club was a private social club that held athletic events, like bicycle racing and other popular sports of the late-19th century. After the club ceased operations, the building survived a couple of years, as it was converted into a building for commercial uses like law offices.

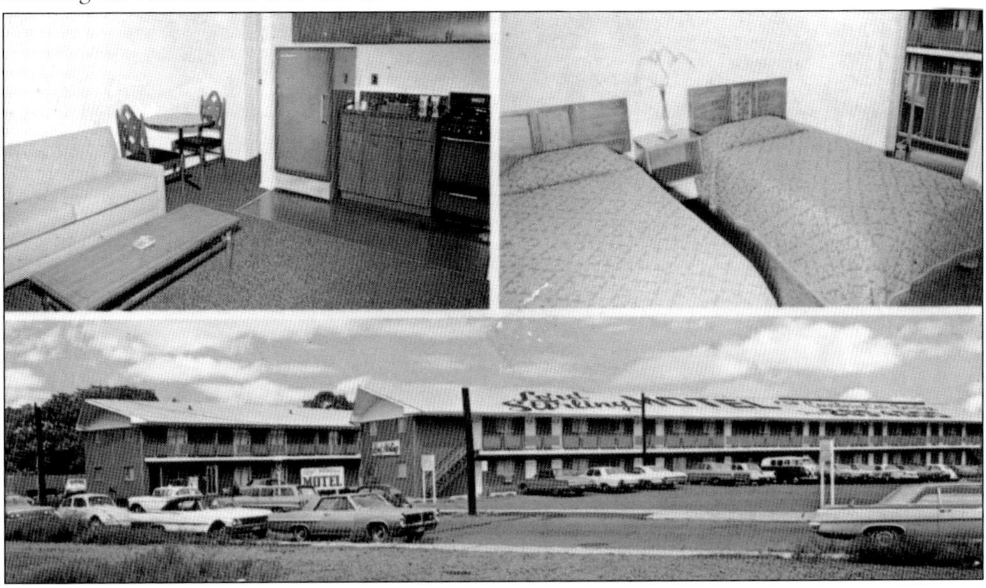

The Lord Stirling Motel was a motel in Elizabeth that ran until the late 1980s. The motel had a bad reputation for being a place where somewhat questionable business exchanges took place. The motel used to be by Cherry Street. Former residents of Elizabeth have negative memories of the motel for being not particularly clean and even dangerous. The motel was likely named after William Alexander, also known as "Lord Stirling," who was a major general in George Washington's Continental Army.

Two

You Learn
The History of Elizabeth

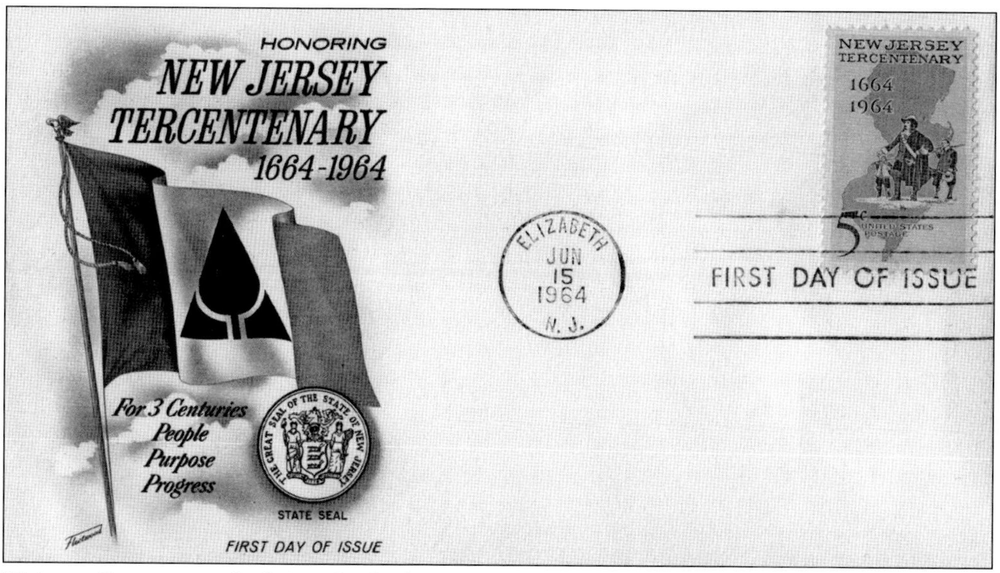

This mailer, postmarked in Elizabeth on June 15, 1964, commemorates the New Jersey Tercentenary, a yearlong celebration of three centuries of existence for the state. New Jersey was founded in 1664 as an English province, although parts of the state can be traced back to earlier New Netherland and New Sweden colonies. The 300-year celebration was marked by projects of civic importance. Many people took a new interest in the history of the state, from the level of historians down to children, who formed many school clubs around the history of the state.

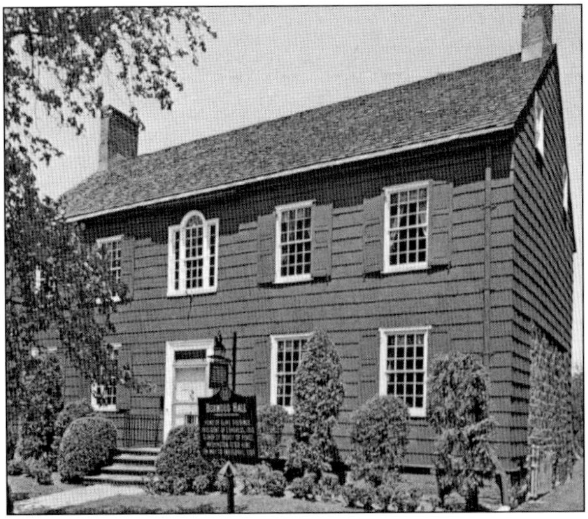

This card shows the historic Boxwood Hall, which stands today as a State Historic Site. The back of the card reads "Boxwood Hall. 1073 E. Jersey St. Elizabeth, N.J. State-owned Historic House. Built about 1750 by the Mayor of Elizabethtown. How, 1772–1795, of Elias Boudinot, Pres. Continental Congress, and 1795–1825, of Jonathan Dayton, signer of the Constitution." The house is built in the Georgian style and was added to the National Register of Historic Places in 1970. Today, the house offers tours and is used for educational displays. (Courtesy of Boxwood Hall).

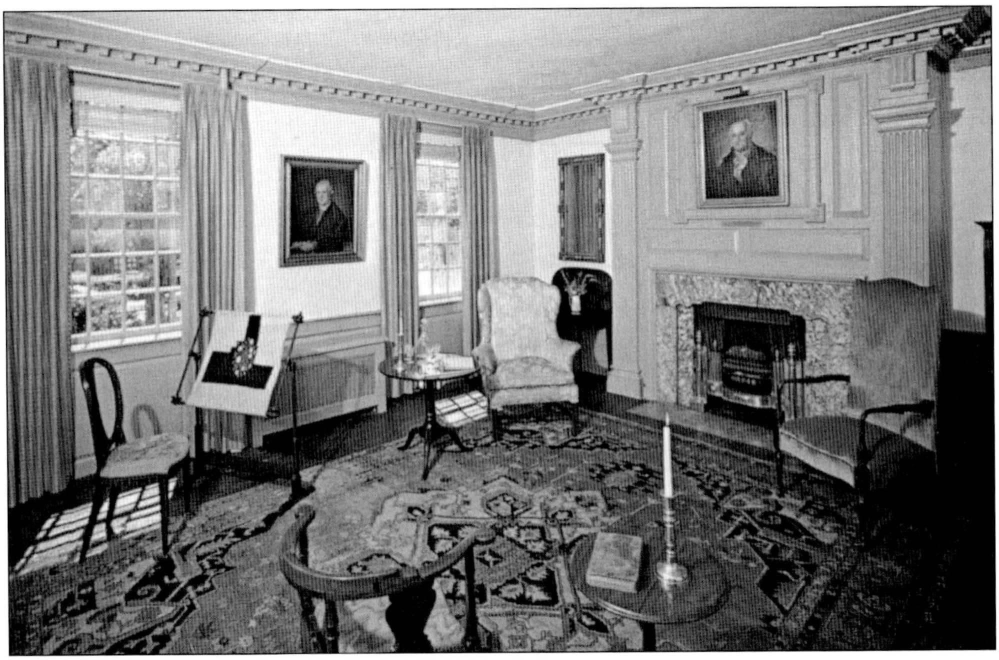

This card shows the interior Boudinot Room at the historic Boxwood Hall. The back of the card reads, "Boudinot Room. Boxwood Hall. 1073 E. Jersey St. Elizabeth, N.J. State-owned Historic House. Home, 1772–1795, of Elias Boudinot, patriot, statesman, and president of the Continental Congress, highest office in the land at the time." In addition to his role as the 10th president of the Continental Congress, Boudinot would serve his state as a congressman as the first New Jersey delegate in the history of the United States and as the first head of the US Mint.

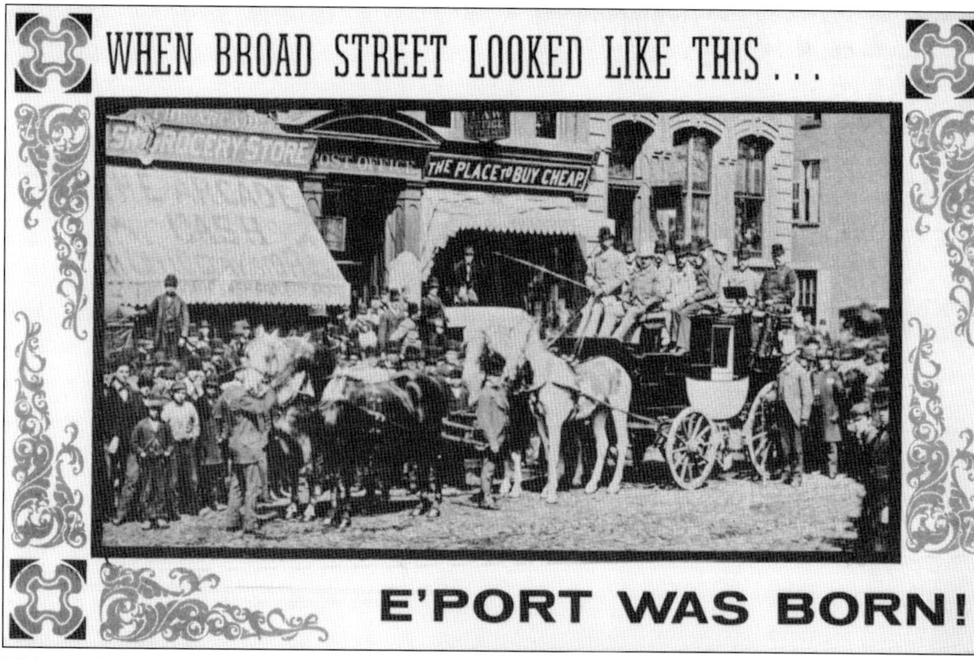

This 1980s reproduction postcard shows Broad Street in Elizabeth around 1889. Several different classes of people are visible in the photograph, including the rich on a stagecoach and the working-class members of Elizabeth's populace. They stand in front of the Arcade Grocery Store and the post office. The back of the card reads, "Elizabeth, N.J.–1889. Things certainly have changed since 1889 when The Elizabethport Banking Company was founded. But through all these long years, one thing has remained constant . . . E'Port's tradition of service to the community."

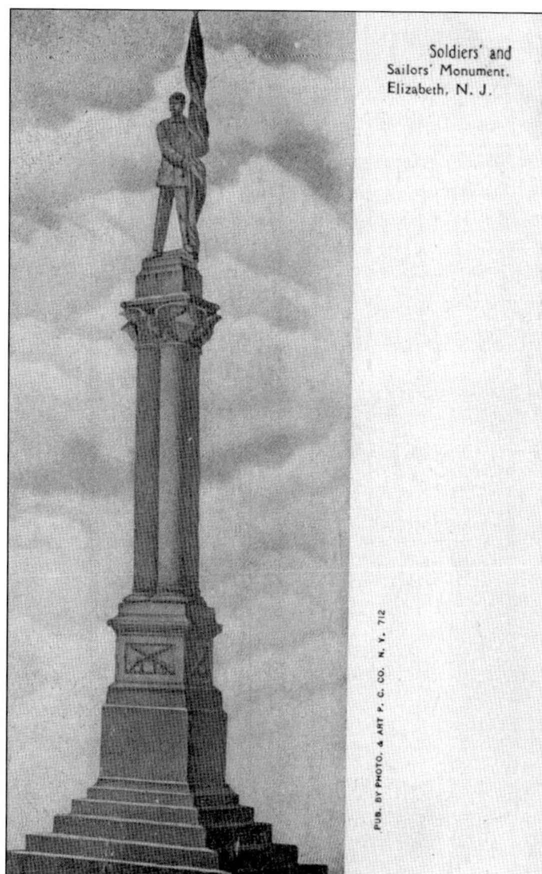

The Soldiers' and Sailors' Monument in Elizabeth is one of the war monuments that would be most recognizable to any resident of the city. As the title of the monument explains, the monument is a tribute to the soldiers and sailors who fought to preserve the Union from 1861 to 1865. The monument was erected by Elizabeth residents on the Fourth of July in 1906.

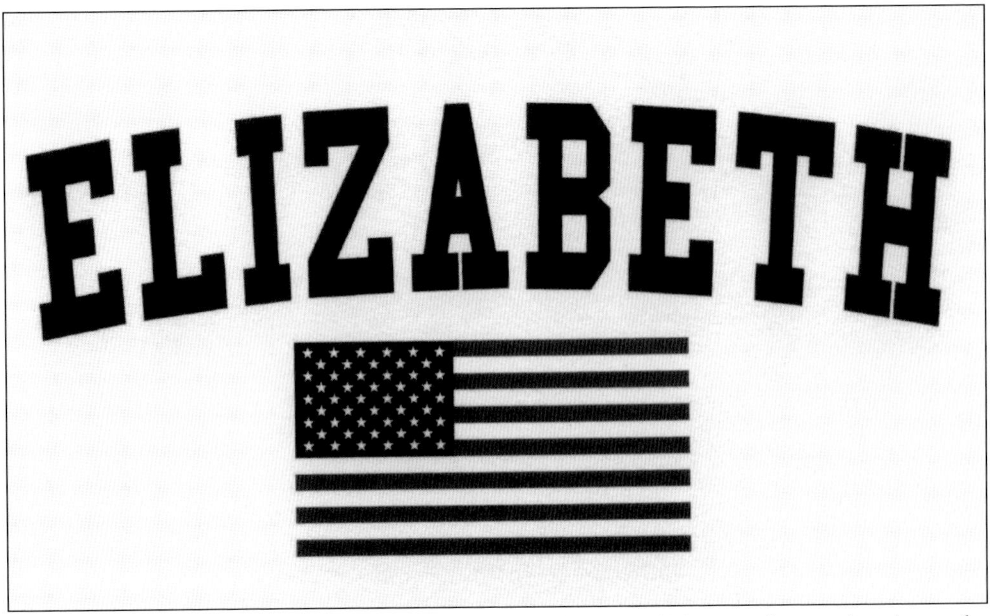

This card, produced in the aftermath of the September 11, 2001, terrorist attacks, shows the name of Elizabeth above an American flag. Such tributes were many and varied across the country, but for Elizabeth, the horror was personal. Of the 60 Union County residents that lost their lives in the attacks, 6 were daughters and sons of Elizabeth: Arcelia "Chela" Castillo, 49; Carlos S. De Costa, 41; Colleen L. Fraser, 51; Margaret S. Lewis, 49; Frankie Serrano, 23; and Anthony Tempesta, 38.

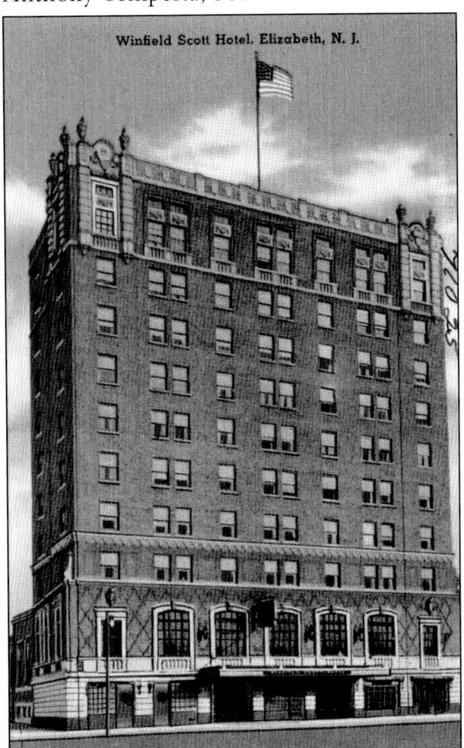

This postcard shows the historic Winfield Scott Hotel in Elizabeth. Today, the Winfield Scott name lives on in the way of the Winfield Scott Ballrooms, which reside at 323 Broad Street in Elizabeth. The facilities contain three ballrooms and are a popular local choice for events such as business meetings, weddings, and parties. They can be reached at 908-354-4424. The hotel's namesake, Winfield Scott, was a decorated war general during the War of 1812, the Mexican American War, and the Civil War in a career that spanned nearly 50 years. He was also the Whig party candidate for president in 1852. (Courtesy of the Boston Public Library Digital Commonwealth.)

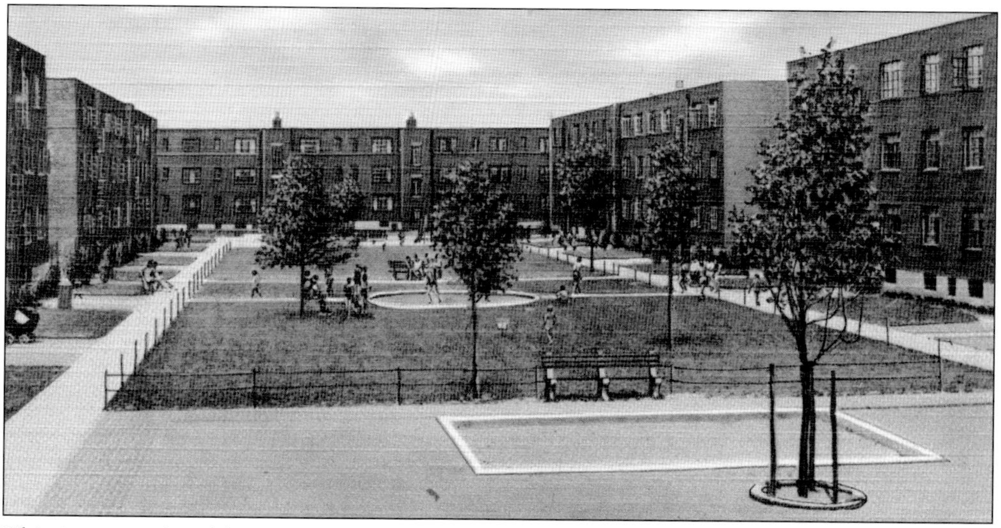

This image, printed between 1930 and 1945, shows Mravlag Manor, one of the first public housing projects to be built in Elizabeth. Located at 688 Maple Avenue in Elizabeth, the complex contains 415 single-family units. Managed by the City of Elizabeth Public Housing Authority, the development is massive, spanning 15 three-story buildings. The property has an extensive waiting list and can be reached at 908-965-2400. In April 2017, the Elizabeth YMCA partnered with the complex to bring low-income residents a mobile market, nutritional education, a children's play area, and access to the Community Paramedic Program. (Courtesy of the Boston Public Library Digital Commonwealth.)

This card, mailed in 1987, was commissioned by the United States Postal service to commemorate the 200th anniversary of New Jersey's statehood. The third state to adopt the constitution (Delaware beat New Jersey by 11 days, and Pennsylvania by six), New Jersey's William Paterson is given credit for the New Jersey Plan, which called for a single legislative body with equal representation and a president elected by Congress from its membership for a single-year term. Elements of the plan were later merged with the Virginia Plan to create the Constitution. This postcard was mailed on September 11, 1987, a mere 14 years before the September 11th terrorist attacks.

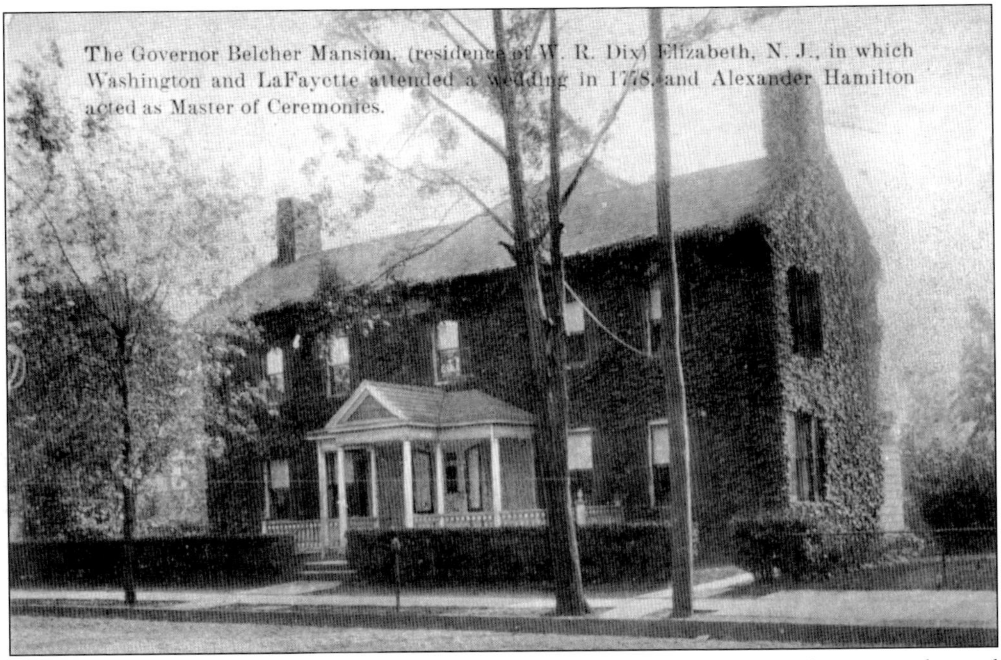

Shown on the front of this postcard is what is now known as the Belcher-Ogden House, located at the corner of East Jersey and Catherine Streets in Elizabeth. This house was constructed in 1742. In its early life, it served as the home of Jonathan Belcher, who had served as the prerevolutionary mayor in New Hampshire, Massachusetts, and New Jersey before his death in 1757. Later, the home was owned by local son Aaron Ogden, who served as the fifth governor of New Jersey. The house was added to the National Register of Historic Places in 1978.

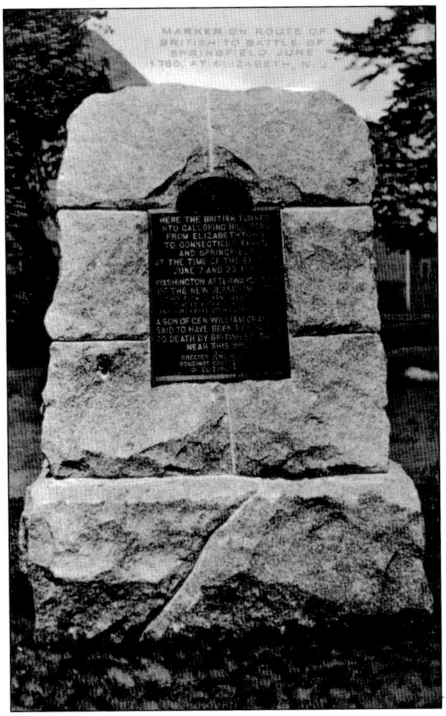

This marker pinpoints the route that the British army took through Elizabeth to the Battle of Springfield, which took place on June 23, 1980. The American rebels, led by Nathaniel Greene, were able to hold off a force four times the size of their own with the help of local militia reinforcements that arrived as the battle progressed on. This battle was a turning point in the war, as it forced forces under Gen. Henry Clinton to retreat and cede New Jersey to the Americans. Of particular note is the fierce bravery and talents of the New Jersey militia, which were noted by George Washington.

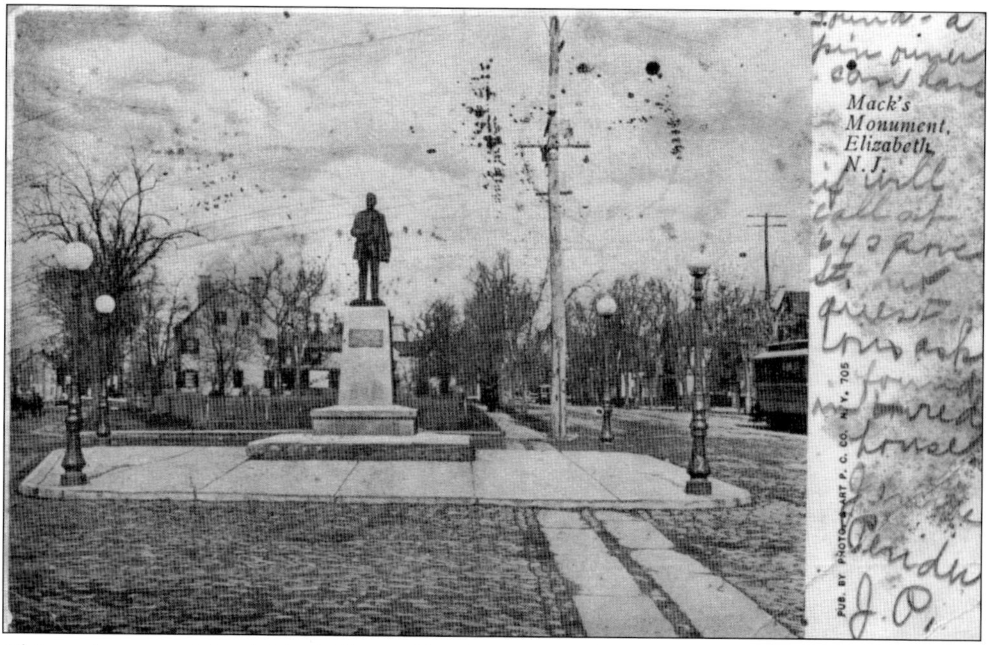

This card, sent on March 30, 1910, to Elisa A. Murray of 103 West Grand Street in Elizabeth, shows Mack's Monument. The statue of Mayor W.A.M. Mack, MD, located at Elizabeth Street and Third Street in Elizabeth, New Jersey, was sculpted by "Frank" and erected by the citizens of Elizabeth in 1904. Mayor Mack died on January 14, 1901. Mack, a doctor, served as Elizabeth's mayor until his death. The address mentioned above is now a part of the Joelle Manor Condominiums, serving the same purpose as it did over a hundred years ago.

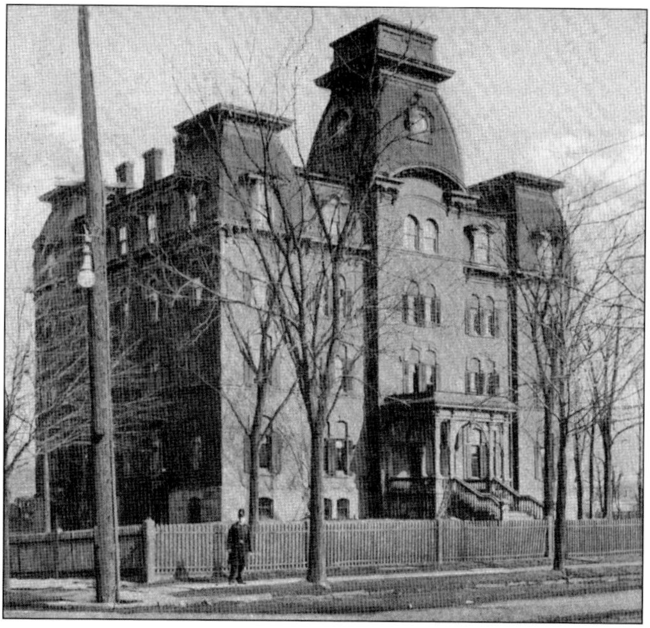

The Elizabeth Orphan Asylum was formed in 1858, which was good timing, given the circumstances of the Civil War, which would break out in 1861. It started out on Broad Street, sheltering 11 children, before moving to a Second Empire–style home on the corner of Murray and Cherry Streets, which is pictured here. The orphanage would later, in 1911, move to Salem Street. Apartment complexes stand where the home once stood. Named the J. William Farley Towers, they were constructed in 1963 and named after a member of the housing authority.

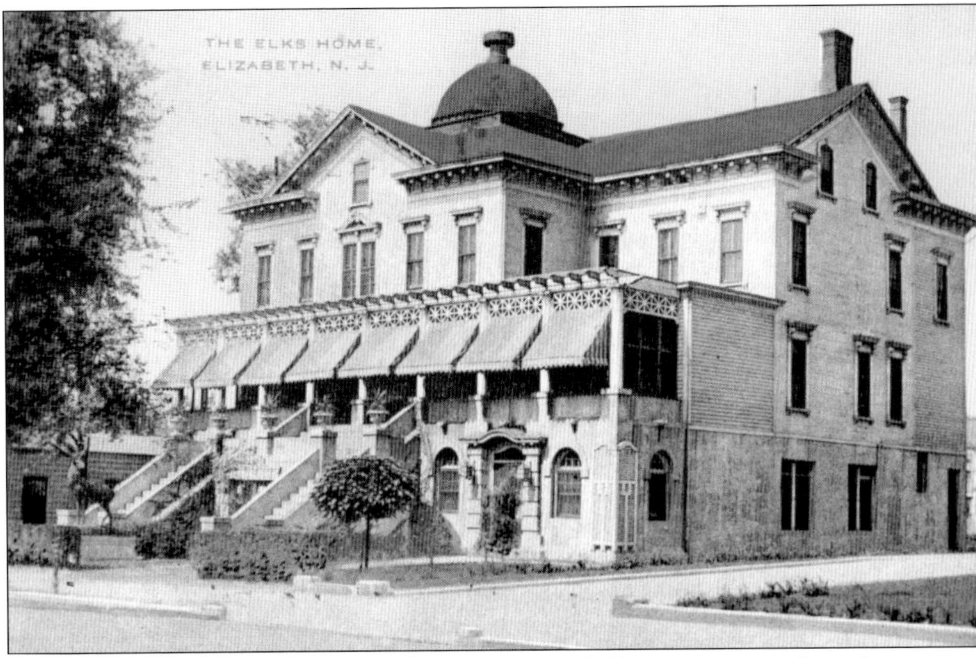

Built in 1911, the Elks Club was constructed on Westfield Avenue, near where the new post office was to be constructed. The building consisted of a one-story foundation with the historic two-story Williamson House set atop it. Later, an auditorium was added. It was in this auditorium that Vice Pres. Calvin Coolidge gave a speech in 1922, in celebration of the liquidation of Elizabeth's city debt, a burden that had existed since the Civil War. Less than a year later, Coolidge would rise to the office of the presidency with the untimely passing of Warren G. Harding. (Courtesy of the New Jersey Public Library.)

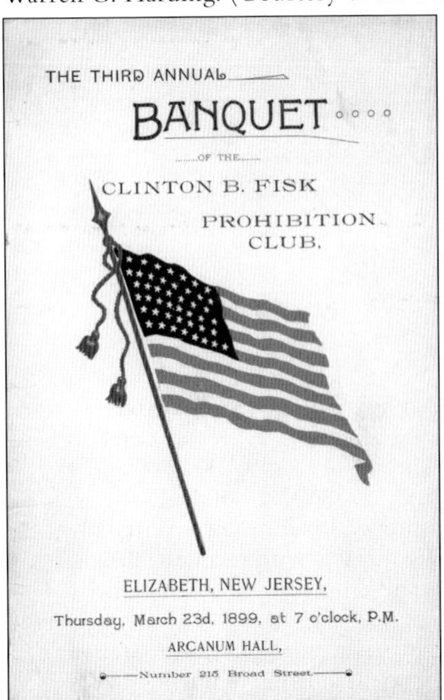

This card was mailed to invite Elizabethans to the third annual meeting of the Clinton B. Fisk Prohibition Society, on March 23, 1899. Fisk was a colonel in the Civil War, serving the Union cause in Missouri and Arkansas. After the war, he was appointed head of the Freedmen's Bureau for Kentucky and Tennessee by President Johnson. He would later endow $30,000 to start Fisk University, serve as the head of the Bureau of Indian Affairs, and run for president in the 1888 election, garnering nearly a quarter of a million votes. (Courtesy of the New York Public Library.)

This invitation, sent to one James Edgar Martine, was sent by the Union County Democratic Committee, one of the oldest branches of the Democratic Party in New Jersey. This event was held at Turn Hall, which was owned by Reinhard Schwarze. The hall was a German social club, located at what was once 725 High Street but is now known as New Point Road. The building still exists today, with a recent tenant being a clothing manufacturer. (Courtesy of the New York Public Library.)

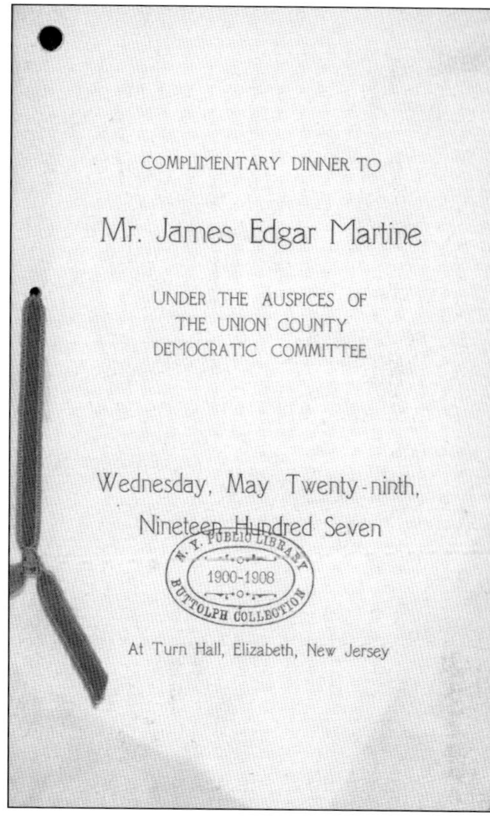

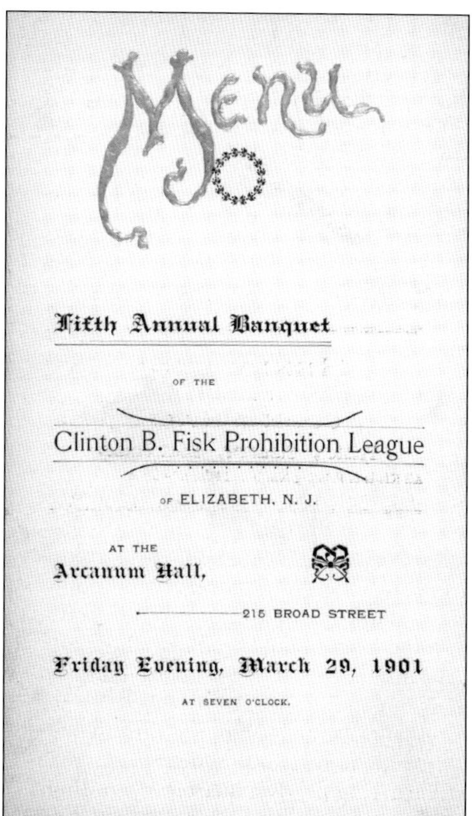

Although Clinton B. Fisk died in 1890, his Prohibition legacy remained strong, as evidenced by his being the namesake of the Prohibition club in Elizabeth, as noted by this 1901 mailed invitation. The hall where the event was located, Arcanum Hall, still stands today, although it has been converted to a mixed-used space, with retail establishments on the ground floor and office, warehouse, and residential space above. The owner of the 215 Broad Street address is now 1 Stop Deli and Grocery. (Courtesy of the New York Public Library.)

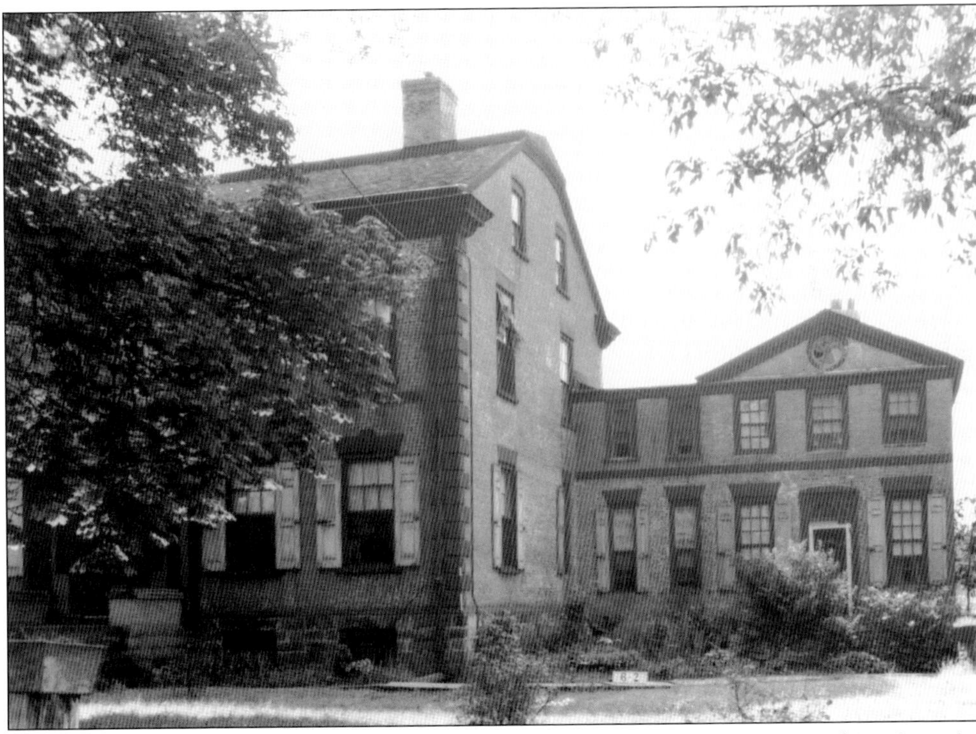

This view of the Cavalier Jouet Mansion provides a more detailed view of its Georgian architecture, with its iconic windows and bricks. The property also featured corner quoins, which were keystones above the main windows that are visible in this picture. Known as "the Old Chateau," it was located at 408 Rahway Avenue, near Grove Street. After Jouet lost the property, Julius A. Fay took told of the mansion in 1845, where he operated a boys' school. After Fay, it is known that the Schmeider family, who were involved in the masonry and construction business, owned the property until at least 1936. The building was remodeled as a commercial building in the 1960s, and it is operated today by the Elizabeth Nursing and Rehabilitation Center.

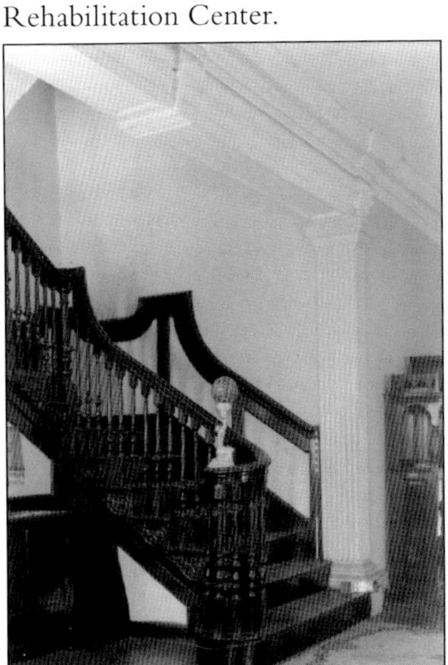

This picture shows the historic interior of the Cavalier Jouet Mansion. This wooden staircase displays the careful design put into the interior of the home when Cavalier Jouet built it around 1760. Note the continuation of the Ionic columns in the exterior of the house, transferred into the interior as a frame for several wall passages. The staircase also displays a small stone sculpture with a marble orb. These postcard images are the visual remains of this historic mansion that once stood in Elizabeth.

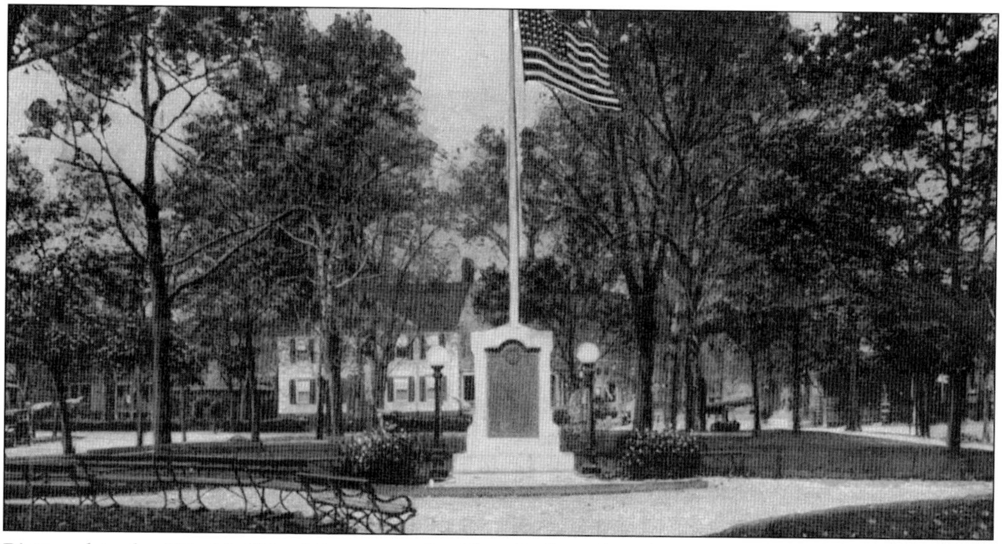

Pictured is the Worlds War Monument in City Hall Park, which is known today as Winfield Scott Park. The monument features a vertical granite slab with corner shoulders as well as a top gable resting on a stone slab base. There is a bronze plaque mounted to the front of the slab, and it has a raised frame and a central arch over the top of the monument. Upon a closer look, one can see the Elizabeth City seal at the top of the plaque. The plaque also contains an honor roll that lists the names of Elizabeth residents who served in World War I. Scott Park is a two-block strip featuring several war monuments, including one to the Vietnam War.

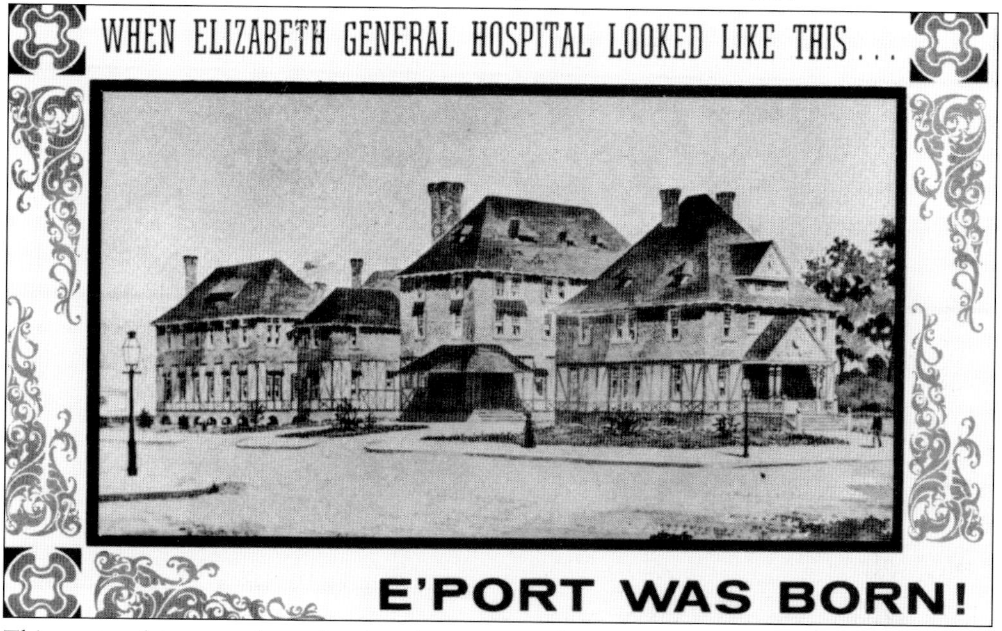

This postcard is part of a series that showcases antique pictures of Elizabeth and of Union County and promotes the Elizabeth Port, which is the part of the city that is closest to the Elizabeth seaport. In this particular postcard, the Elizabeth General Hospital is featured, and the text on the card reads, "When Elizabeth General Hospital Looked Like This . . . E'Port was Born!" "E'Port" is the nickname given to Elizabeth Port, and the text on the postcard is meant to emphasize the contrast between the Elizabeth of back then and the Elizabeth of now.

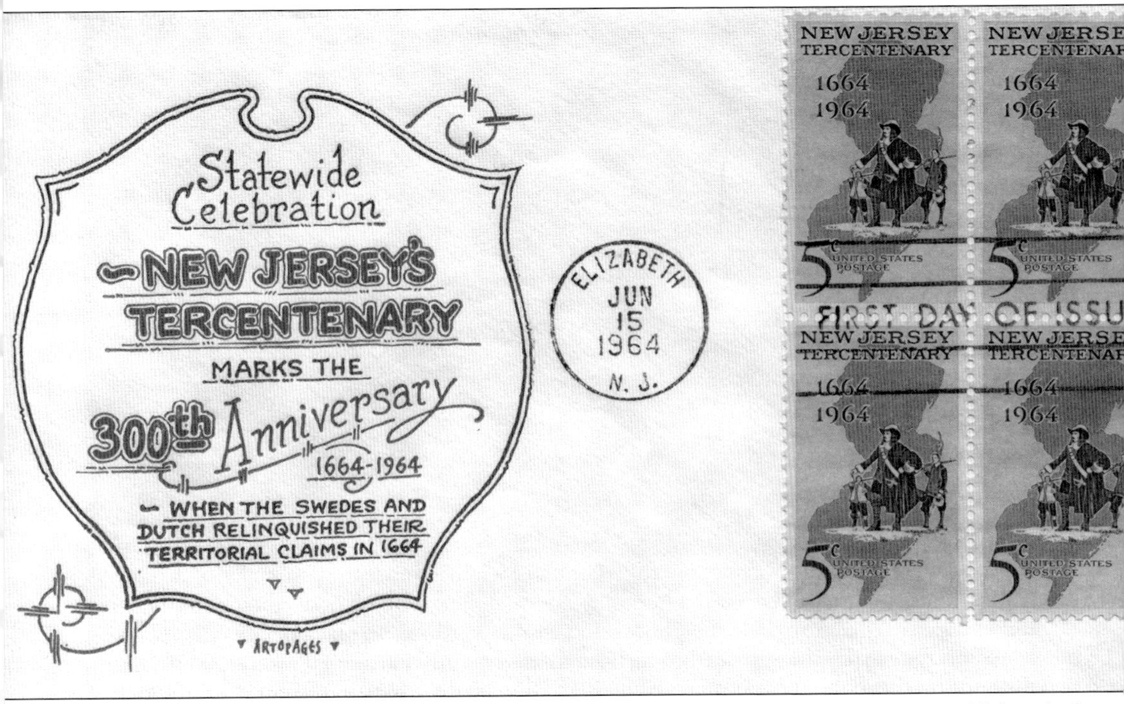

This envelope also commemorates the New Jersey Tercentenary. This important and historical event was part of a yearlong celebration to recognize the three centuries of New Jersey's existence as a state, and it was celebrated through a series of projects of civic importance. As we know, New Jersey was founded in 1664 as an English province, but its roots as a collective territory run much deeper, back when it was a part of the New Netherland and New Sweden colonies. The bottom of the envelope reads, "When the Swedes and Dutch relinquished their territorial claims in 1664."

Three

We Didn't Start the Fire
The People of Elizabeth

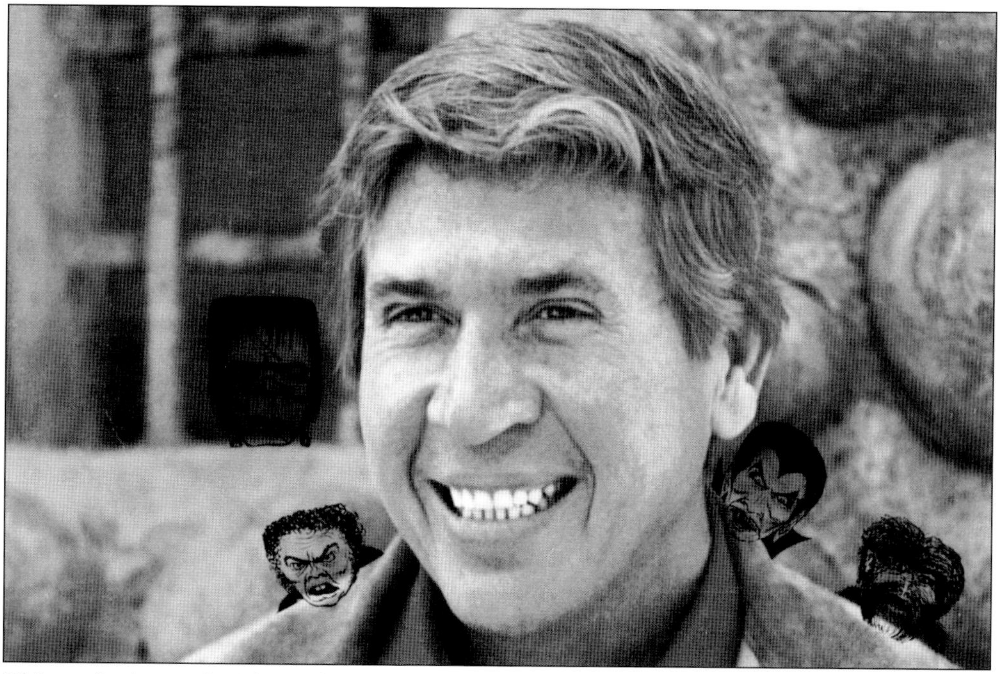

This card, plastered with Buck Owens's smiling face, was sent by the former Record Wagon store at 303 Morris Avenue in Elizabeth. Owens was one of the founders of country music's "Bakersfield sound," named in honor of the hometown of both he and Merle Haggard: Bakersfield, California. A whopping 21 of Owens's singles would top the Billboard country music charts, and Owens would later go on to host the popular television show *Hee Haw*. Record Wagon has closed, and in its place stands Jersey Ink, Tattoos and Piercings.

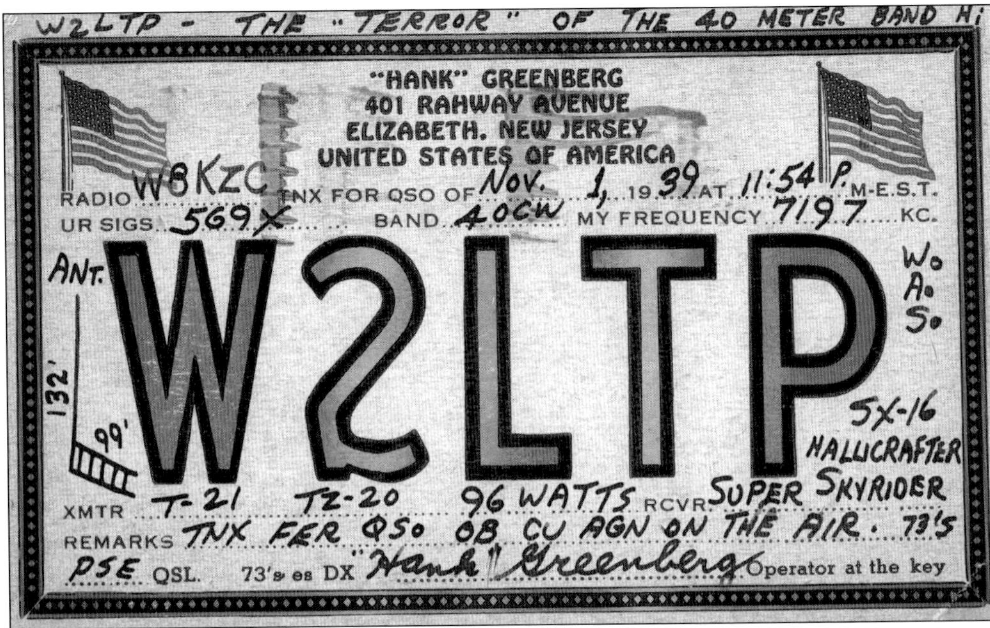

Postmarked on November 4, 1939, this preprinted postcard is just one of a great number of samples of cards that private-brand radio operators would send back and forth to one another. Elizabeth resident "Hank" Greenberg sent this one to Toledo, Ohio, operator M.E. Roller, presumably after a conversation had between the two on November 1 of that year. Greenberg details his rather expensive setup, as well as the height of his tower and technical details. While census records give no indication of Greenberg's fate, we do know his address at 401 Rahway Avenue is now a Walgreens pharmacy.

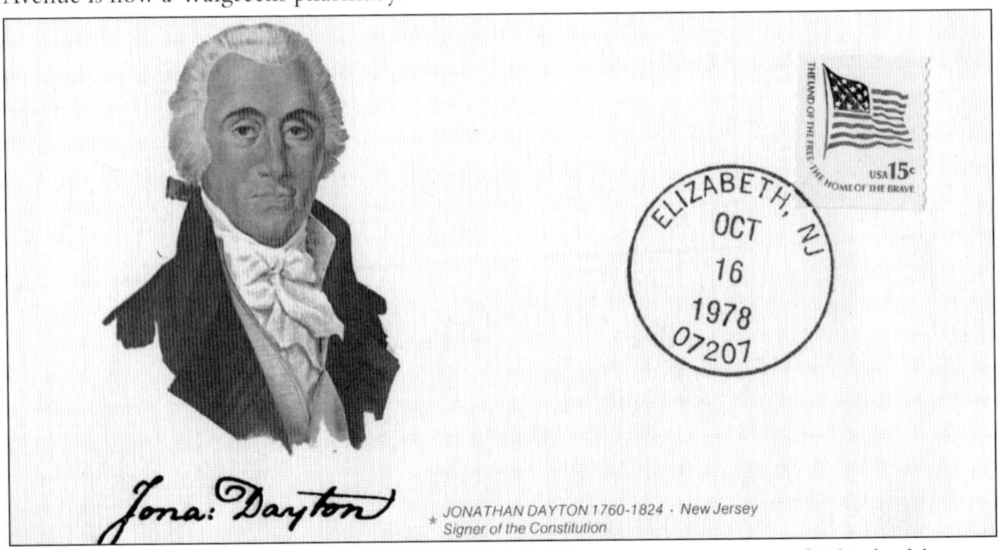

As one of the signers of the Constitution, Jonathan Dayton remains of Elizabeth's most famous sons. Born on October 26, 1760, Dayton was 16 years old when the War for American Independence began. Just 15 years old, he fought both under his father and George Washington for the duration of the war. He would see action at the Battles of Brandywine Creek and Germantown. He was a delegate to the Continental Congress and would go on to serve as a senator and Speaker of the House during his political career. He died in Elizabeth in 1824.

Known as "the Toy Bulldog," Mickey Walker is perhaps the most successful athlete to come out of Elizabeth. Born on July 13, 1901, Walker would, in his storied career, win world championships at both welterweight (1922) and middleweight (1926) before later challenging for the light-heavyweight title, a title he nearly won when he fought champion Mike McTigue to a no-decision in 1925. In 1931, he fought soon-to-be world heavyweight champion Jack Sharkey to a 15-round draw while weighing less than 150 pounds. Walker would die on April 19, 1981, leaving behind a career record of 131-25-5, with 61 knockouts.

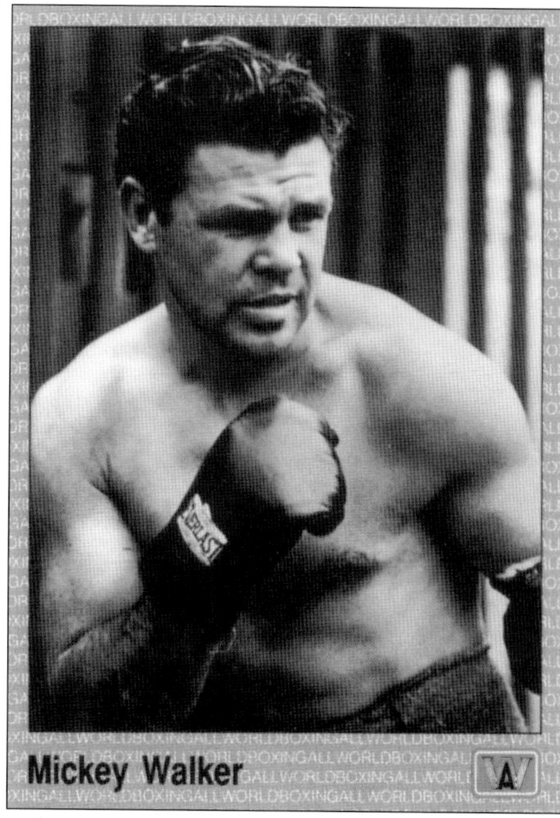

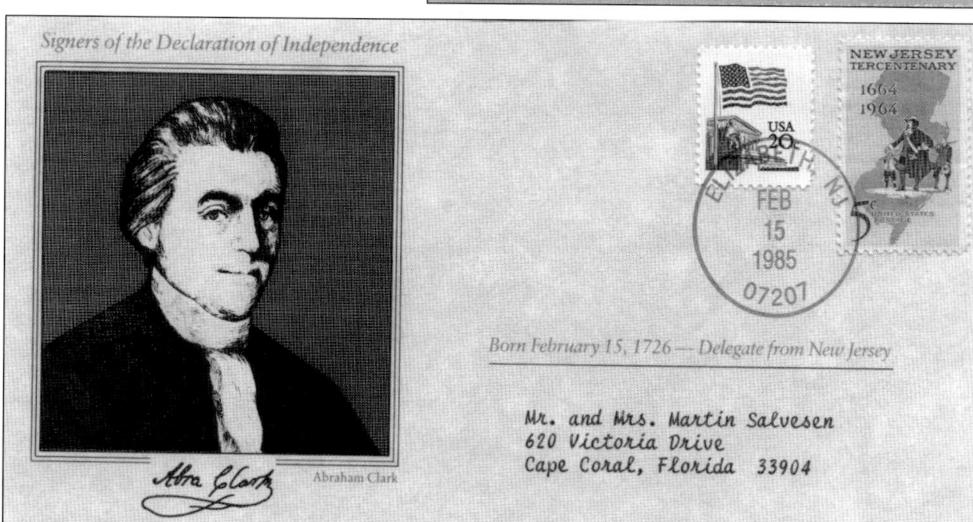

Abraham Clark was one of the New Jersey delegates that met in Philadelphia on July 3, 1776, to draft a declaration addressed at the colonies grievances against England's King George. The document that followed would change the course of world history upon its signing on July 4. Clark, the father of 10 children, would see two of his sons tortured by the British, ultimately refusing to turn his back on the American cause. After the war, Clark would serve as New Jersey's first congressman in the House of Representatives. Born in Elizabeth in 1726, he would die there in 1794.

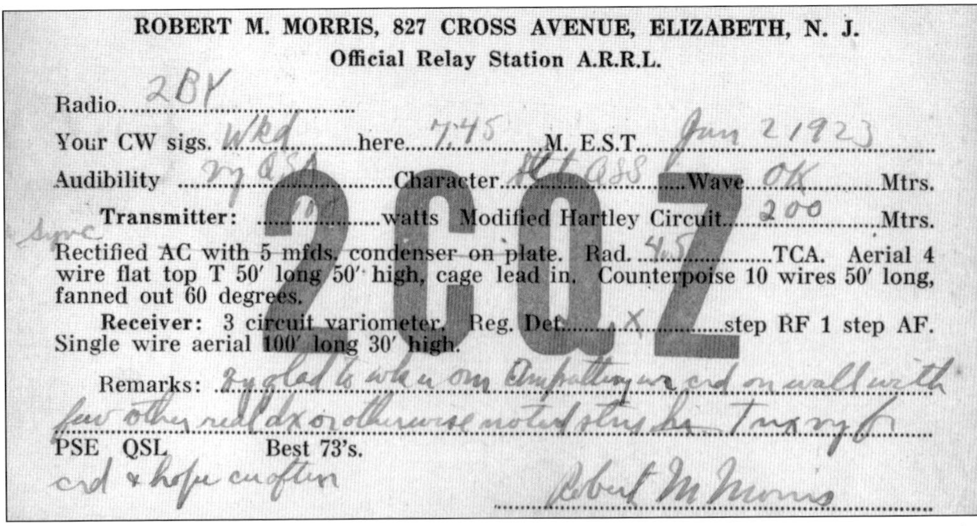

This card, mailed on June 2, 1923, was sent by amateur radio operator Robert M. Morris, who lived at 827 Cross Street in Elizabeth. According to census records from 1920, Morris lived, at age 25, with his mother in Elizabeth. Morris, a descendant of German parents, worked as an electrician, which would make his fascination with amateur radio a sensible one. His equipment was powerful enough to allow him to serve as a relay station. The house at 827 Cross Avenue still stands as a single-family residence.

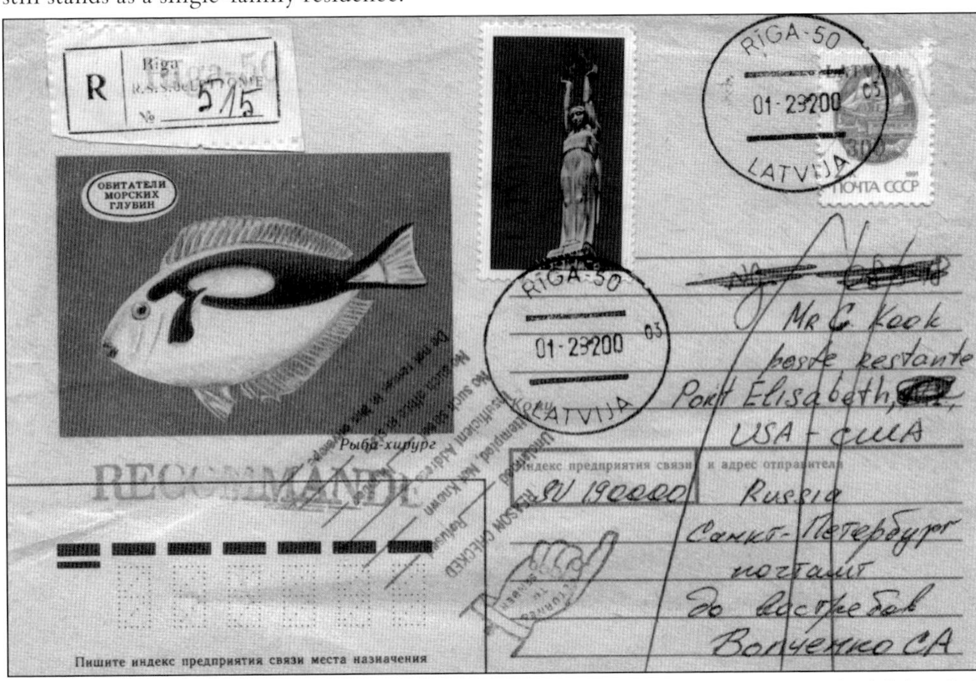

While this card never reached its destination of (Port) Elizabeth [spelled "Elisabeth" here], it nonetheless serves as a fascinating artifact in the history of the Cold War. Sent from Latvia, just before the breakup of the Soviet Union, the back of this card shows the familiar hammer and sickle imagery of the world's last great superpower. The New York City Latvian Community Association serves Connecticut and New Jersey as well, which, given Elizabeth's size, suggests a robust Latvian community in the area.

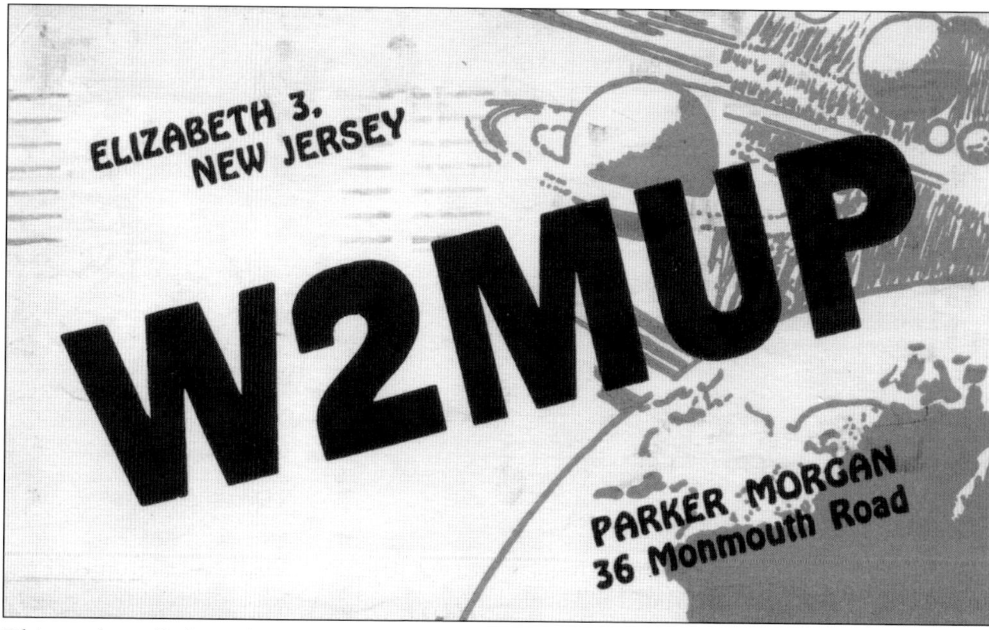

This card, mailed on August 1, 1953, shows the private station W2MUP, hosted by Parker Morgan of 36 Monmouth Road. Morgan, according to census records, had lived at the address since his childhood and, at age 46, was a lawyer in private practice. He was married to Jeanne. Shockingly, Morgan was a CIA operative for the early part of his practice, and much of his later work was with one L. Ron Hubbard, the founder of the Scientology cult. He was a graduate of Lafayette College and New Jersey Law School.

This card, mailed on June 15, 1964, memorializes the 300th anniversary of Philip Carteret's arrival at Elizabethtown. The envelope notes that this is the closest post office to the actual landing spot. Carteret served, from 1665–1673, as the first governor of New Jersey and, from 1674–1682, as the first governor of the colony of East Jersey. The town of Elizabeth is named after his cousin George's wife. It was Carteret who designated Elizabeth as the first capital of New Jersey, and he served the area until his death in December 1682.

Before the era of the postcard (much less the telegram, wire, fax, telephone, or e-mail), Americans would often communicate through letters, communicated through a series of postal offices. This letter, mailed by an unknown sender from Elizabeth on May 27, 1886, was sent to Kate Stoneman of Albany, New York. As the address on the letter alludes to, Stoneman was a schoolteacher, having taught at the State Normal School in Albany, the capital of neighboring New York. Stoneman would later achieve fame after she became the first female lawyer in the state of New York as well as the first to have graduated from Albany Law School.

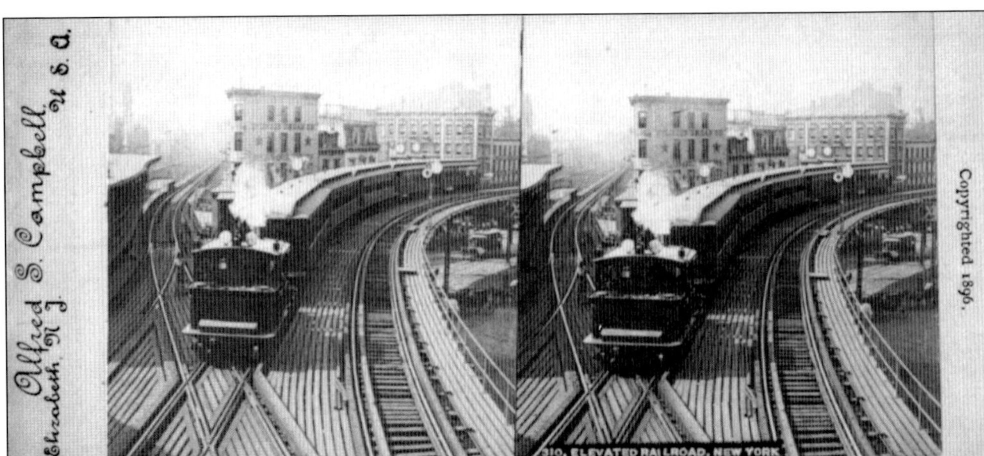

Although this card shows an elevated railroad in New York, the photographer is more important than the subject of this image. Alfred S. Campbell was an English transplant whose art photography for cards of all stripes was much desired. After a failed partnership in New York dissolved, Campbell relocated to Elizabeth, setting up shop a few scant miles south of New York. Campbell used his business in Elizabeth to gain a monopoly on printing cigarette cards, printing for every brand in America at some point. Campbell would remain one of the most accomplished printers of art photography until his death in 1912.

This card features George Washington, the first president of the United States. Washington's roots in Elizabeth are deep; for example, Elizabeth served as one of Washington's base camps during the Revolutionary War. Elizabeth's location helped Washington track British equipment movement up and down the Hudson River. After marching his troops through Elizabeth in 1776, Washington would return in 1778 to attend Elisha Boudinot's wedding. He would return again in 1789, on his inauguration tour, to have lunch with Boudinot.

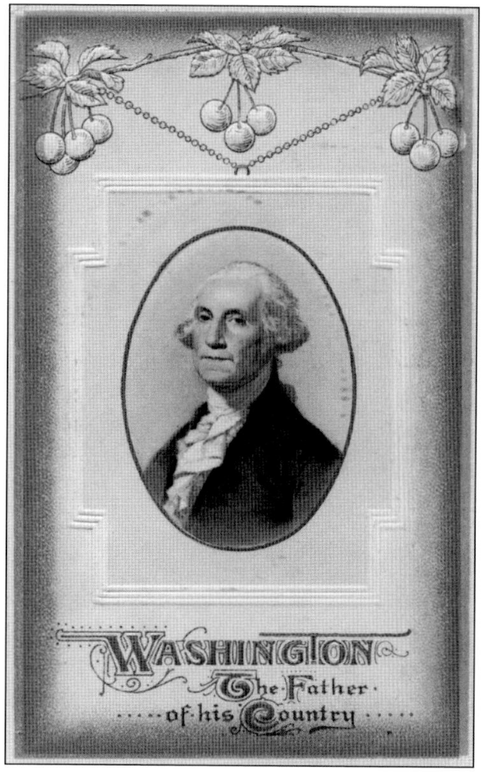

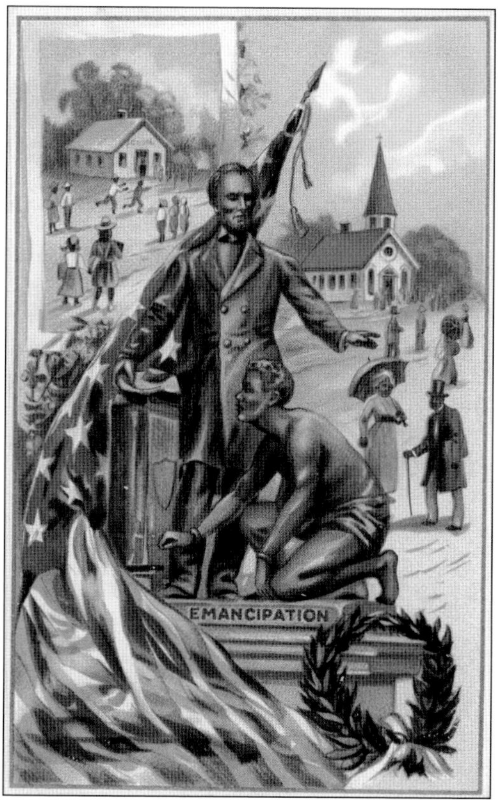

Shown on the front of this card is Abraham Lincoln, the 16th president of the United States. Lincoln made many visits to New Jersey, including a stop in Elizabeth. In 1861, on his way to Washington after his election, he stopped in Elizabeth to give some unrecorded, impromptu remarks to about 15,000 bystanders. He was introduced from the train by J.J. Chetwood. Today, the Abraham Lincoln Elementary School stands in Elizabeth as a monument to the many great acts and deeds performed by Lincoln as he served as president.

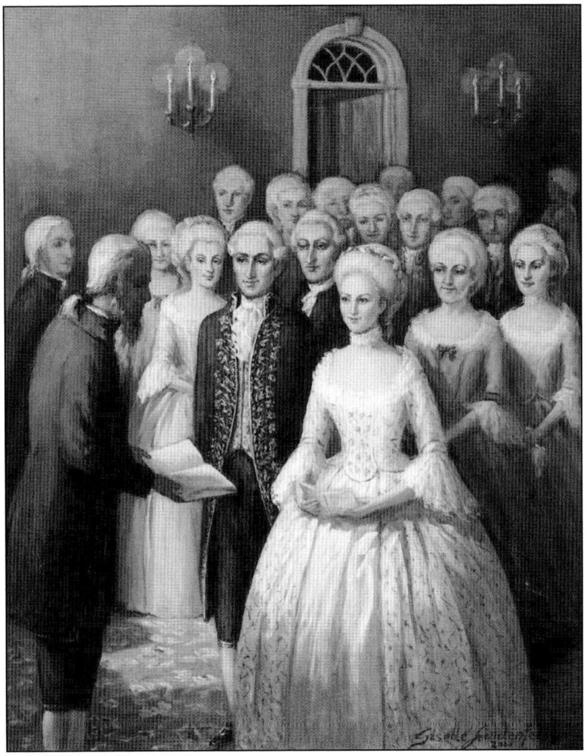

Shown here is the wedding of Elizabethan Sarah Livingston, the daughter of New Jersey governor William Livingston (who died and is buried in Elizabeth), and John Jay, who served as the first chief justice of the Supreme Court, the second governor of New York, and the first secretary of state. Jay was a signatory of the Treaty of Paris that ended the Revolutionary War. This postcard, a replica of the oil painting produced in 2000 by Giselle Lindenfeld, depicts the 1774 wedding between Jay and Livingston.

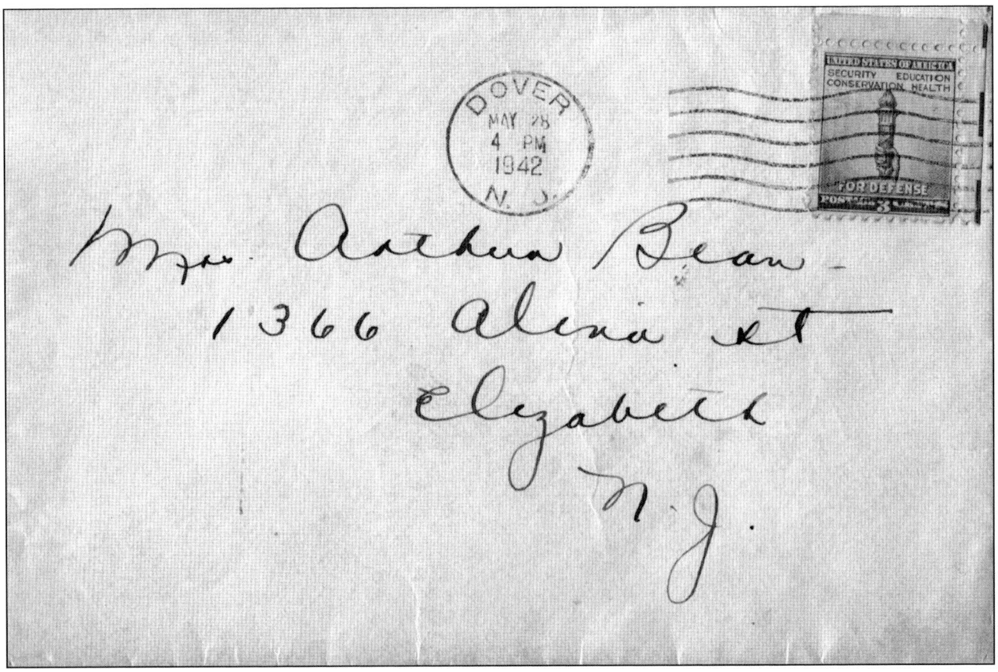

This cover is addressed to Arthur Bean of 1366 Alina Street in Elizabeth. Bean, according to the 1930 US Census, lived in Elizabeth with his wife, Lillian, their daughter Gloria, his mother-in-law, Josephine Middlesteadt, and her son Ernest, who would have been Gloria's brother and Arthur's brother in law. The house at 1366 Alina Street still stands as a duplex.

This cover is addressed to a J(osephine) Middlesteadt of 1366 Alina Street in Elizabeth. Middlesteadt, according to the 1930 US Census, lived in Elizabeth with her daughter Lillian, her husband Arthur, their daughter Gloria, and her son Ernest, who would have been Gloria's brother and Arthur's brother-in-law. The house at 1366 Alina Street still stands as a duplex.

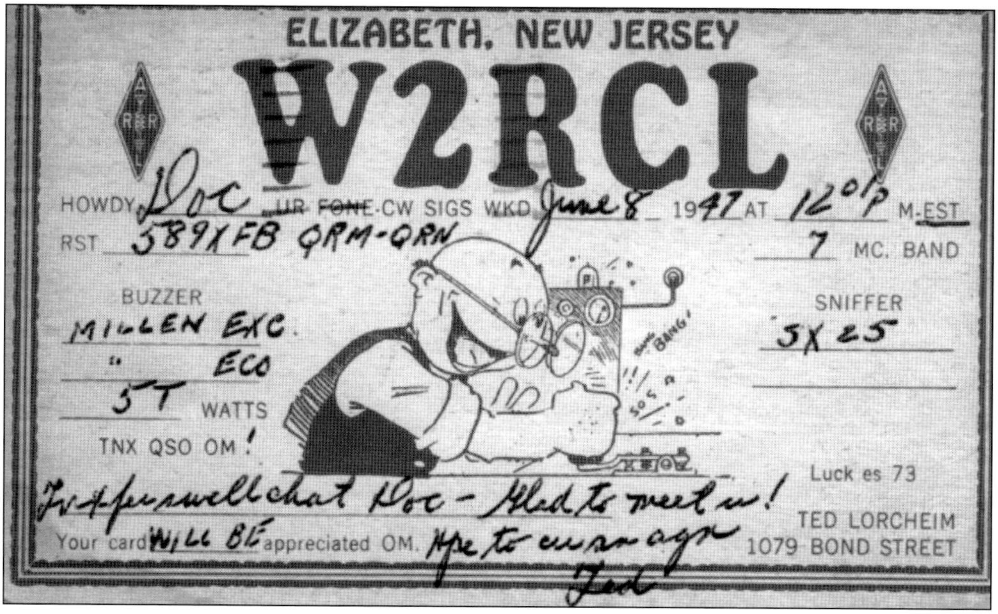

This card was sent in on June 8, 1947, by one Theodore "Ted" Lorcheim, who, according to his son's 2006 obituary, had a 19-year-old son, Wilbur, when this card was sent in 1947. Wilbur would marry Mildred and die in 2006. This card was sent from 1079 Bond Street in Elizabeth. This card was sent to G.E. Meeker, who operated amateur radio station WZADV in Elmira, Kentucky. All that remains of 1079 Bond Street is an empty lot with a garage.

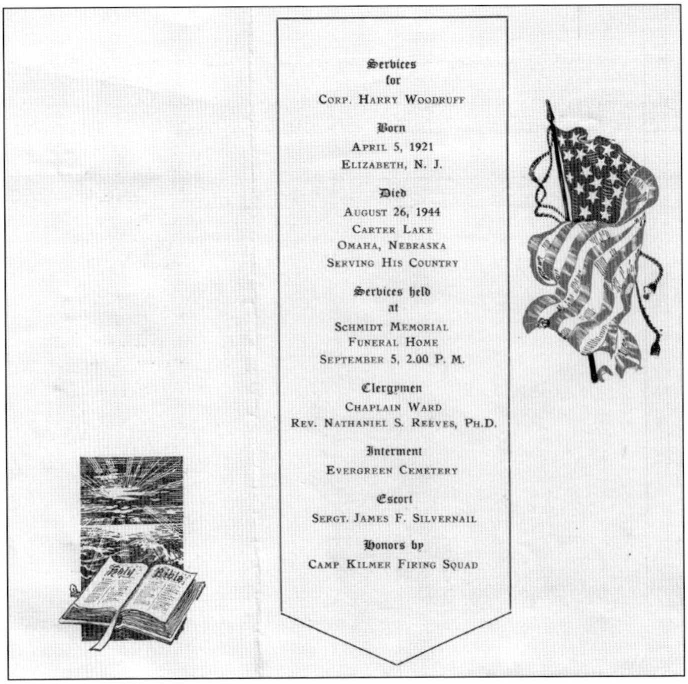

Services
for
Corp. Harry Woodruff

Born
April 5, 1921
Elizabeth, N. J.

Died
August 26, 1944
Carter Lake
Omaha, Nebraska
Serving His Country

Services held
at
Schmidt Memorial
Funeral Home
September 5, 2.00 P. M.

Clergymen
Chaplain Ward
Rev. Nathaniel S. Reeves, Ph.D.

Interment
Evergreen Cemetery

Escort
Sergt. James F. Silvernail

Honors by
Camp Kilmer Firing Squad

This card announces funeral services for Cpl. Harry Woodruff, one of many soldiers who died in bizarre accidents during military drills during exercises in Omaha, Nebraska, in 1944. There was a great deal of new equipment being tested for use in the war, sometimes with catastrophic results. The 1930 Census tells us that Harry, then age nine, lived with his parents, Clarence and Dorothy, and his siblings Frank and Dorothy in a house on Van Buren Street. Woodruff is memorialized in the National Archives for his service to his country.

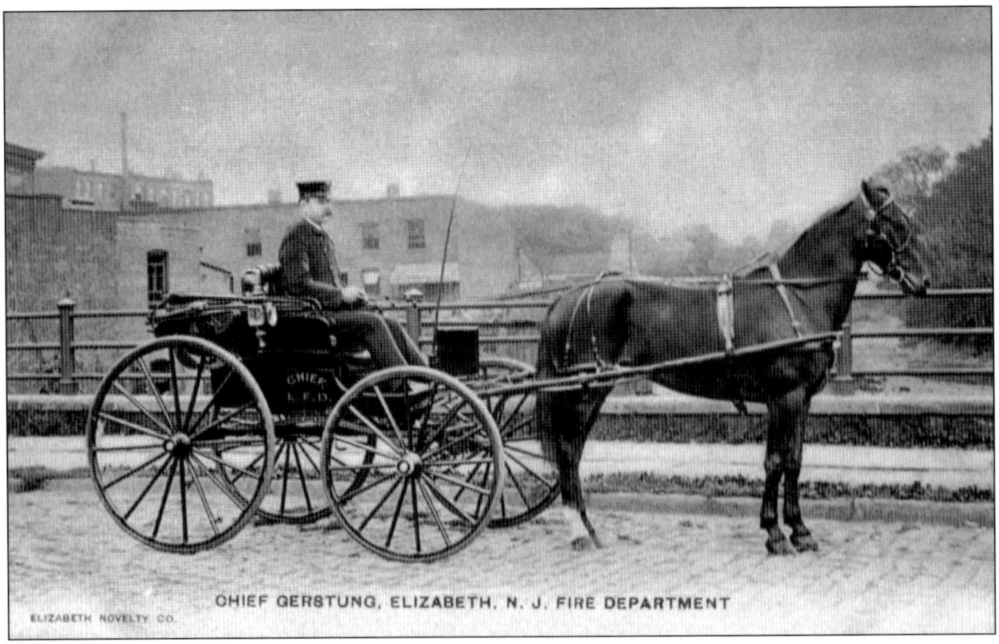

Shown here is fire chief August Gerstung, a later chief of Elizabeth's first fire company, which was established at 24 Broad Street back in 1789. The fire company was renamed the Protection Engine Company P, No. 1 in 1837. Gerstung would become chief of the brigade in 1902, when the fire brigade went from volunteer firemen to paid ones, as the demands of a much-larger city necessitated a full-time fire force. Gerstung would serve until 1931, leading the shift from a horse-powered brigade to an engine-driven one.

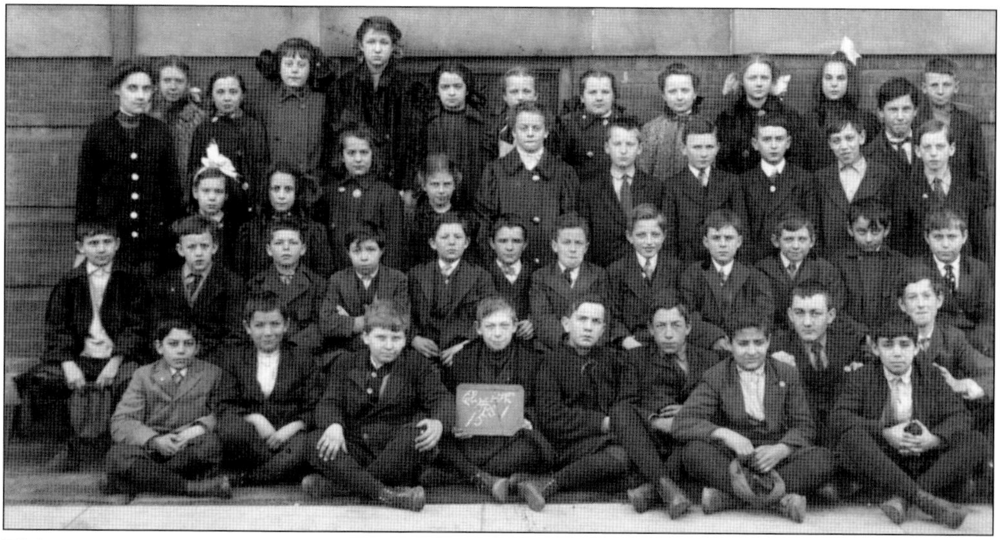

This unique postcard shows the fifth-grade class of what was then known as Public School No 1. The back of the card has handwritten text that reads, "Room 15, Fifth Grade, Public School No. 1. George Foy. 11 years old. February 1, 1911." Sadly, the card does not show us which student is George Foy. Public School No. 1, however, would go on to become George Washington Elementary School. The school was built on Third Street in 1855 and was replaced with a larger building in 1906. The final version was built on the corner of Third Street and Broadway in 1971.

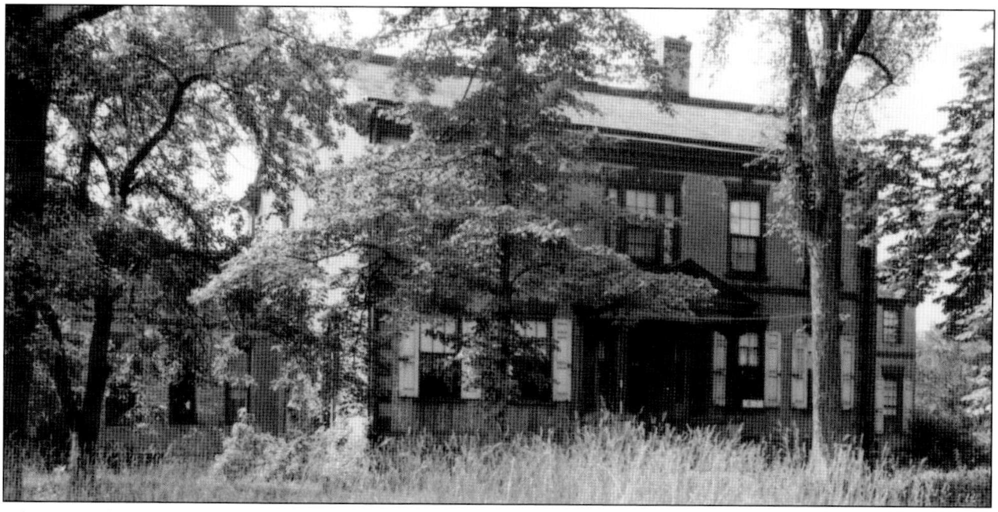

The Cavalier Jouet Mansion, built in 1760, is the only remnant of a fully developed Georgian-style mansion in New Jersey with a central unit, symmetrical flanking wings, and Ionic columns at the entranceway. The property was 18 acres. This type of scheme was more commonly used in houses in Maryland and Virginia. The mansion is named after its owner, Cavalier Jouet, who was arrested and his property confiscated in 1778 due to his unpatriotic sympathies and known affiliation with the Tory party. Jouet was born in the West Indies in 1734, and he was a vestryman at St. John's Church and one of the wealthiest men in Elizabethtown. The mansion was consequently put up for auction in 1779 by the Commissioners of Forfeited Estates of Essex County. This postcard shows the facade of the house and provides a good view of its symmetrical flanking wings.

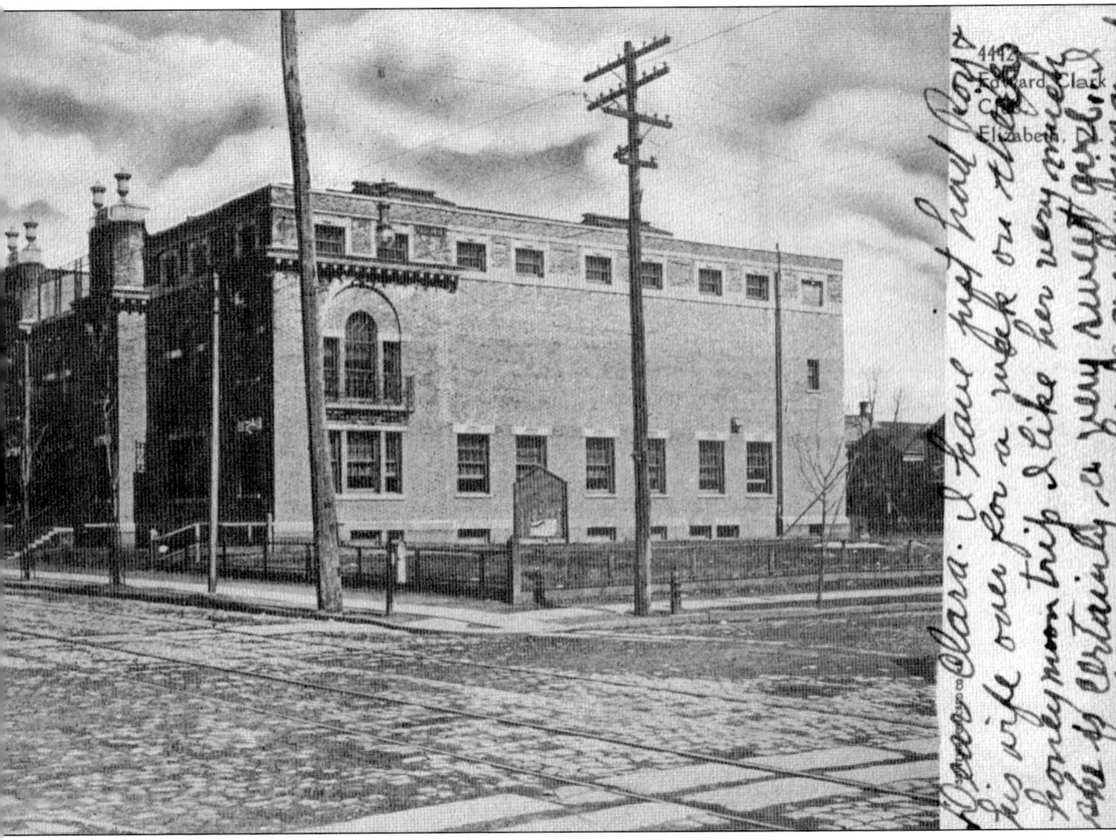

This postcard version of the Edward Clark Club shows the same image from two of the other postcards featuring the location. The text on this postcard reads, "Dear Clara, I have just had Roy and his wife over for a week on their honeymoon trip I like her very much she is certainly a very sweet girl. I am well as usual. We are having grand fall weather out here. Love, J.H. Rem." Often, many of these postcards were meant to highlight important parts of the city of Elizabeth, but it is important to remember that the primary purpose for these postcards was to keep in touch with loved ones.

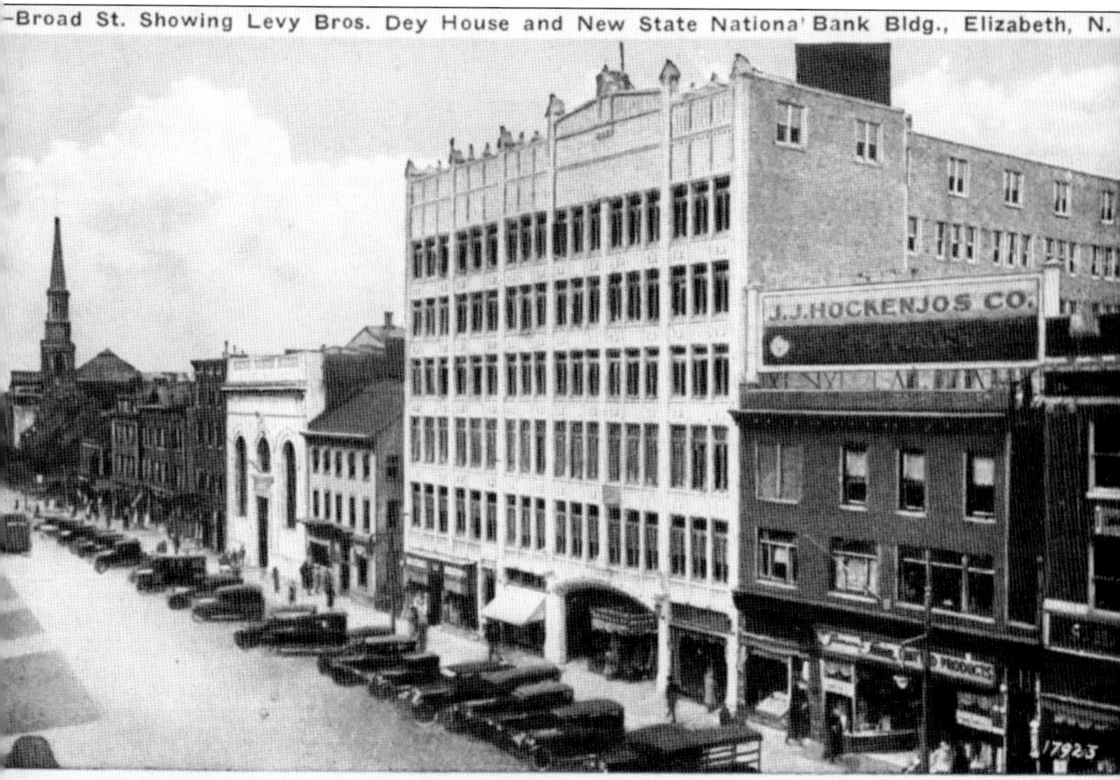

The Levy Brothers was a department store in Elizabeth. The chairman of this department store was a man by the name of Milton Levy, an incredibly accomplished Elizabeth resident. His obituary in the *New York Times* described him as the "chairman of the Levy Department Store and a leader in Jewish community activities." Levy died on November 11, 1970, at the age of 66, in Beth Israel Medical Center in New York after a short illness. He was a graduate of New York University and of the University of Pennsylvania, and he enlisted in the Army in 1942 and became a major in 1944. Levy was also the first president of the Jewish Educational Center in Elizabeth and a director for 25 years at the Elizabeth General Hospital. His department store business started as a women's clothing store but grew in the 1920s into a full-line department store.

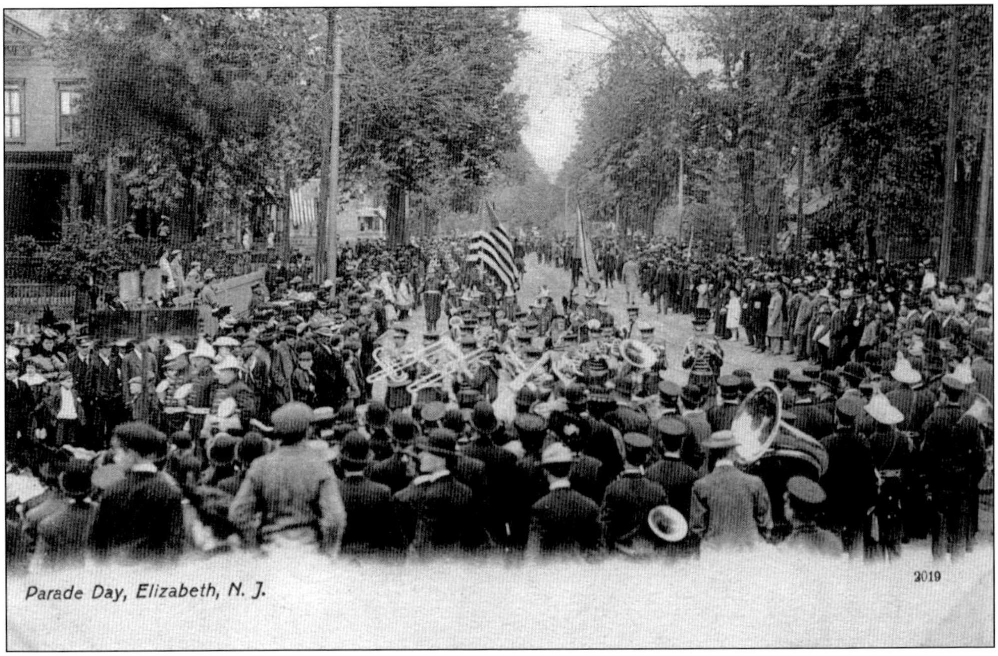

This postcard shows a parade that is taking place on what appear to be residential streets in Elizabeth. There is a marching band playing music as they walk down the street. Parades were a typical way for new and longtime neighborhood and city residents to celebrate important events. The event for this parade is unknown. The tradition of Elizabeth parades, however, has remained; Elizabeth today is popular for its annual Portuguese Day Parade, Cuban Day Parade, and Colombian Day Parade.

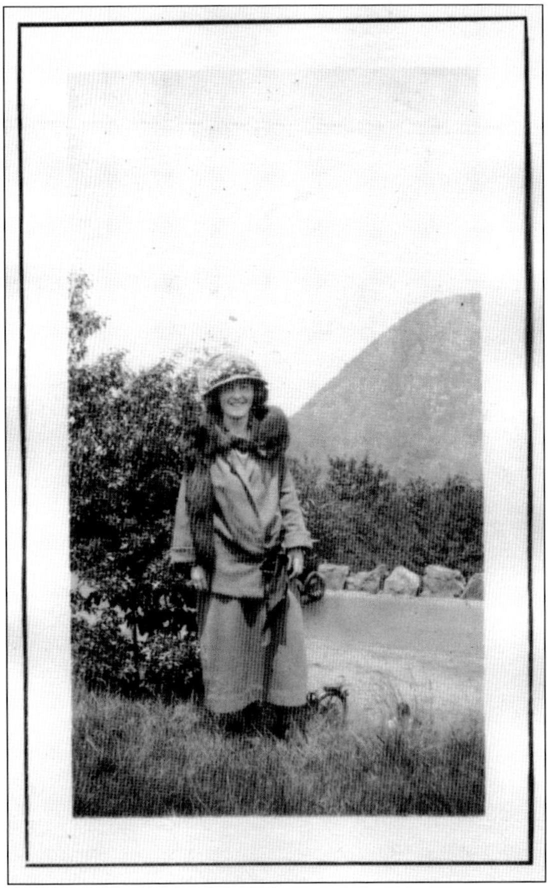

The woman in this photograph wears a mink shawl. The picture is postmarked Elizabeth and was sent in 1921. The American mink, which is larger than its European counterpart, has been used in clothing since the settlement of Jamestown nearly 400 years ago. As minks would fight to the death, even in trapped situations, the inhumane nature of the trade was brought to life, and the trapping of wild minks was abandoned for the farming of stock for their use in clothing. The animal is now bred to be a pet.

Four

Corridor of Time
Places and Spaces of Elizabeth

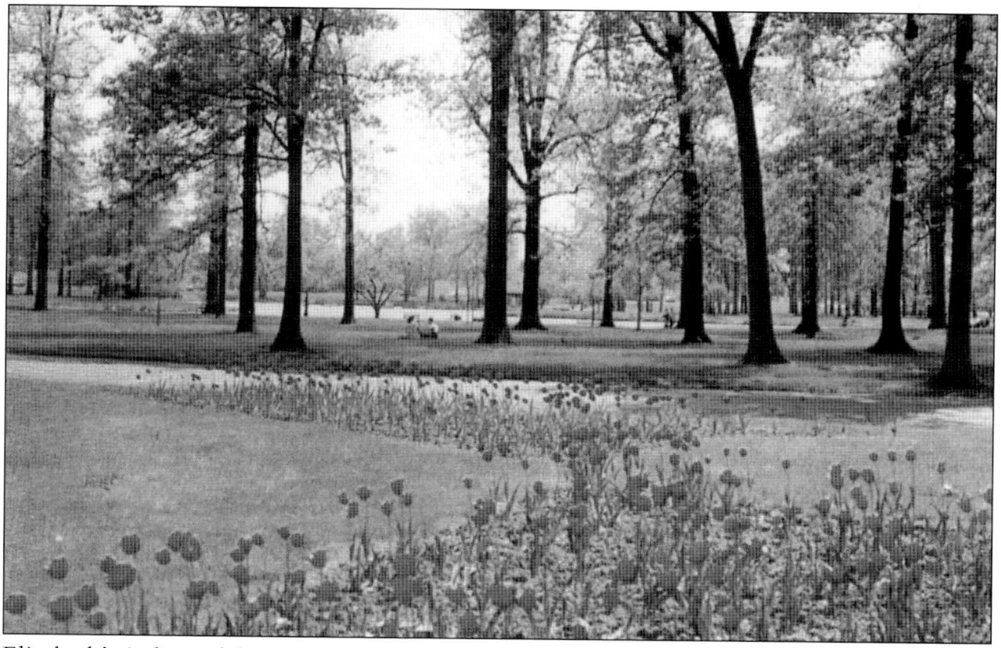

Elizabeth's industrial history means that public parks were essential for the community as places of leisure and recreation. Warinanco Park remains Elizabeth's largest public park, known and recognized for its plentiful trees, scenic lake, and walkways. The view from this postcard depicts Warinanco's small but beautiful flower garden. The scene shows the garden decorated with tulips, though the gardeners change the flowers year-round and surprise locals and visitors alike with their arrangements of flowers. In the distance, one can see the park's lake, which is a central point of the park.

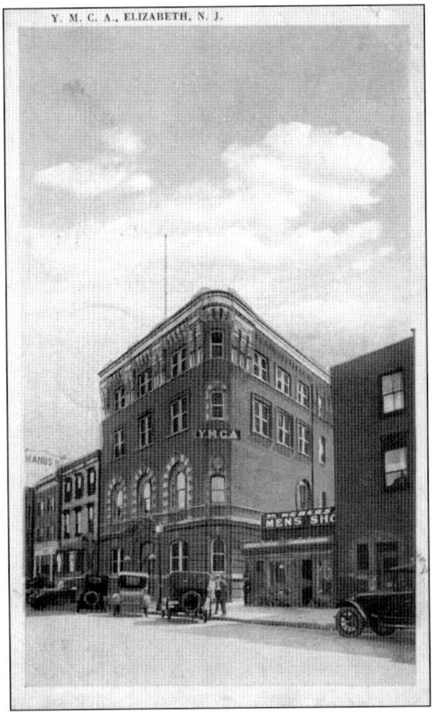

The Young Men's Christian Association has been around in Elizabeth for many years and remains an important community center up to the current day. The building's facade as it is depicted in this postcard has changed dramatically as the building expanded and renovated its exterior, but it still serves the same function as a place of recreation and community building for young boys and girls and young men and women living in the city of Elizabeth.

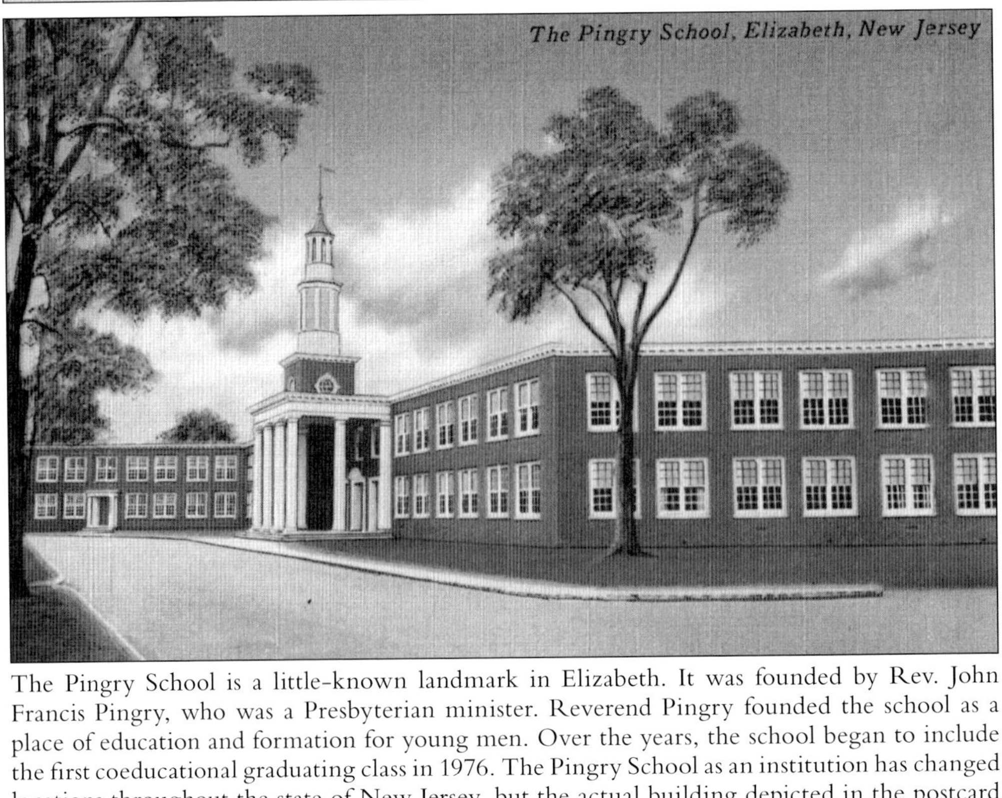

The Pingry School is a little-known landmark in Elizabeth. It was founded by Rev. John Francis Pingry, who was a Presbyterian minister. Reverend Pingry founded the school as a place of education and formation for young men. Over the years, the school began to include the first coeducational graduating class in 1976. The Pingry School as an institution has changed locations throughout the state of New Jersey, but the actual building depicted in the postcard still exists today as a part of Kean University.

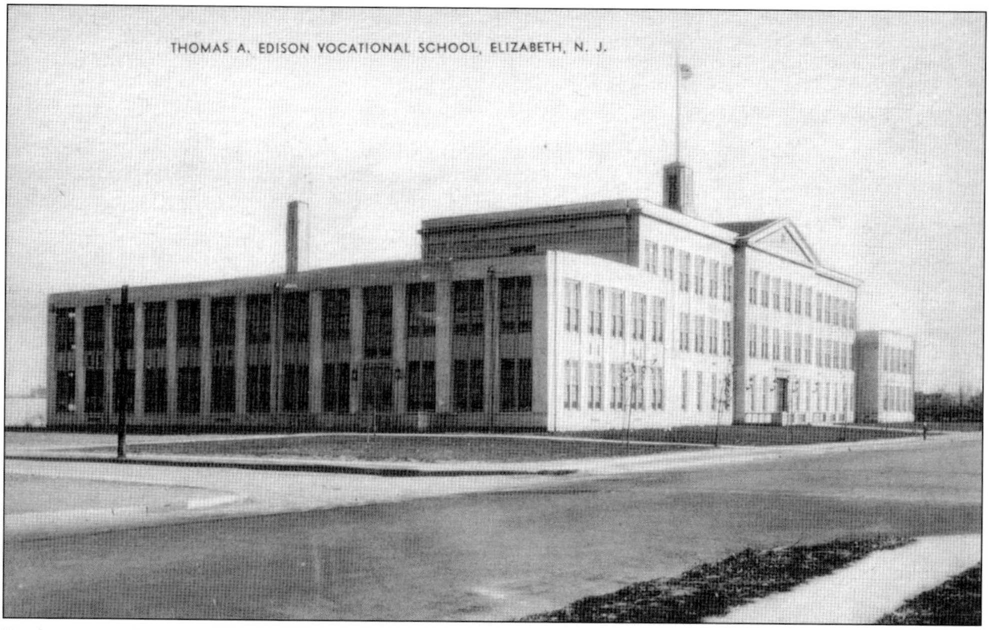

"Edison High School," as it is called by locals, is one of the high schools in the Elizabeth Public Schools system. The school is named after the famous inventor, whose important inventions were developed and created in the state of New Jersey in a nearby town—today called Edison. From its beginnings, up to the present day, the school is focused on vocational and technical education for its students. The school is also home to Williams Field, which is the city's main football and track field.

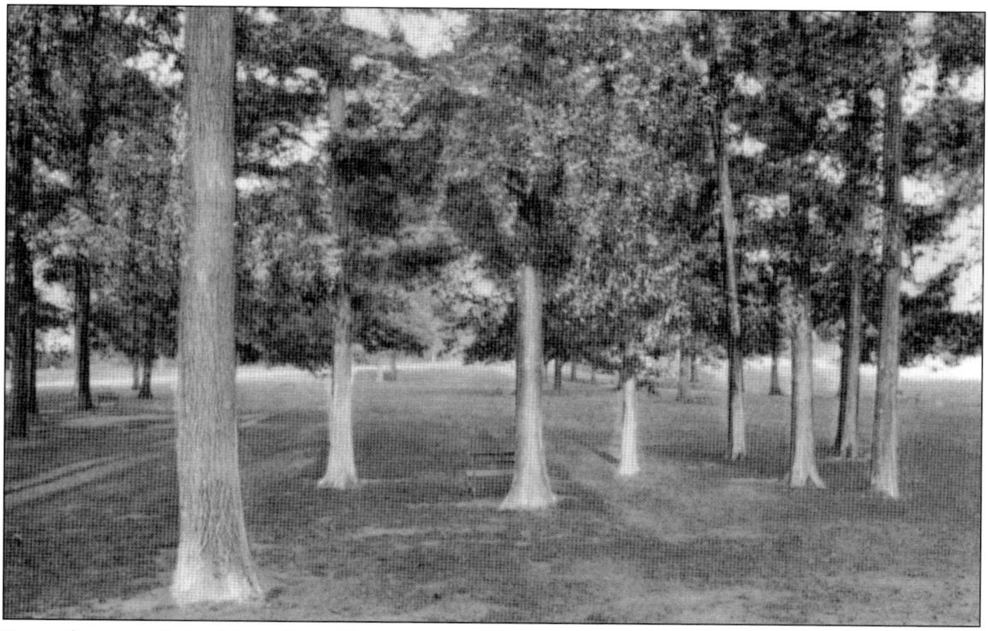

Several postcards in this series offer variations of locations in Warinanco Park. The fact that so many postcards existed that were meant to highlight the city's park demonstrates how important the place was for locals and tourists alike. This postcard, titled "Picnic Grove," shows a tree-lined part of the park that, as the name implies, was popular as a picnic destination.

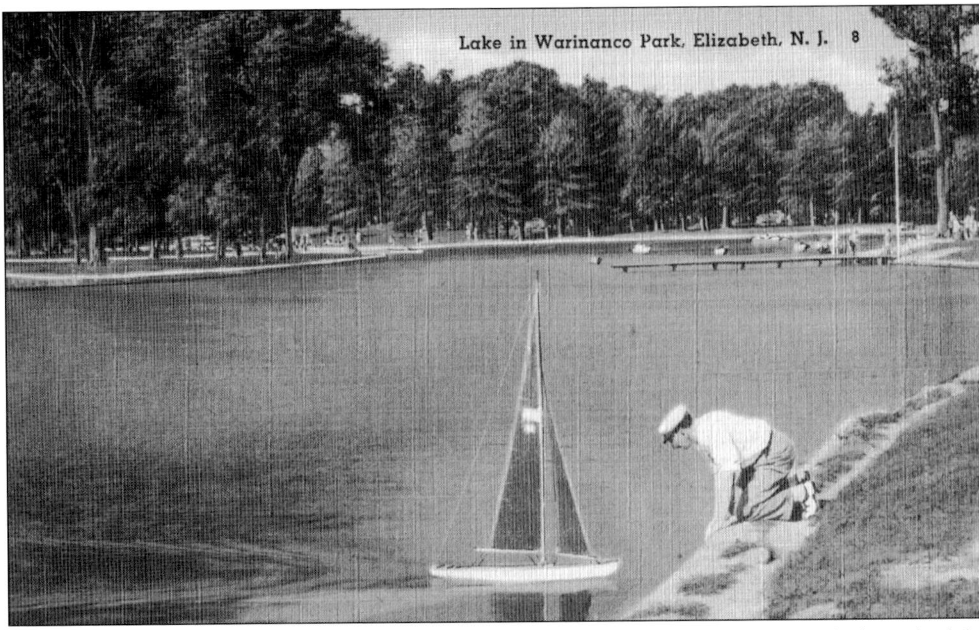

The lake in Warinanco is one of the most popular locations within the park. Back then, the lake was used for small recreational purposes like toy-boat sailing, as this postcard shows. Today, the lake still serves a similar purpose but also installed paddleboats. It is a medium-sized lake with a lovely trail that people strolling the park can easily circumvent in order to observe all the various vantage points that the lake offers.

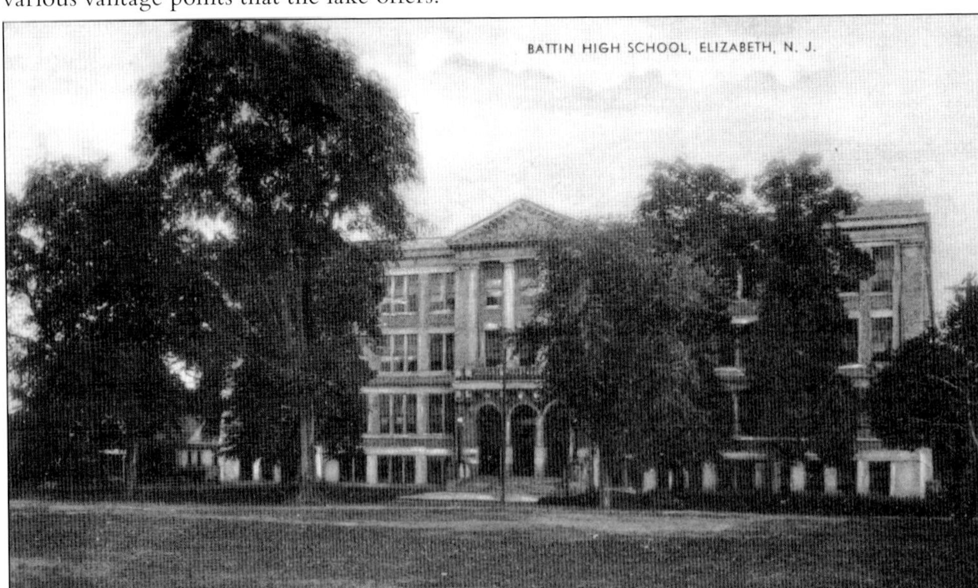

Battin High School was originally built in 1889 for the Elizabeth Public Schools system. It became an all-girls school in 1929 and remained this way for 48 years. Before becoming a coeducational institution in 1977, Battin High School was one of the only two public high schools in the state of New Jersey that separated male and female students. The building was originally the mansion of Joseph Battin, who was president of the Elizabethtown Water Company. Battin donated his mansion to the city, and it is named after him to this day.

St. John's Church is an Elizabeth institution. Located at 61 Broad Street, the building served as the home of both the Episcopalian and Catholic congregations in the area until 1855, when St. Mary of the Assumption was erected. The current edifice was built in 1860. The church is the marriage site for the parents of the first American Catholic saint, Elizabeth Ann Seton, and below the church, in an unmarked grave, rest the remains of Jonathan Dayton, the youngest signer of the Constitution, and an Elizabeth native. The church was added to the National Register of Historic Places in 1995.

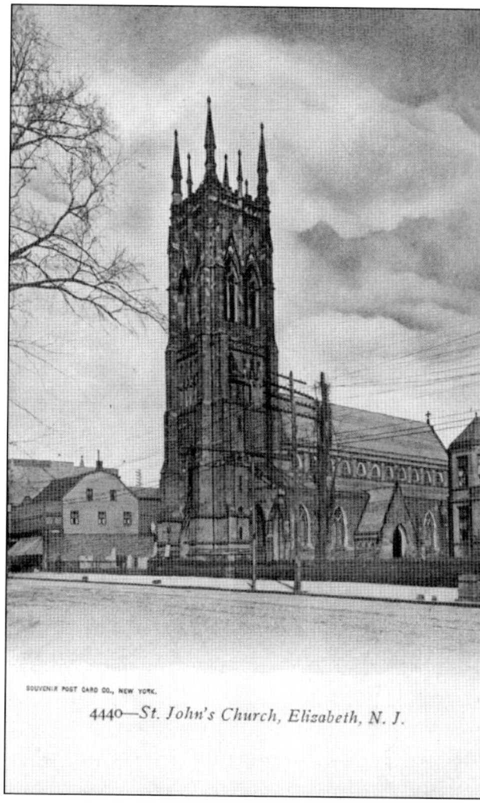

The US Post Office had, up until July 1, 1971, been a part of the executive branch, with the president responsible for selecting postmasters as cabinet members. This envelope marks the date in time that the postal service was spun off into an independent agency. This was brought about by a massive 1970 strike of postal workers that started in New York City and spread to over 200,000 postal workers across the country. This action allowed workers to unionize and eventually win rights to collectively bargain with the government.

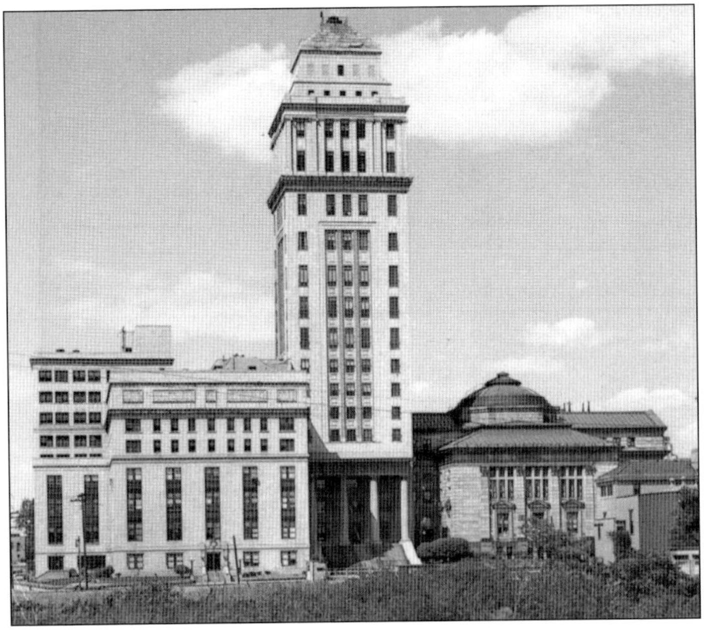

This postcard, published in 1962 by the Scheller Company in nearby Hackettstown, shows the Union County Courthouse on a sunny day. The back of the card reads, "Erected in 1903, this building is the tallest structure in Elizabeth, New Jersey, and it can be seen from many miles disant. Elizabeth is one of New Jersey's largest cities." Today, the courthouse stands at 2 Broad Street and is home to divisions dedicated to criminal, civil, family, finance, municipal, and probate law.

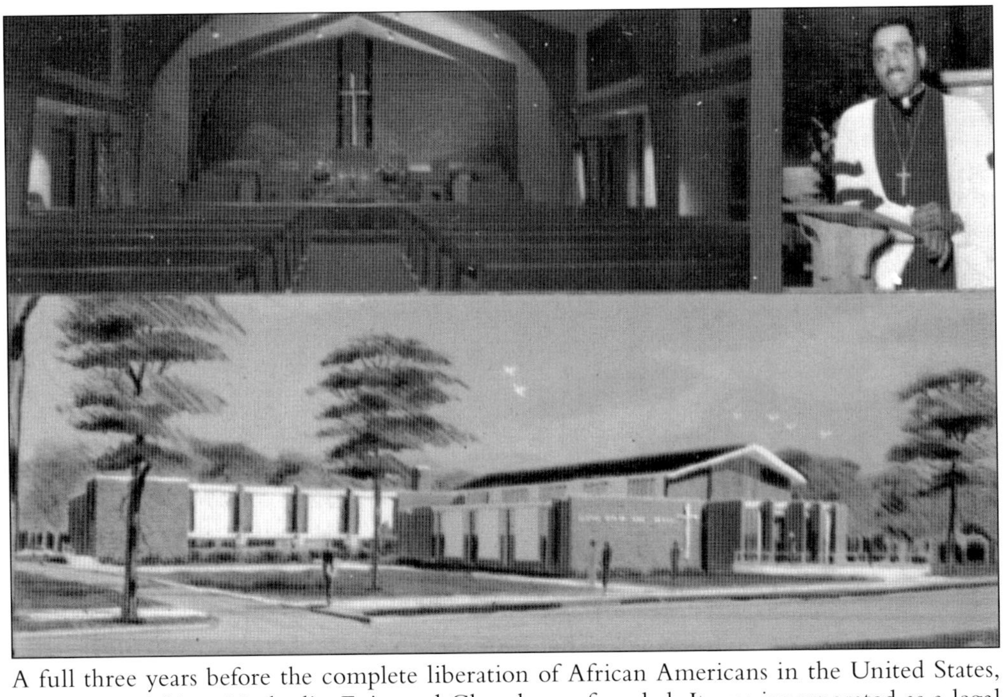

A full three years before the complete liberation of African Americans in the United States, Mt. Teman African Methodist Episcopal Church was founded. It was incorporated as a legal entity in 1884, with the articles of incorporation bearing the signature of two of the original founders. This 1960s postcard shows both the interior and exterior of the church's new (at the time) home on 160 Madison Avenue, where the church remains today. It also shows Minister Lasalle Marshall Watts, whose fundraising efforts made the new structure possible.

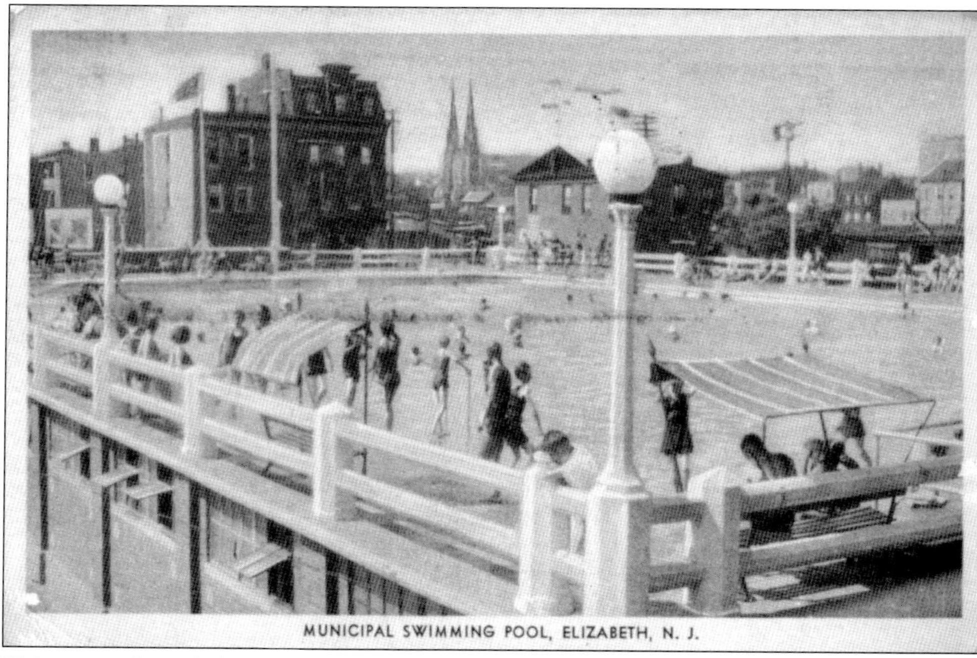

This postcard, mailed on December 6, 1933, shows the municipal swimming pool in Elizabeth. Despite its station along the north of New Jersey, Elizabeth does see its share of warm days, averaging 87 degrees in July and 85 degrees in August. Today, the sole publicly operated pool in Elizabeth is now an indoor pool, which runs from the Fourth of July to Labor Day. The pool is staffed with certified lifeguards and is open from Monday to Friday from 12:00 p.m. to 6:00 p.m.

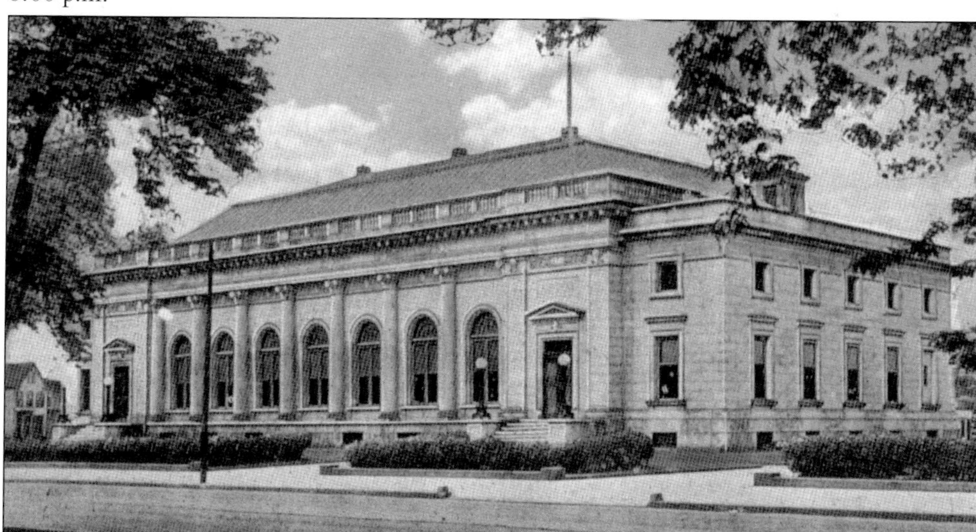

Built in 1911, the Elizabeth Post Office stands as a testament to early-20th-century ingenuity and architectural prowess. Covering a whopping 136,000-square-foot lot, the building has been responsible for the delivery of mail in the area of over 100 years. It was designed by supervising Treasury architect James Knox Taylor. Inspired by the Beaux Arts movement, it features columns, bas-relief eagles on each end of the lobby, arched windows, and 12 customer service counters. The building was placed in the National Register of Historic Places in 1982.

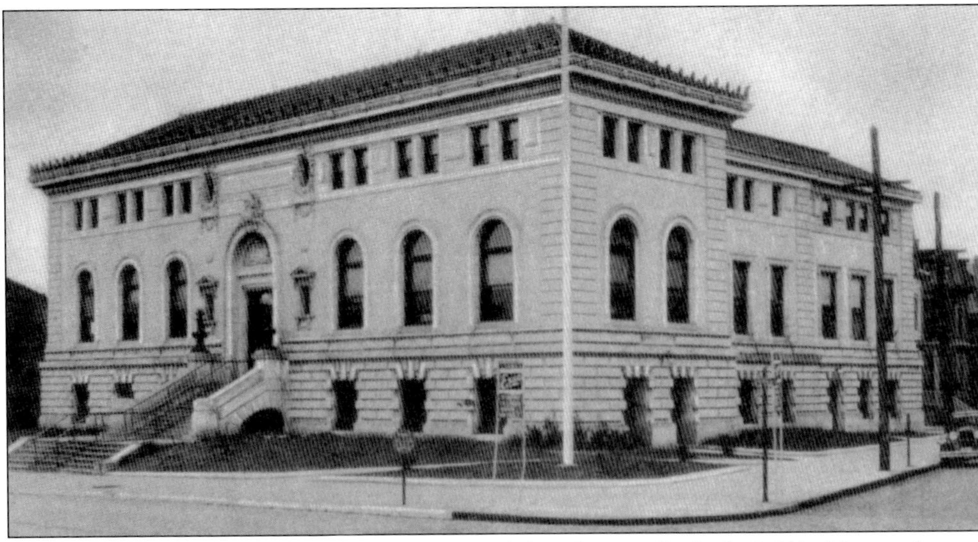

Completed in 1912, this postcard shows the edifice that is Elizabeth Public Library, known then as the Free Public Library of Elizabeth. The construction of such libraries began in the early 20th century, as part of a movement by Charles N. Fowler. The collections at the library contain nearly 350,000 pieces, and currently serves a population of over 125,000. The library was added to the National Register of Historic Places in 1982 and to the New Jersey Register of Historic Places in 1995. The construction was financed by Andrew Carnegie, and the building was designed by Edward Lippincott Tilton.

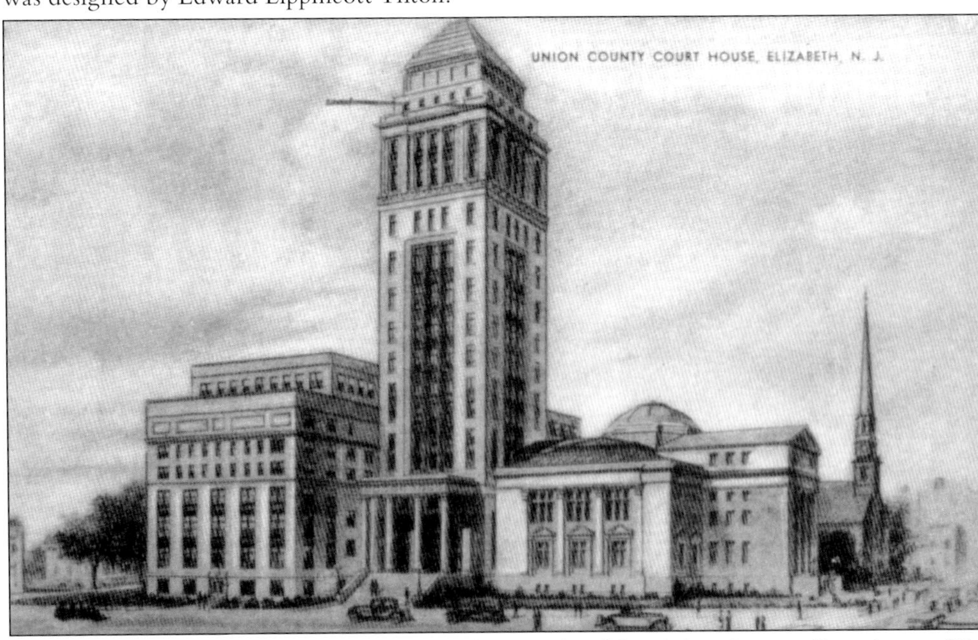

This card, postmarked April 8, 1942, shows the outside of the Union County Courthouse. The card was printed by the Mayrose Company Publishers for exclusive sale in the Court House Cigar Store at 13 Broad Street, a block away from the physical building itself. The courthouse, built in a Neoclassical style, started construction in 1925 and was completed in 1931. The cost was $1.2 million, or nearly $31 million today. It stands 17 stories, or 238 feet high, and is the tallest building in Elizabeth.

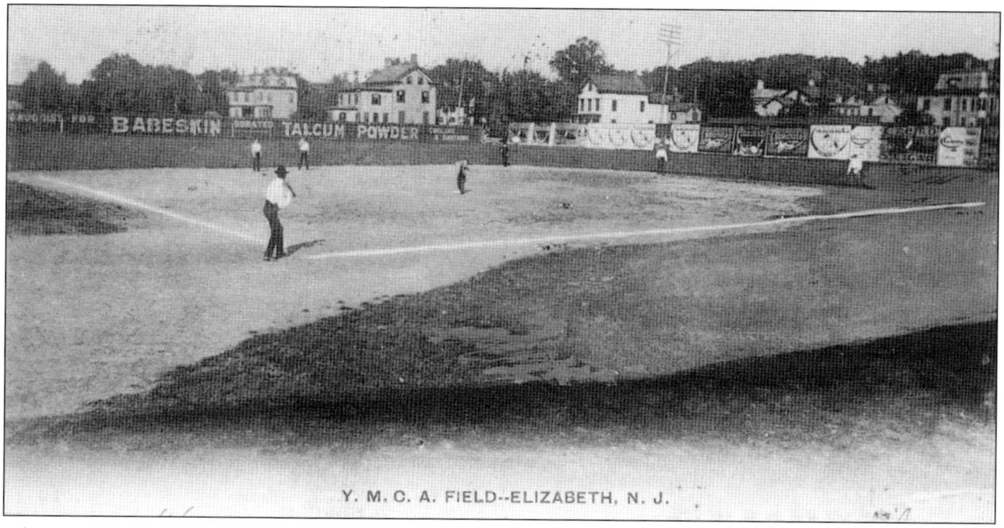

This c. 1907 card shows the YMCA baseball field in Elizabeth. This card was an advertisement, of sorts. Postmarked October 1907, the typeset text on the back reads "We are expecting you on for Old Home Week, October 6–12, 1907. Great doings. Carnival. Parades and parades. Biggest time ever. Latch string is on the outside. Railroad fares reduced. Ask the agent. You'll have the best time of your life. Honest. Industrial Exposition and Gigantic Water Carnival. Everything to contribute to your enjoyment. Betsytown will be at her best." (Courtesy of the Boston Public Library Digital Commonwealth.)

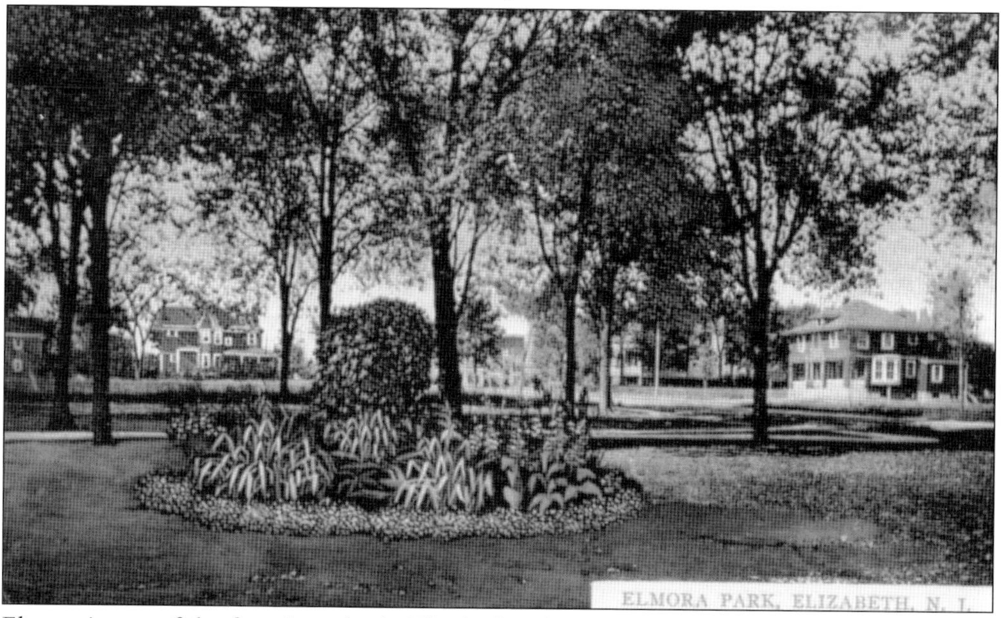

Elmora is one of the five zip codes in Elizabeth. This postcard shows a view of Elmora Park, which is also located in a mainly residential area in Elizabeth. The houses in the background of this postcard are all built in a Victorian style, many of which still remain with similar facades today. The park itself has been renovated since this postcard to include a children's playground, and the flower and plant centerpiece in the middle of the postcard has been replaced with more turf in order to accommodate playing children, since the park is conveniently located behind the Abraham Lincoln school, part of the Elizabeth Public Schools system.

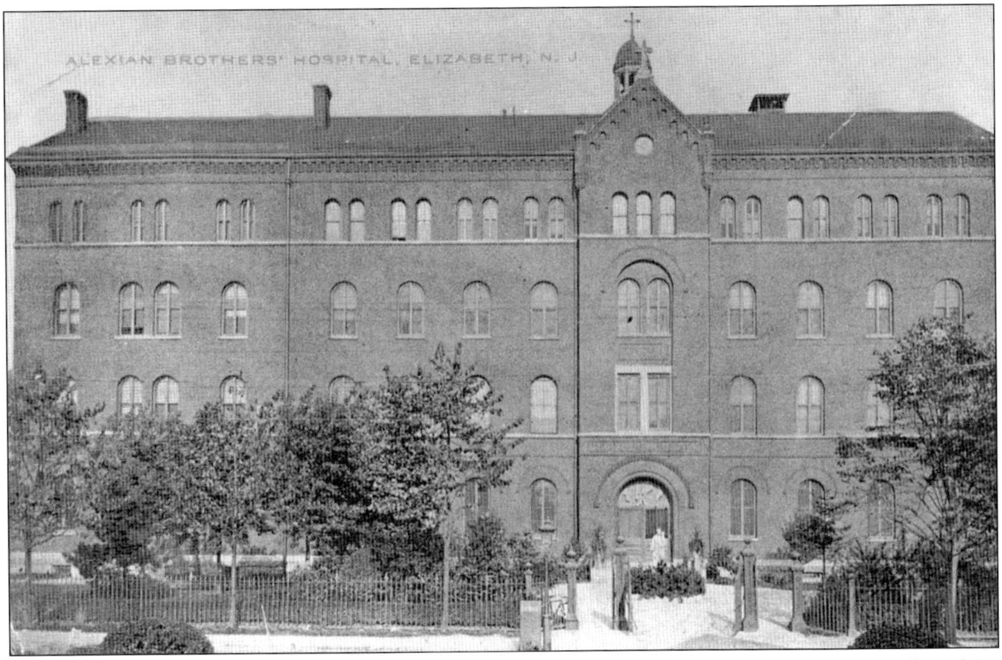

This image shows the Alexian Brothers Hospital, constructed in 1892. The hospital and its assets became a part of the Trinitas Regional Medical Center in 2000. The Alexian Brothers, as a religious organization, have served the ill for nearly nine centuries. The first written account of their existence dates to 1259, as providers of care for those stricken by the plague. In honor of their patron, St. Alexius, the brothers worked toward rehabilitating Europe as half of the world's population was wiped out. Pope Sixtus IV officially recognized the work of the Brothers, making them an official order under the purview of St. Augustine in 1472. (Courtesy of the New Jersey Public Library.)

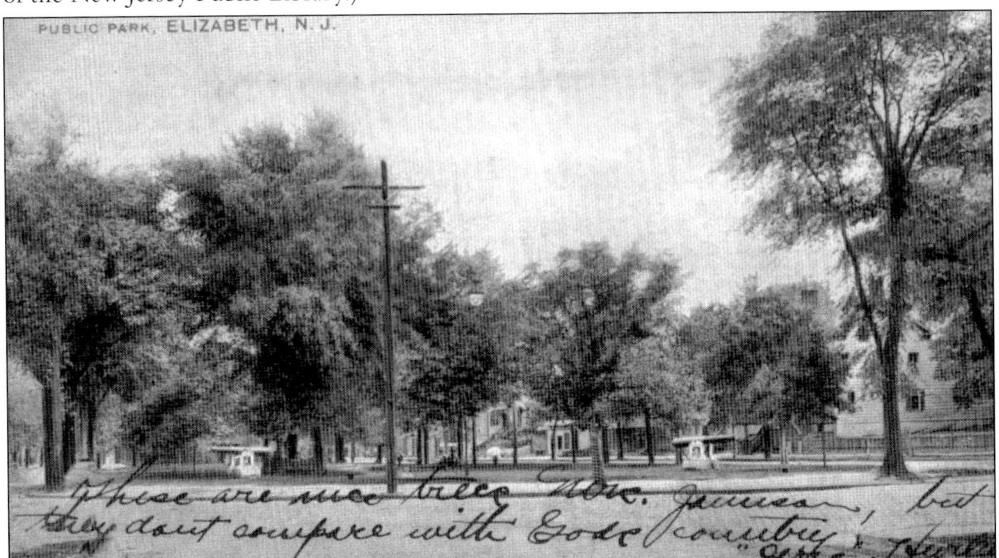

The printed caption for this postcard reads, "Public Park, Elizabeth, N.J." The handwriting on the front reads, "These are nice trees Mrs. Jamison, but they don't compare with God's country." This could be one of many small public parks in Elizabeth.

Shown here, sometime before 1907, is the First Presbyterian Church of Elizabeth. The church was built in 1783 at its current location, 14-44 Broad Street. Constructed of brick and white painted wood, the church is built in the Gothic Revival style that was popular at the time. In 2013, a Bible inscribed with the date of 1699 that belonged to church founder James Ogden was returned to the congregation. The building was added to the National Register of Historic Places in 1977.

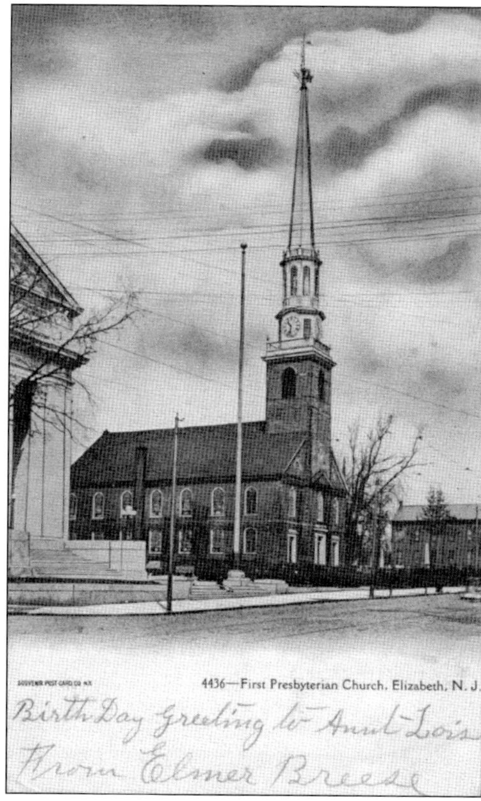

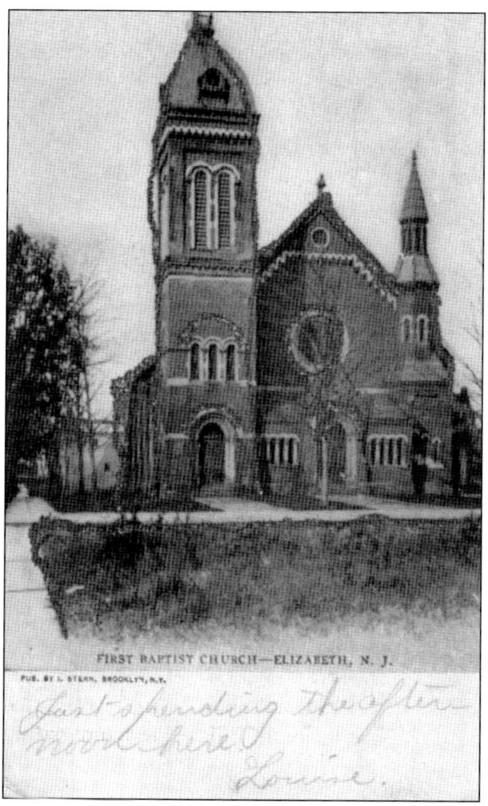

This glitter card, sent on November 25, 1906, to Margie Walters of 3127 Front Street in Philadelphia, shows the First Baptist Church of Elizabeth, located at 402 Union Avenue in Elizabeth. The church is now known as the First Baptist Church of Cranford/Elizabeth. The church is a member of American Baptist Church USA. The church can be reached at 908-352-0519. Their mission statement reads, "First Baptist Church is a church for all people who has been around for over 100 years."

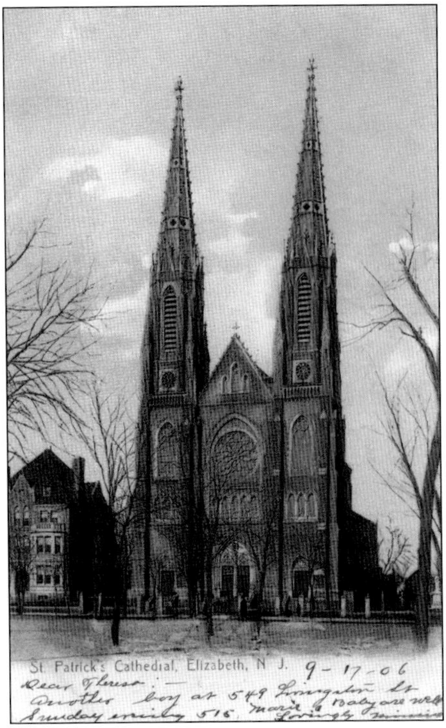

Constructed between 1889 and 1901, St. Patrick's Cathedral was built as a scaled down copy of the great cathedral of Cologne. At the time of its construction, it cost $400,000, which would equate to nearly $12 million today. The interior can seat up to 1,600 people. Its construction was overseen by Reverend Martin Gessner, who encouraged parishioners to carry stones to the site to aid in reducing construction costs. Fran Mulligan was the builder responsible, and the interior marble statues were done by sculptor Joseph Sibbel. The towers are 212 feet tall.

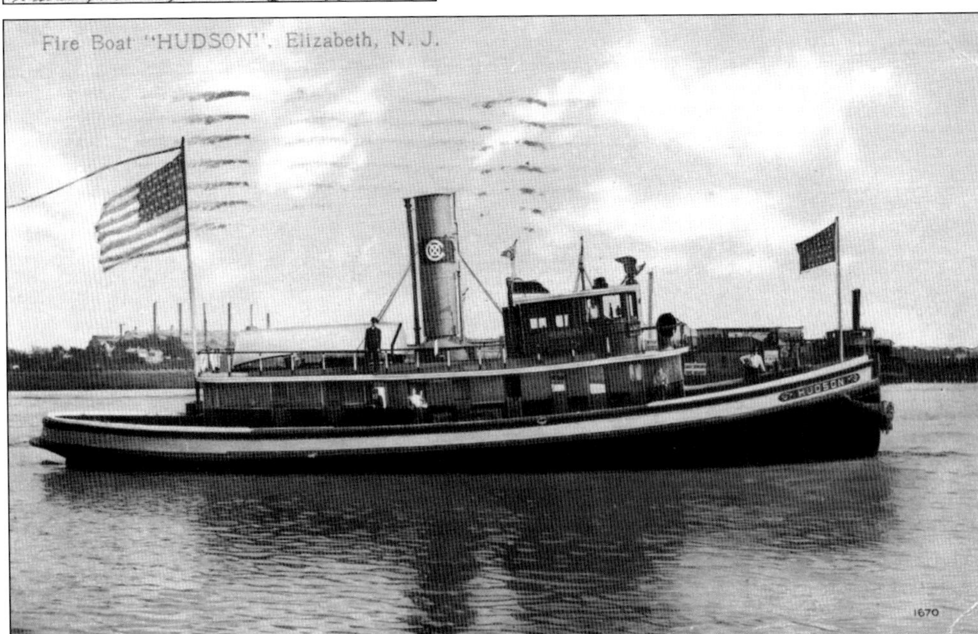

Shown here sometime around 1911 is the fireboat *Hudson*, part of the joint efforts of several fire departments on the Hudson River to fight fires. Most fireboats were either wooden-hulled steamers modified for service or boats built with the explicit purpose of carrying pumps and hoses directly to the scene of fires along the river. This particular card was mailed from Elizabeth on August 12, 1911, and served as a friendly dialog between two mothers, discussing their mothers and the toys with which their children played.

Destroyed by fire in 1992, this pre-1907 postcard shows the Greystone Presbyterian Church. The congregation started life as a Congregational church, founded in 1836. However, the church soon switched to the Presbyterian denomination and became the Marshall Street Presbyterian Church, in 1846. The church would rename itself again in 1896 when the structure pictured was erected, and the congregation was, aptly, renamed the Greystone Presbyterian Church. Today, all that stands at the mission's former location of 228 Elizabeth Avenue is a parking lot used by the adjoining Subway franchise.

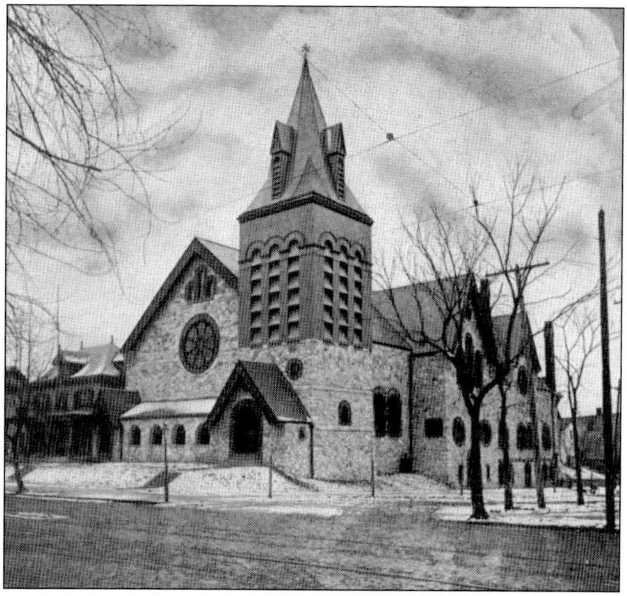

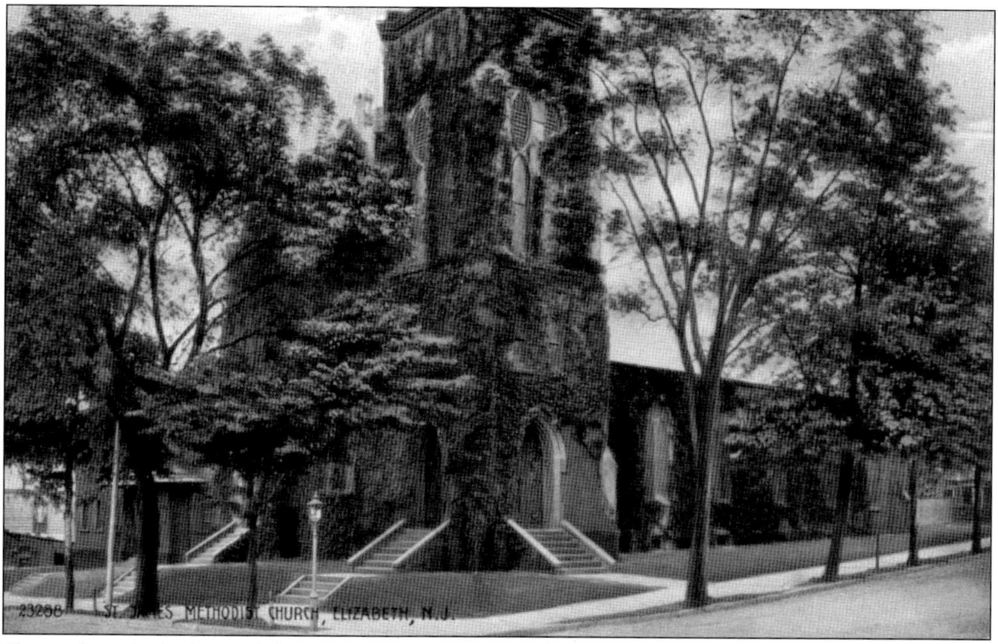

Shown here is the long-defunct St. James Methodist Church of Elizabeth. The building pictured started life in 1904, serving as the home of the unified congregations of the Elizabeth Avenue and St. Paul's Methodist churches in the area. The congregation had been through no less than three homes before the pictured one was occupied. The church, as with many churches on the East Coast, no longer stands, as the congregation merged with two others to form the First United Methodist Church of New Brunswick in 1960. The building, at 36 Broad Street in Elizabeth, is now occupied by the Haitian Bethany Baptist Church.

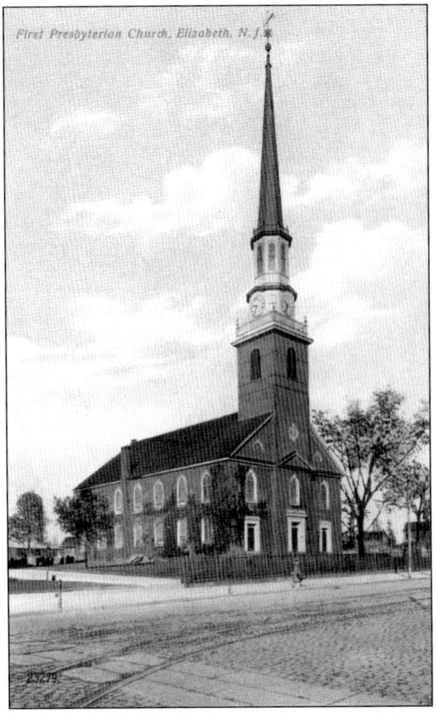

First Presbyterian Church, shown here sometime between 1907 and 1915, has a unique place in the history of America. On its site was where the first English-speaking church in New Jersey began. It claims no less than three former governors on its membership rolls, as well as Abraham Clark, signer of the Declaration of Independence. The steeple was replaced in 2006, replacing the one destroyed in 1946. Jonathan Dickinson, who served as pastor from 1707 to 1747, was the original founder of the College of New Jersey, which would later become Princeton.

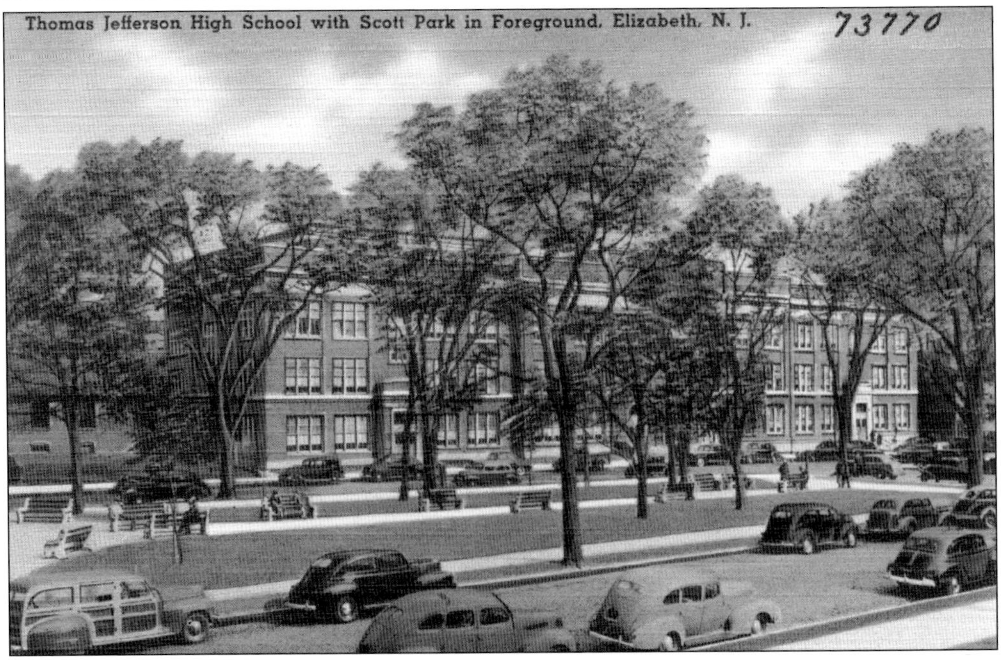

Until 1977, Elizabeth had one of the last set of separate public schools for boys and girls in the New Jersey area. The boys' school was known as Thomas Jefferson High School, named for the nation's third president. The school opened in 1929. The buildings that made up Thomas Jefferson High School were integrated into the new Elizabeth High School, which opened as a co-ed facility for the 1977–1978 school year. The project to combine the schools cost nearly $30 million. (Courtesy of the Boston Public Library Digital Collections.)

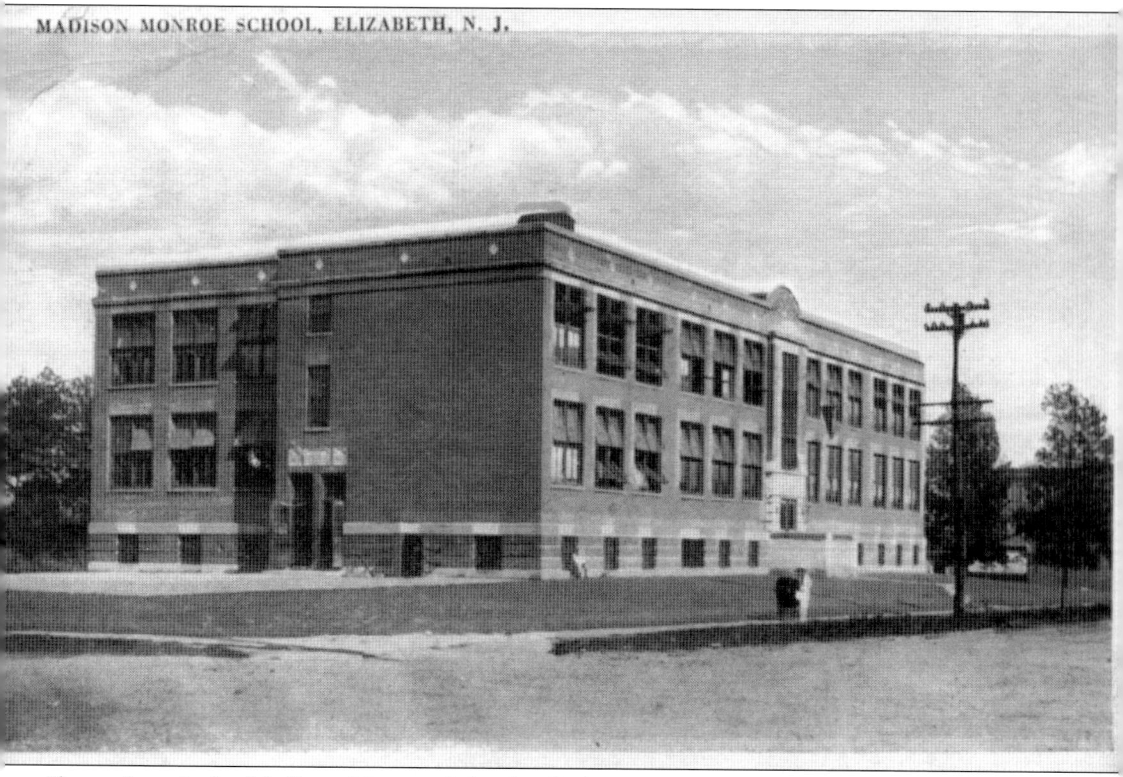

Shown here is the Madison-Monroe School, which serves today as Elementary School 16 in the Elizabeth School District. This card, mailed on June 23, 1937, was sent by a Noel Yarling to June Gregg of Ohio. Today, the Monroe-Madison school serves grades first through eighth. The message on the card reads. "Thanks for the Capitol view. Hope this one will be O.K. Come again. Sincerely, Noel Yarling." Such cards, with white borders, were popular during the Great Depression, as the white borders helped printers save on colored ink. The school is currently located at 1091 North Avenue.

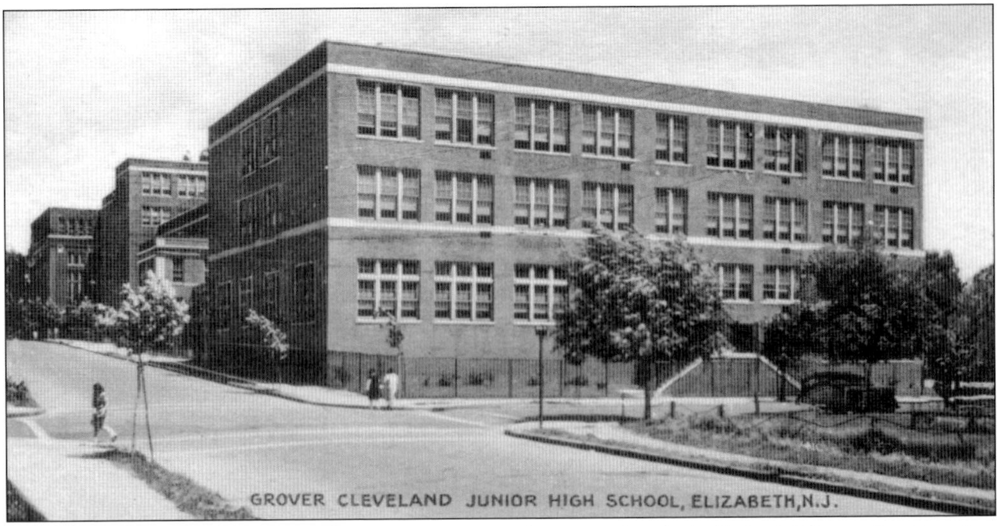

Grover Cleveland Junior High School was one of many schools built in 1923, as the Roaring '20s brought on both a glut of tax dollars and the need to improve society. Built in 1923, the school consumed an entire city block and was designed by famed designer C. Godfrey Poggi, who designed other schools in Elizabeth, such as Battin High School, Roosevelt Junior High School, and the Elmora School. The first principal was Joseph O'Brien, a Seton Hall graduate, who was in charge from 1924 until his death in 1942.

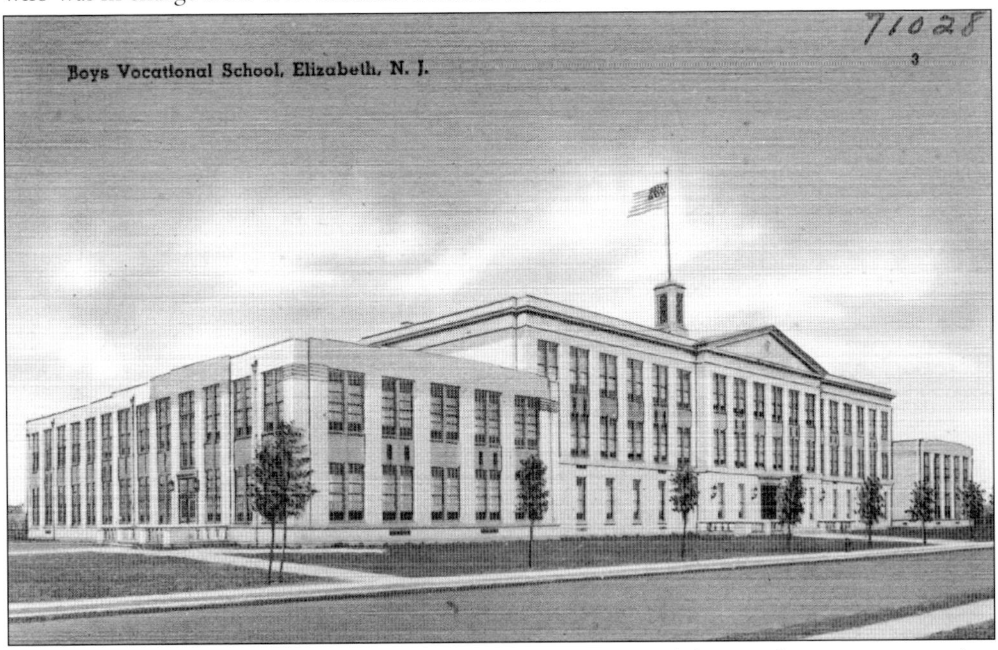

Now named after Thomas A. Edison, a somewhat controversial figure who was purported to have stolen ideas from inventors such as Nikola Tesla, this card shows the Boys Vocational School, which was built in 1935 at its present location on Summer Street. The school currently services nearly 700 kids with nearly 70 teachers. The curriculum focuses on four trades: construction technology, health science, automotive technology, and hospitality and retail services, with different disciplines assigned to each. The school serves grades 9 through 12. (Courtesy of the Boston Public Library Digital Collections.)

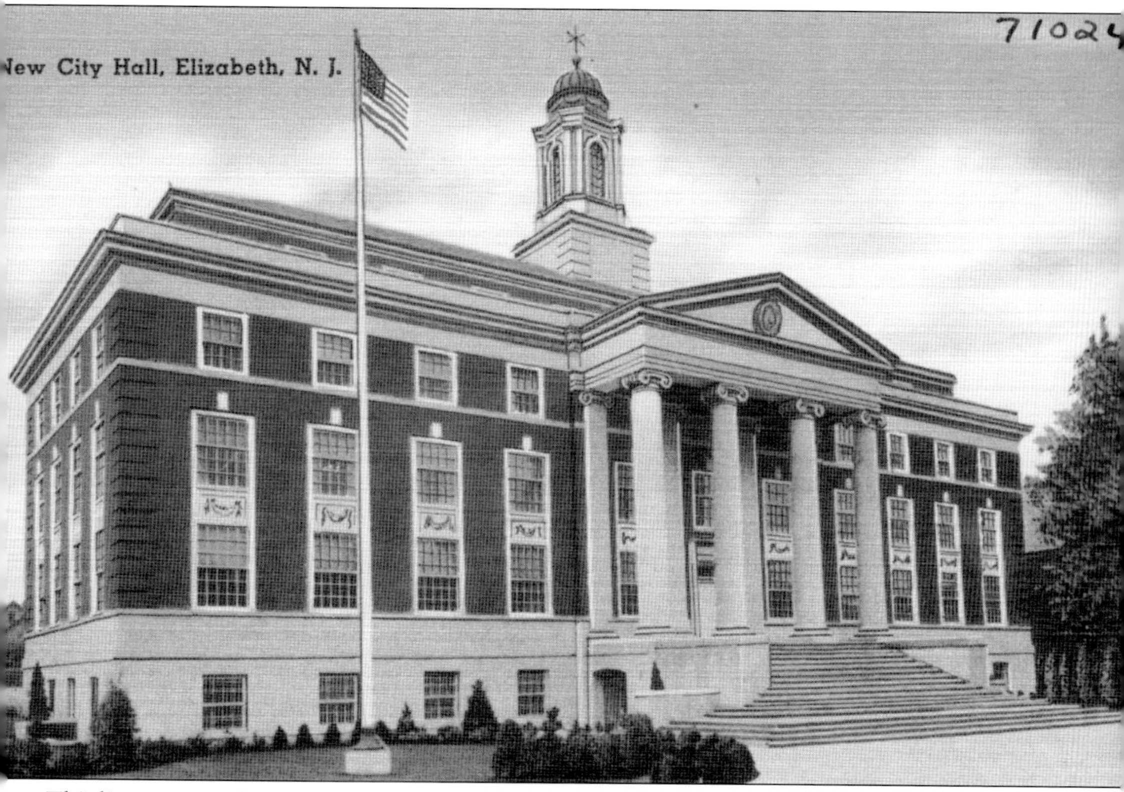

This linen postcard was printed sometime after 1940, as the version of city hall pictured was not complete until that date. This version of city hall was designed and constructed by Eggers and Higgins, who were given some degree of infamy for how they had been chosen to complete the Thomas Jefferson memorial a year prior. The group is still in existence, albeit as a part of the much larger RMJM Hillier Group, a larger firm based in London. City hall contains the mayor's office, where Christian J. Bollwange is serving his eighth term as mayor. (Courtesy of the Boston Public Library Digital Collections.)

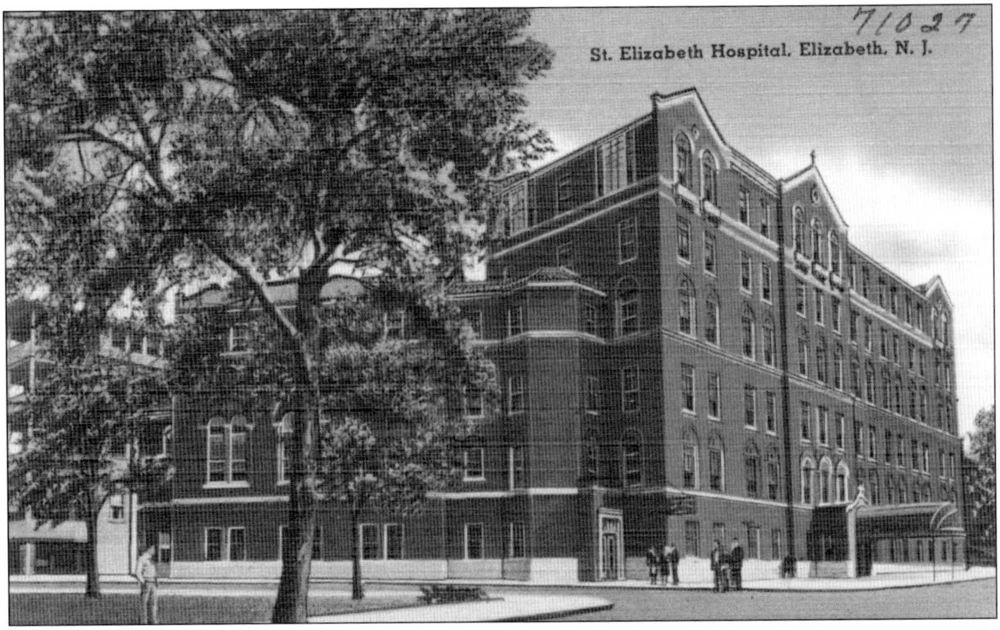

Founded 27 years after Elizabeth General Hospital, St Elizabeth's Hospital was a charitable endeavor arranged by the Sisters of Charity of St. Elizabeth, under the guidance of Bishop John J. O'Connor of Newark. A residence was purchased at 204 South Broad Street in Elizabeth and renovated for this purpose, serving up to 25 patients at its inception. In 2000, Elizabeth General merged with St Elizabeth's, and the two entities, now known as Trinitas, serve the public, with a campus still located at the South Broad address. (Courtesy of the Boston Public Library Digital Collections.)

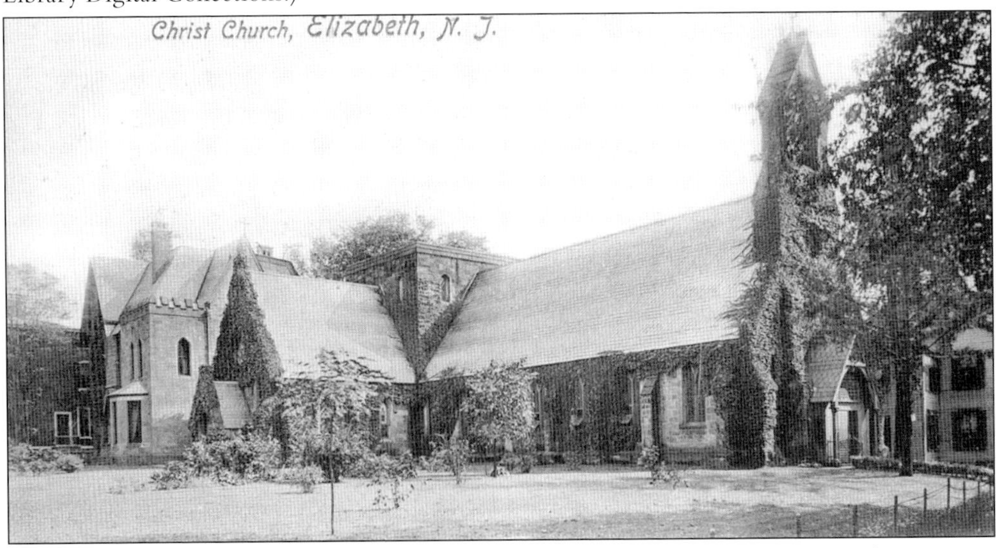

Established in 1853, the Christ (Episcopal) Church was stationed at the corner of East Jersey Street and East Scott Place. The church is shown here, pre-1907, with Gothic-style architecture, covered with English Ivy along its facade. Flames consumed the building on January 16, 1987. An early member was Charles Townsend, who was a glue industry titan in New York. He served as an early secretary of the church. Dr. Richard Bayley Post served as the assistant rector from 1896 until his death in 1905. (Courtesy of the New Jersey Public Library.)

The Presbyterian presence in Elizabeth has always been strong, as evidenced by the events of 1851, when 75 members of the First and Second Presbyterian Churches organized to spin off a third congregation, the Third Presbyterian Church. The cornerstone was laid in 1852, and the church was dedicated in 1855. With the ability to seat 1,000 people, the church prospered, yet closed when the congregation merged with the Westminster Presbyterian Church on North Avenue. From 1995 to 2004, the property operated as the Elizabeth Playhouse. (Courtesy of the New Jersey Public Library.)

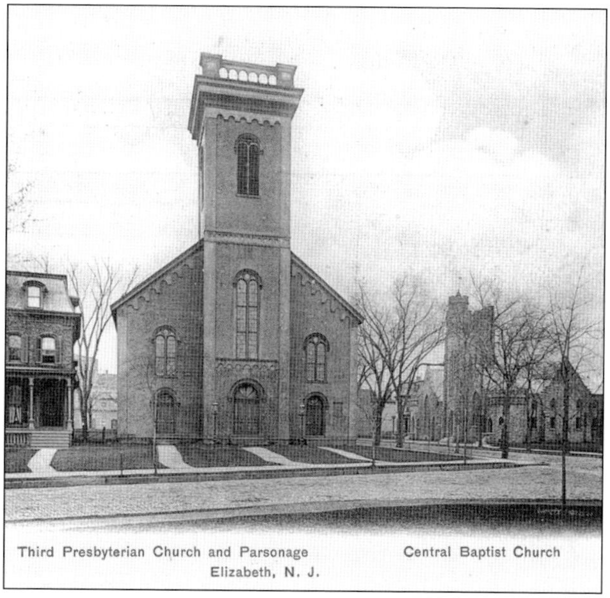

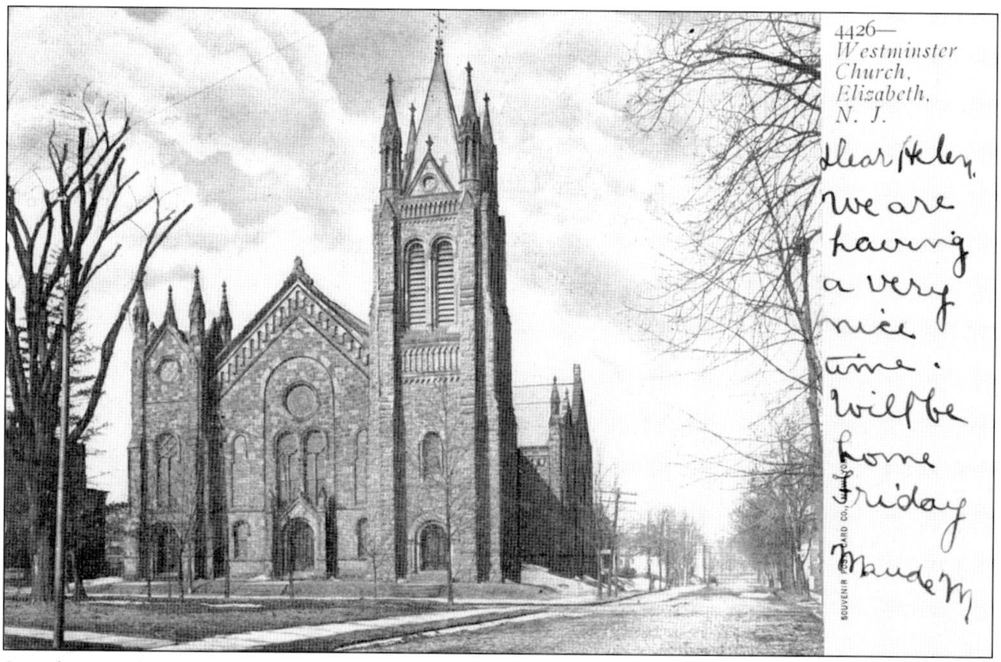

Standing at the corner of Westminster Avenue and Prince Street, the Westminster Presbyterian Church was erected between 1866 and 1877, as a way to accommodate the increasing numbers of Presbyterians in northern Elizabeth. Built in the Norman style of architecture, the massive building has a seating capacity of 1,100. Rev. William C. Roberts served as the first pastor. The building was destroyed by fire in 1944 and was rebuilt at the corner of North and Salem Avenues in 1949. The church merged with the Third Presbyterian Church and is now known as the Third-Westminster Presbyterian Church. (Courtesy of the New Jersey Public Library.)

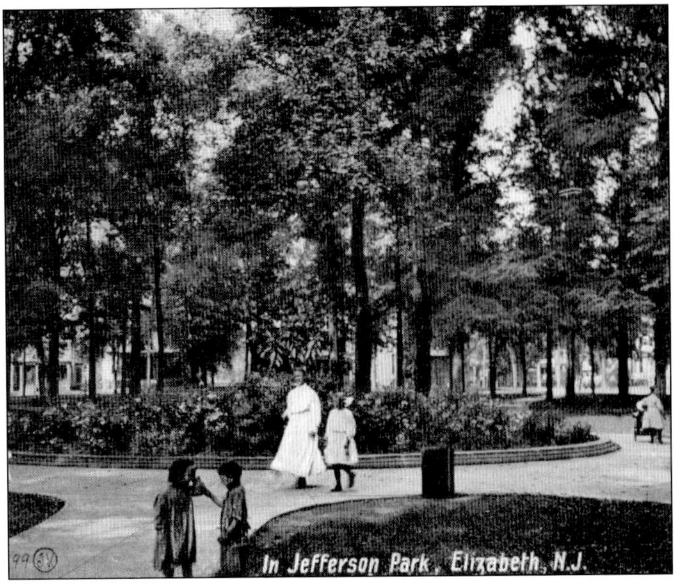

The plot of land that would become Jefferson Park (shown on this 1912 postcard) was given to the City of Elizabeth by famous real estate developer Edward N. Kellogg in 1855. The park is bounded by Jefferson and Madison Avenues, and Mary and Anna Streets. The park began life as a swampy part of Pierson's Woods and contained many fine examples of large oak trees. Nearby are several Victorian homes, and the park was planned by its benefactor before donation.

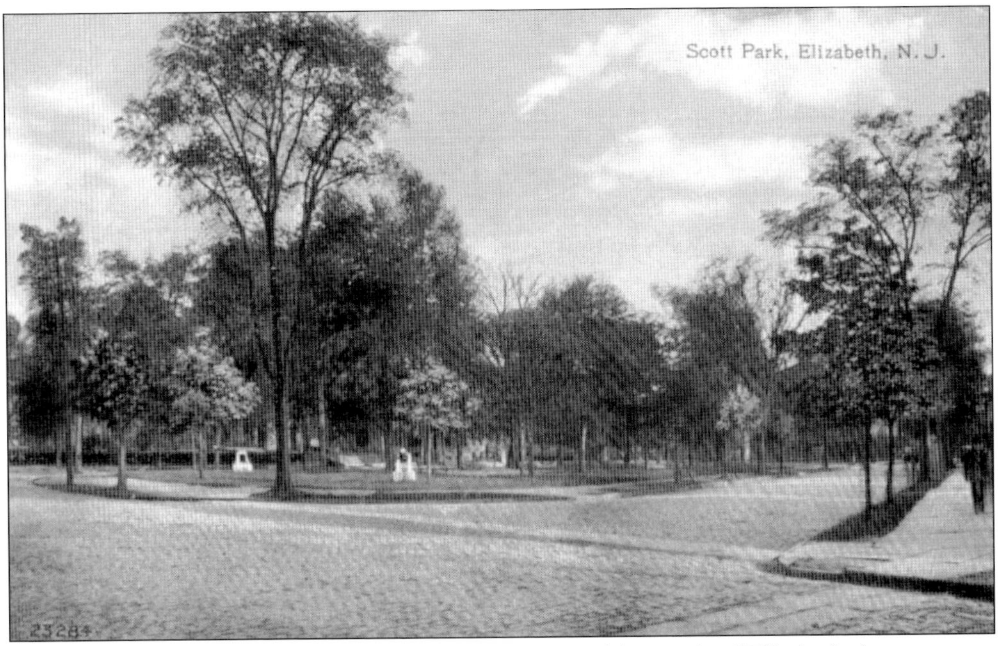

Scott Park, before it rose to its lofty status as a park, was like much of Elizabeth: low, swampy land. Before it became Scott Park, it was known as Horse Hollow and even had a small stream that ran through it, although the stream was later drained to run sewer lines. The park is home to several war monuments, including a set of cannons that were used in the Mexican War, a tablet made by Tiffany & Company to memorialize war dead, and a monument placed in the park to honor all of Elizabeth's war dead up until World War II.

The Union County Courthouse is located in Elizabeth, and it is the main courthouse for the county. The structure was completed in 1931 and features a Neoclassical architectural design. The front of the court has the inscription "Vox Populi Vox Dei—the voice of the people is the voice of God." The building is 17 stories tall, and it is the tallest building in the Elizabeth skyline. This postcard shows the courthouse as it looked when it was first finished and is likely meant to showcase this impressive building.

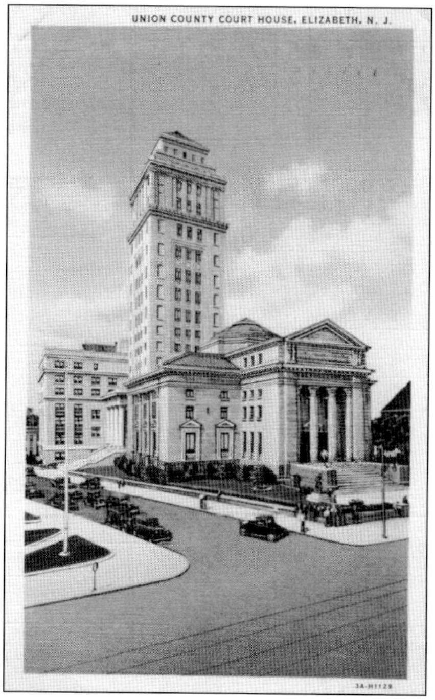

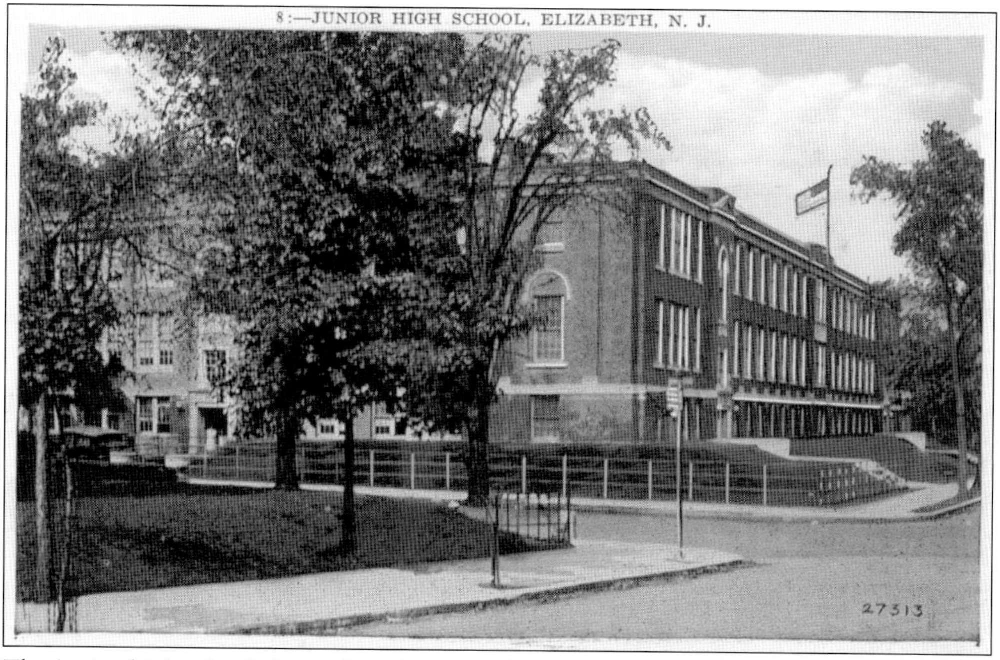

The junior high school shown in this postcard is today known as the Alexander Hamilton Preparatory Academy, part of the Elizabeth Public Schools system. It was originally known as the Alexander Hamilton Middle School until 2008 when it became a high school; it is named after the famous president who was once a one-time resident and student in the city of Elizabeth. The postcard shows a view of the school behind a small park and some trees, hinting that the image in the postcard was taken some years back since the park and trees are no longer a part of the school's landscape.

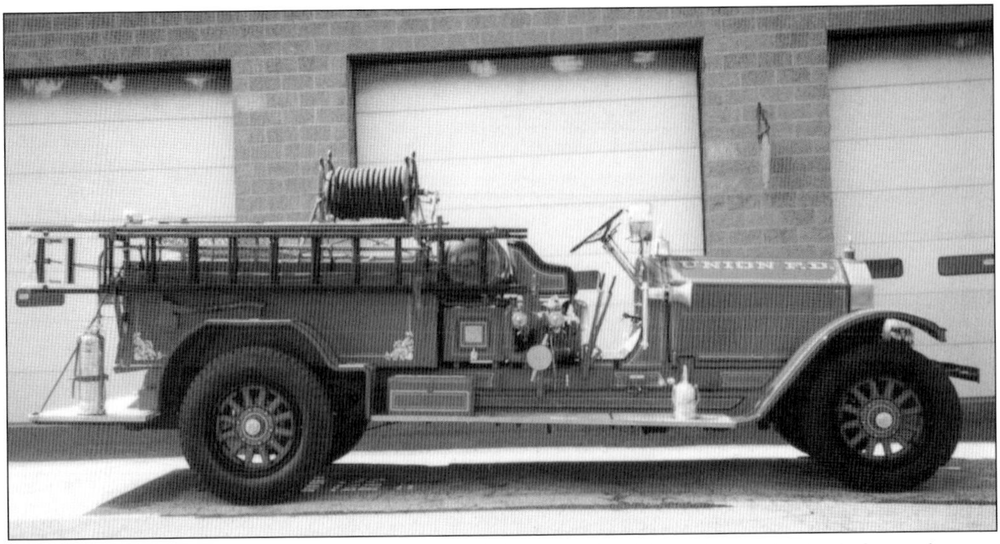

This postcard, taken in 1928, shows a fire truck from Union Township. Elizabeth formed a part of Union Township (now Union County), and so this image is historically significant for the city's history because it shows what a fire truck in the early 1990s would have looked like. The location of the specific city where this picture was taken is not known, but these are the types of fire trucks that would have responded to any city crisis that fell under the responsibility of the fire department.

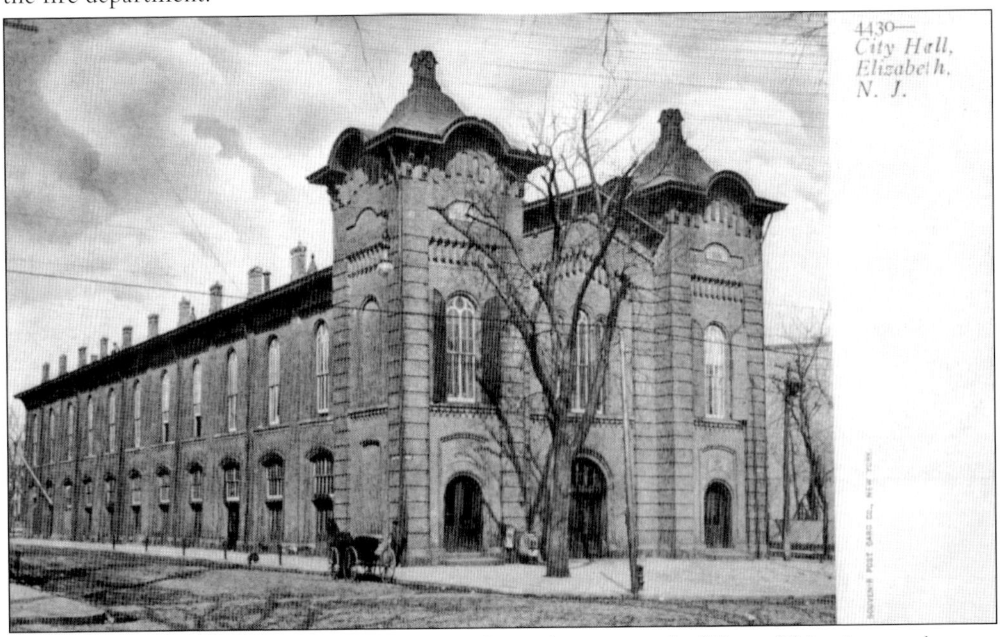

City hall before 1907 looked very different from the current building. This picture shows a rare view of the old city hall, a two-story building erected in 1865 that shared a space with the police department and the jail and armory of the 3rd Regiment. The current city hall was built in 1940, which is also when the old city hall was closed in order to transition into the new, four-story building that we know today. The old city hall was completely demolished in 1947, leaving behind only photographic evidence of this historical building. The old city hall was located on Elizabeth Avenue, between East and West Scott Places.

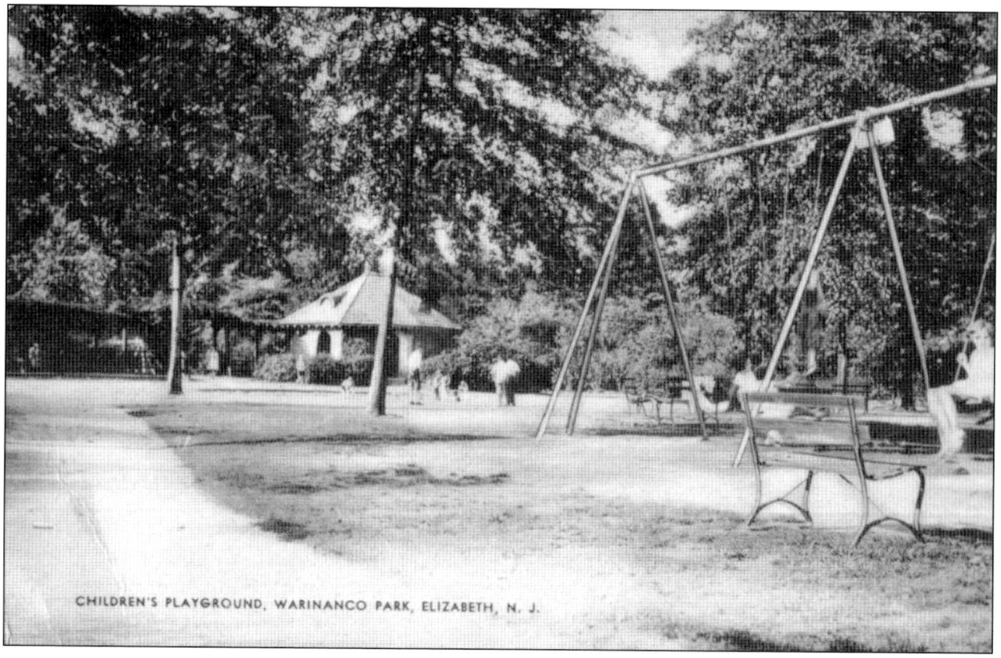

Warinanco Park, spanning 204 acres, is Elizabeth's largest recreational park. The park was designed by the landscape design firm Olmsted Brothers, the founder of which famously designed New York's Central Park. The park is named after the indigenous Lenape tribal leader of this region, and his name was recorded by the English colonists in 1664 as "Warinanco." This children's playground shows a glimpse into what the recreational life of an Elizabeth native would have looked like. The vast size of the park meant that many residents and visitors alike could bask in the park's green fields.

The First Presbyterian Church of Elizabeth was built in 1783, though its origins date back to the founding of the town in 1664. It is a historic church for the history of the state. The church was constructed in a Gothic Revival style. The church was the first of its type that was organized for worship in English, and it remained a Congregational church until 1717. In that same year, Presbyterian articles of faith were adopted, and it became affiliated with the Presbytery of Philadelphia. The First Presbyterian Church received its charter from King George II in 1753, and it has been rebuilt twice, once in 1786 after British soldiers set fire to it during the Revolutionary War and in 1946, after another fire that destroyed most of the church. The writing on this postcard shows how the church was a significant and historical edifice that identified Elizabeth.

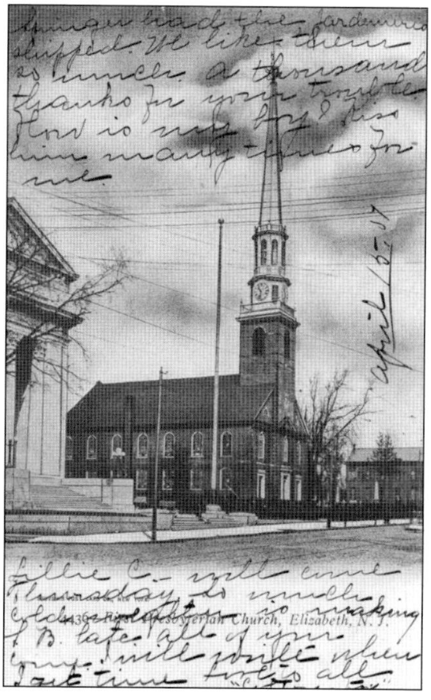

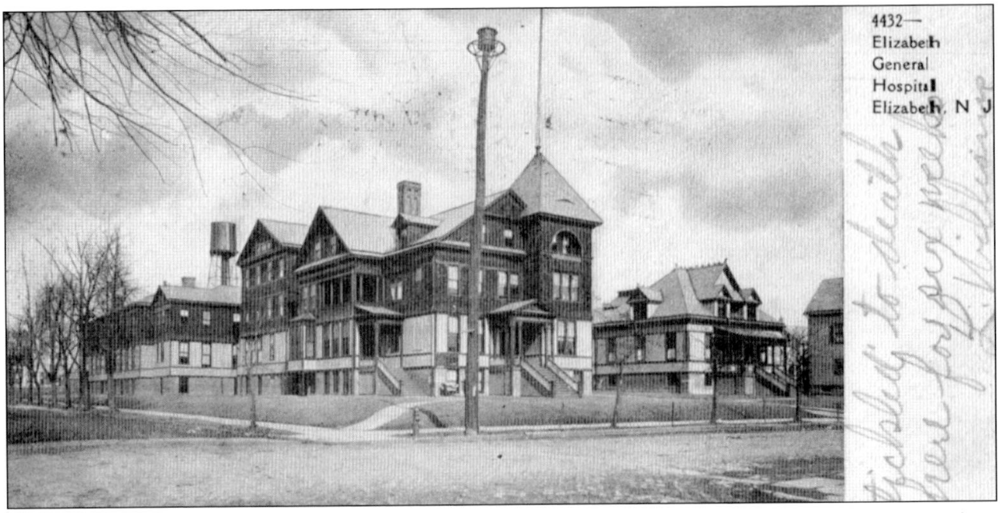

The Elizabeth General Hospital was the first medical facility in Elizabeth, established by four physicians in 1877. This historic picture shows the original building, a two-room surgical clinic with 22 beds, located in a home on Jacques Street. As the need for healthcare in the city grew over the years, a property on the corner of East Jersey and Red Street was eventually bought, and a large hospital was built.

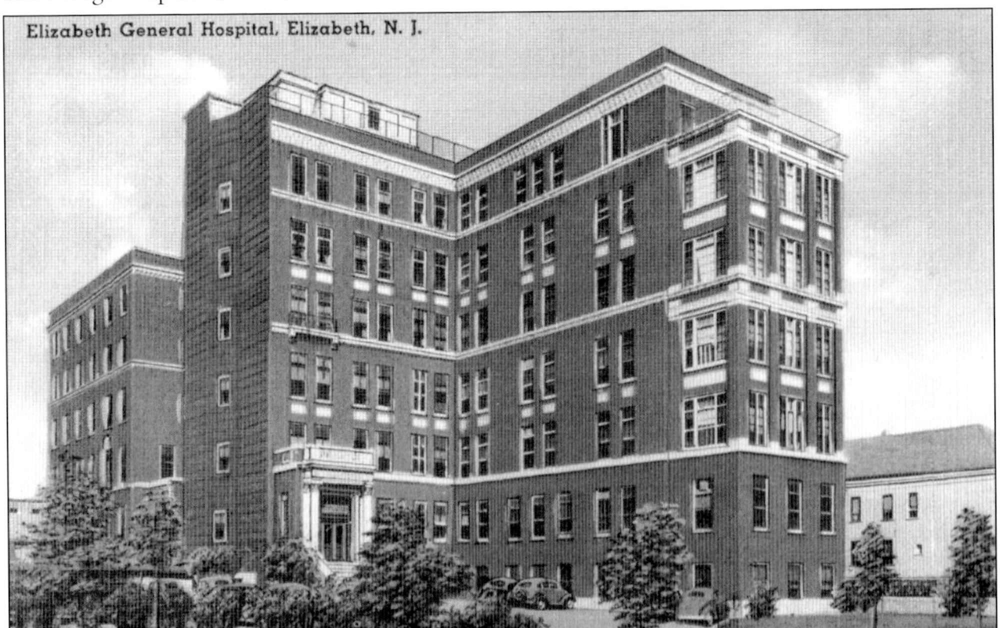

The Elizabeth General Hospital was a large, brick building covering roughly 350,000 square feet. The hospital expanded greatly and grew from its humble origins as a two-room surgical clinic. In the 1950s through the 1960s, a new wing was added to the hospital to include a maternity ward. In the year 2000, the hospital merged with the St. Elizabeth Hospital, and they formed the Trinitas Regional Medical Center. As some years passed after this union, most of the hospital operations were moved to St. Elizabeth's campus; thus, the original building gradually became obsolete, until its eventual closure in the early 2000s and its first partial demolition in 2012.

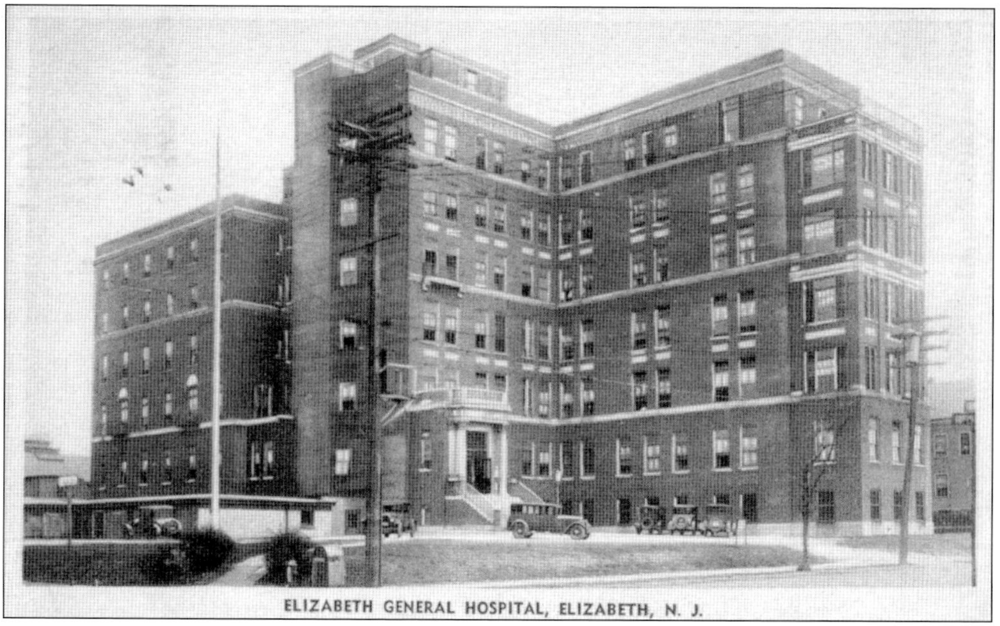

This postcard also depicts the Elizabeth General Hospital during the time that it was fully operational. Much like the other iconic buildings featured in this postcard series, the Elizabeth General Hospital was, for many years, an important hospital for the city and for Union County at large. This black and white depiction of the hospital shows what the hospital looked like before the new wing for the maternity ward was added.

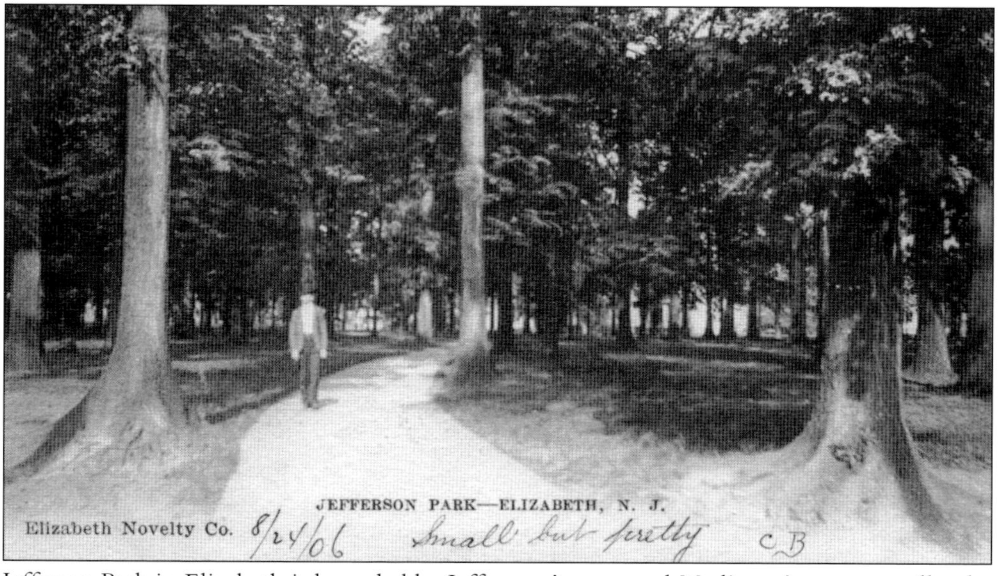

Jefferson Park in Elizabeth is bounded by Jefferson Avenue and Madison Avenue as well as by Mary and Anna Streets. The park was given to the city in 1858 by the prominent real estate developer Edward N. Kellogg. As the picture on the postcard shows, the park originally had many large oak trees because it was part of Pierson's wood. Current residents of Elizabeth who frequent the park might be surprised to know that the park was quite swampy back in the day. In handwriting, the card is dated August 24, 1906, with the succinct message, "small but pretty," and the initials "C.B."

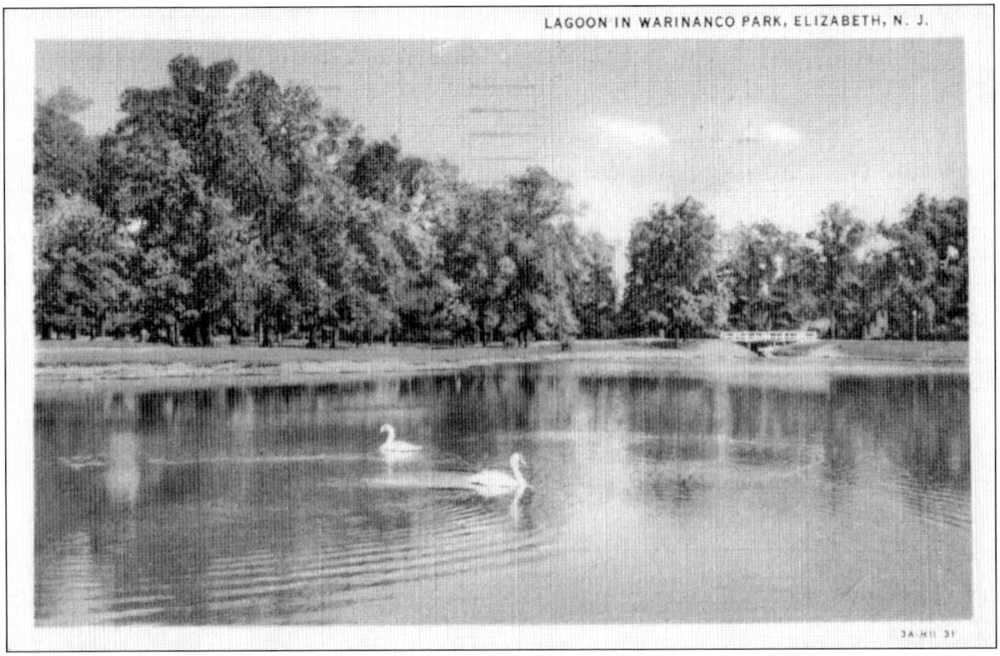

This postcard shows a view of the lagoon in Warinanco Park. Warinanco Park was a popular location for image postcards sent from Elizabeth because it was the largest park in proximity to the city. Many residents and visitors would visit the park as a quick leisurely getaway from the hustle and bustle of Elizabeth. This image shows some swans swimming in the lake, and although they are not as common today in Warinanco, the park lagoon is still home to ducks and geese.

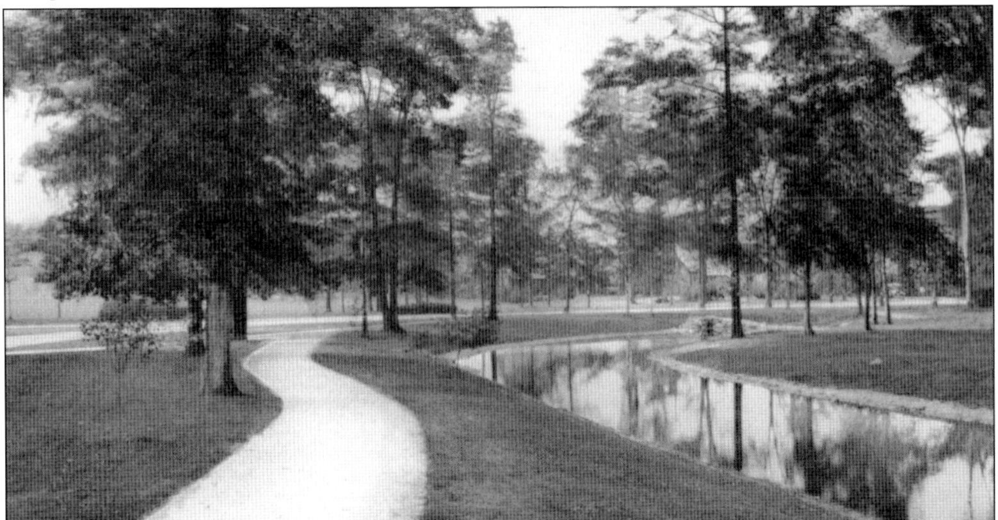

Another view of a lagoon in Warinanco Park, this postcard shows an old water source that could be found in the park that ran alongside one of the walking paths. That little stream has since then been removed, but the postcard image of this view of Warinanco still captures the same tranquility of the park that has remained over the years. To date, Warinanco Park is still a popular place for leisure and recreation among residents of surrounding cities and among visitors.

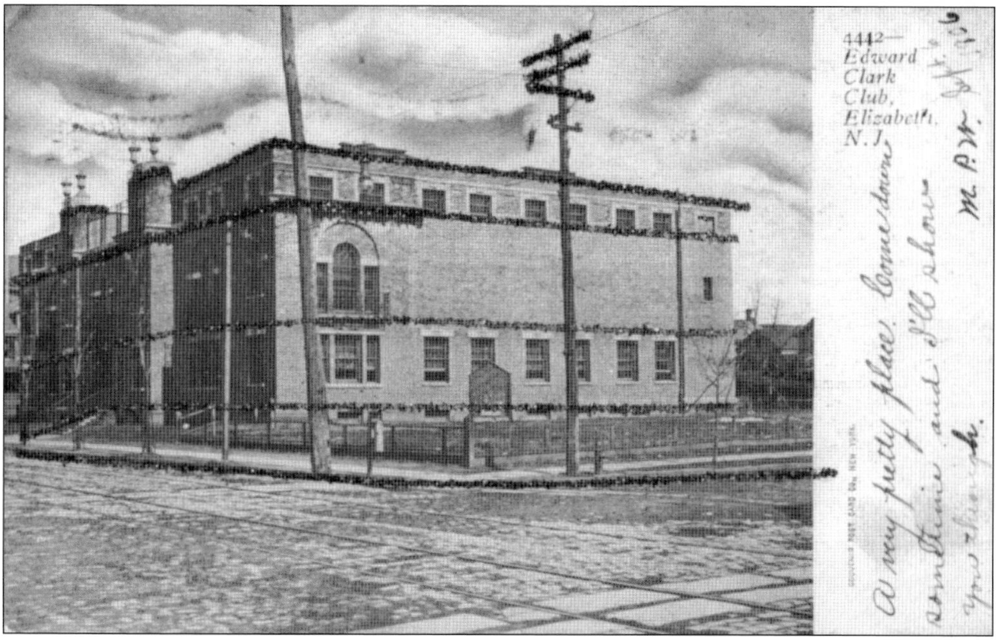

The Edward Clark Club in Elizabeth was a social institution that strove to build and strengthen community ties—much like the YMCA. The club was built in 1904 on the grounds of what used to be the Grace Episcopal Church on 221 East Jersey Street. Most of the members of the club were workers from the Elizabethport industries, which demonstrates that the club served as an important recreation and leisure place for many of the city's employees. The building eventually became a church again, The Immaculate Heart of Mary, which later merged with St. Patrick's Church.

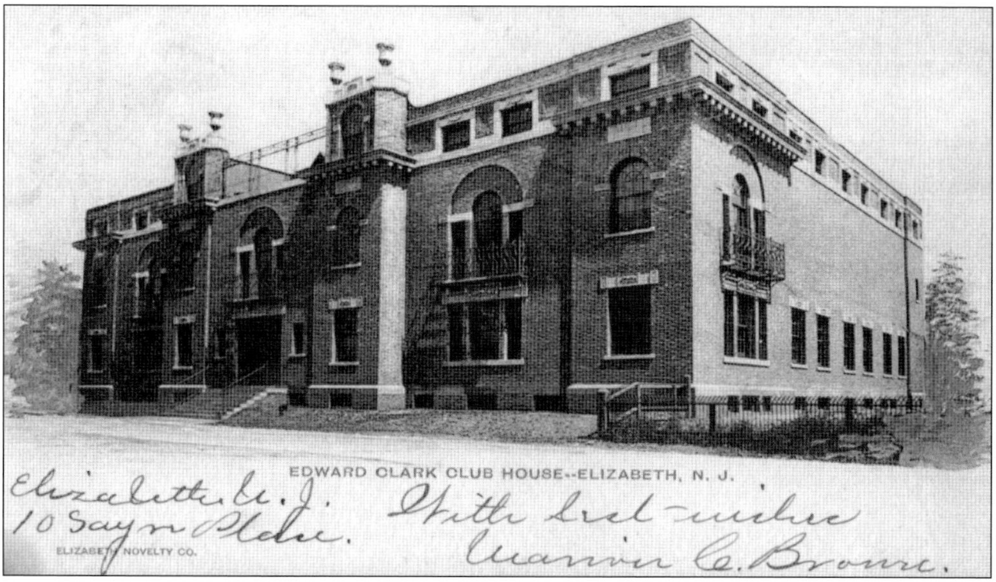

The view of the Edward Clark Club on this postcard is different from the other two. This view shows the facade of the Clark Club, which is decorated with several large windows and an ornate brick arrangement. Since the Edward Clark Club was a social institution, it was important for the space to be conducive for interaction and camaraderie.

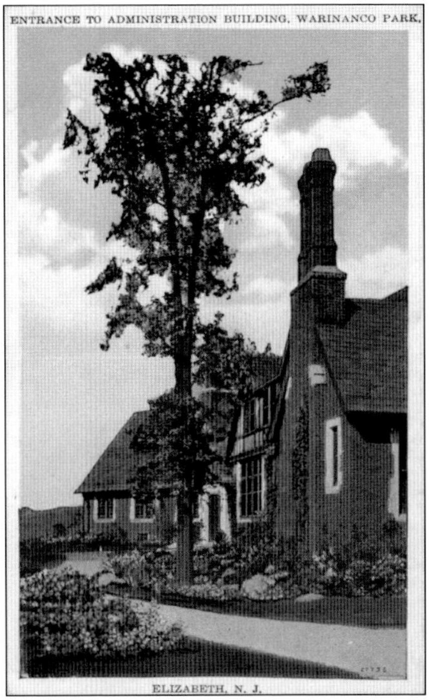

This portrait-oriented image of a beautiful home is the entrance to the administration building in Warinanco Park. The building was completed in 1925, by the architect C. Godfrey Poggi. This unique home was designed in a Tudor Revival architectural style and is still standing today. Poggi's buildings are featured around Elizabeth and Union County at large; he also famously designed the Singer Recreation Building, Battin High School, Grover Cleveland Junior High School, and several commercial buildings and factories.

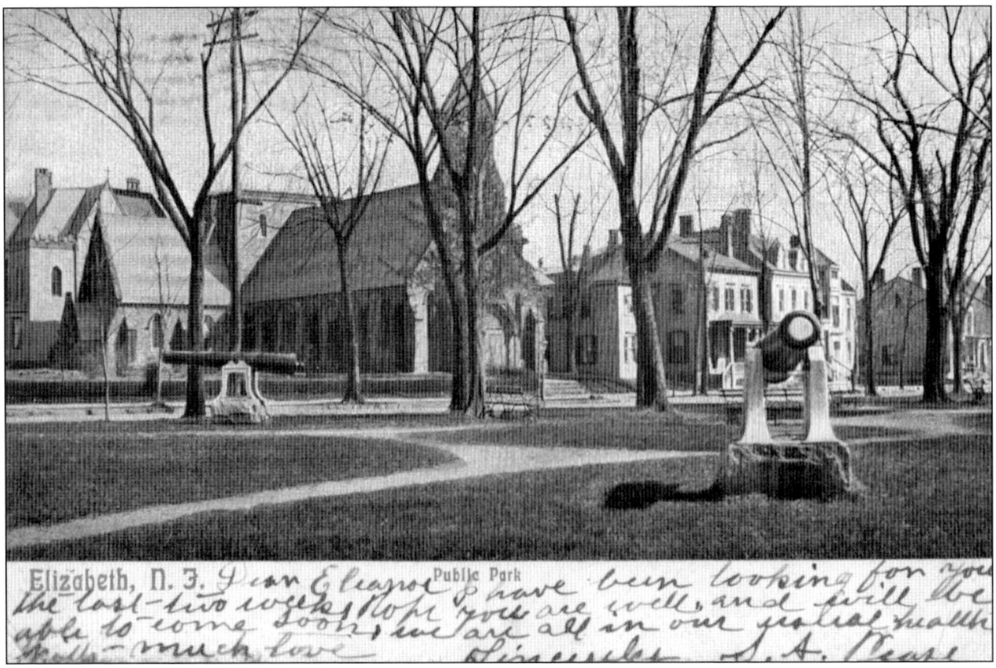

The image on this postcard is of a public park in Elizabeth. The park shows some historic cannons that stand as monuments on the grounds. In the background of the park, a church is visible, as well as some traditional houses. The church in the background can be recognized as Trinity Church, an Episcopal church. The writing on the bottom of the postcard reads, "Dear Eleanor, I have been looking for you the last two weeks, hope you are well, and will be able to come soon, we are all in our usual health—much love."

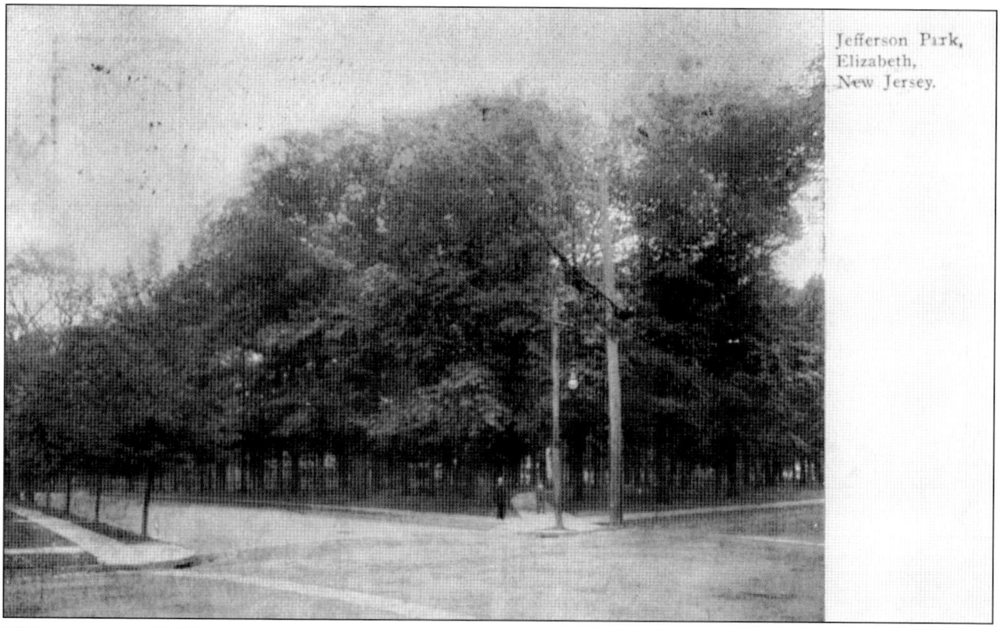

This image of Jefferson Park shows two people enjoying the park's paths. The postcard image was likely captured around the 1900s. Today, the park would be recognized as Kellogg Park, named after the real estate developer Edward N. Kellogg, who gave the park to the city in 1858. Kellogg Park is right next to the Madison & Monroe School, and it is often used by the school as a place for recreation for the young students.

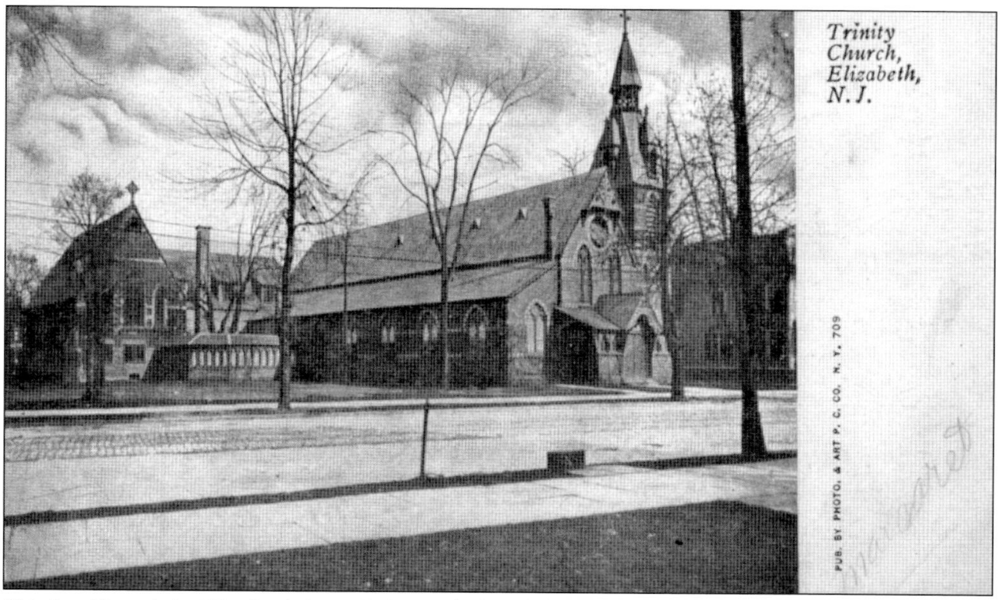

Trinity Church in Elizabeth is an Episcopal church located on the intersection of North Broad Street and Chestnut Street. The church started as a chapel in 1866, and the final church product, seen in this image, was finished in 1871. Trinity Church was designed by the leading architect of Gothic Revival style, Richard Upjohn. Upjohn also designed the Trinity Church in New York and the Grace Church in Newark. The lower right-hand corner of the postcard shows the name "Margaret" in faint pencil.

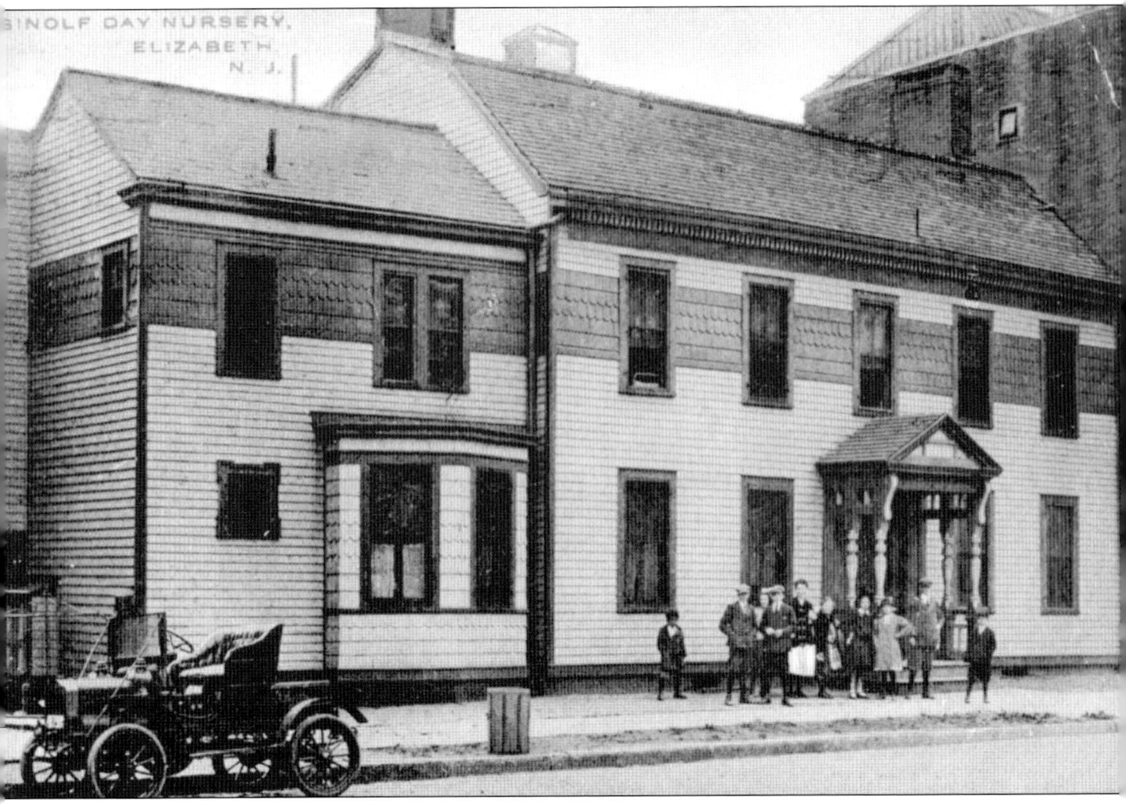

The Eginolf Day Nursery in Elizabeth, now known as the Early Childhood Center, is over 125 years old. It was also called the Elizabeth Day Nursery, and it was created in 1890 by a group of well-known women who were residents in Elizabeth and wanted to improve the welfare of children while their mothers were at work. The nursery was named after Peter and Lena Eginolf, the couple that donated the house for the day nursery. The center is still up and running today, though it has been highly renovated. In 1995, the center became the first child care program in Elizabeth that was accredited by the National Association for the Education of Young Children. The center provides early childhood education to over 100 children in the city.

Five

Where the Streets Have No Name
The Roads of Elizabeth

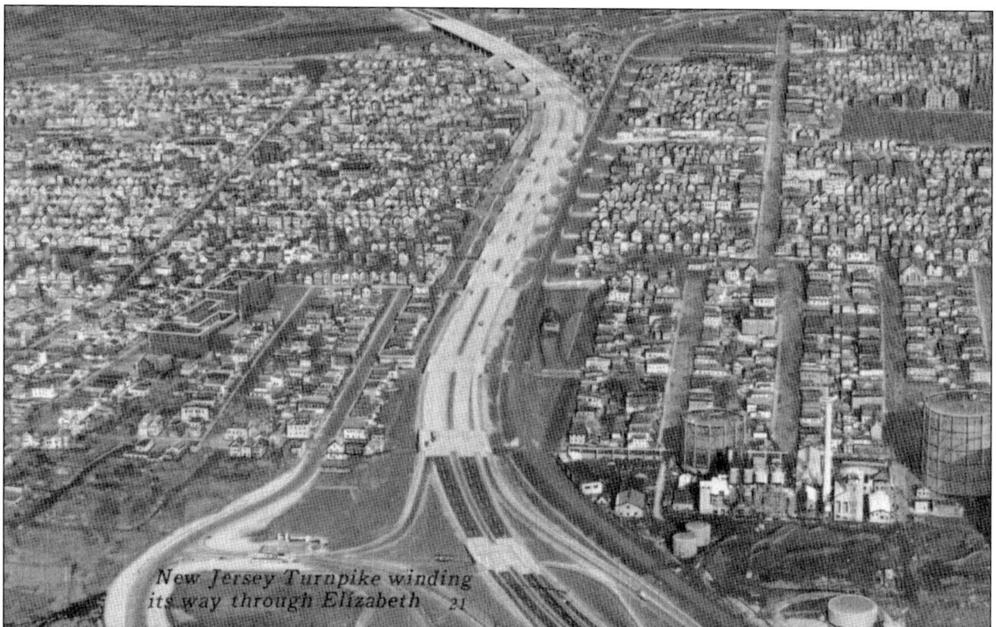

"The Turnpike" is one of New Jersey's toll roads, connecting it to the surrounding states of New York, Pennsylvania, and Delaware. The aerial view from this postcard shows the Turnpike that dissects the city of Elizabeth into two recognizable halves. The road was constructed through a residential area, so as to avoid destroying businesses and homes. One of the Turnpike's major junctions is in the city of Elizabeth, and it is known for its high volume of traffic, mainly due to its proximity to the city of New York, Newark International Airport, and the Elizabeth/ Newark Sea Port.

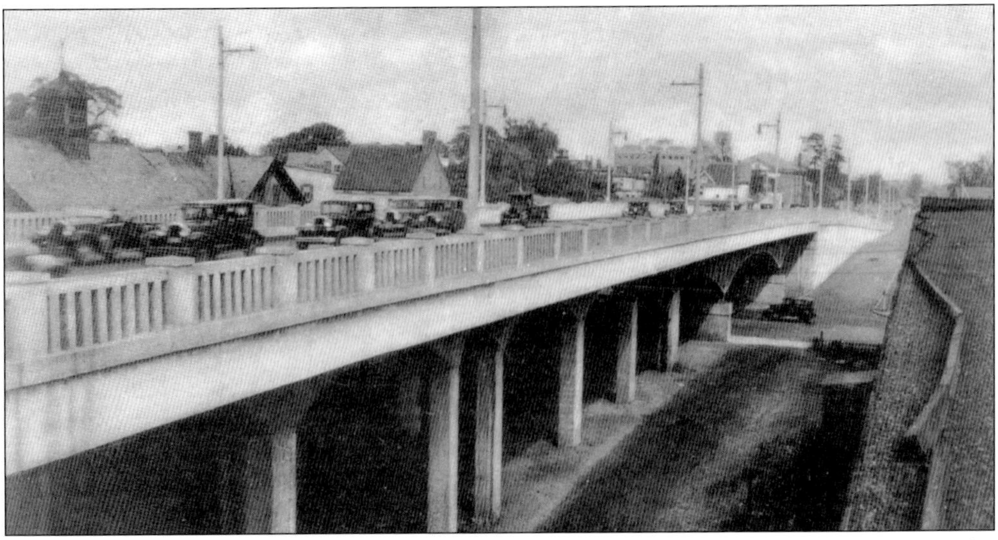

Elizabeth Avenue is one of Elizabeth's main commercial strips, along with Broad Street. The Super Highway Bridge was constructed to go over Elizabeth Avenue in order to allow for easy passage through the town while avoiding the bustling commercial streets. The bridge still exists today and serves much of the same purpose and is a part of St. George's Avenue, a main transportation route in Union County. From the vantage point of this photograph, one can see Battin High School in the distance.

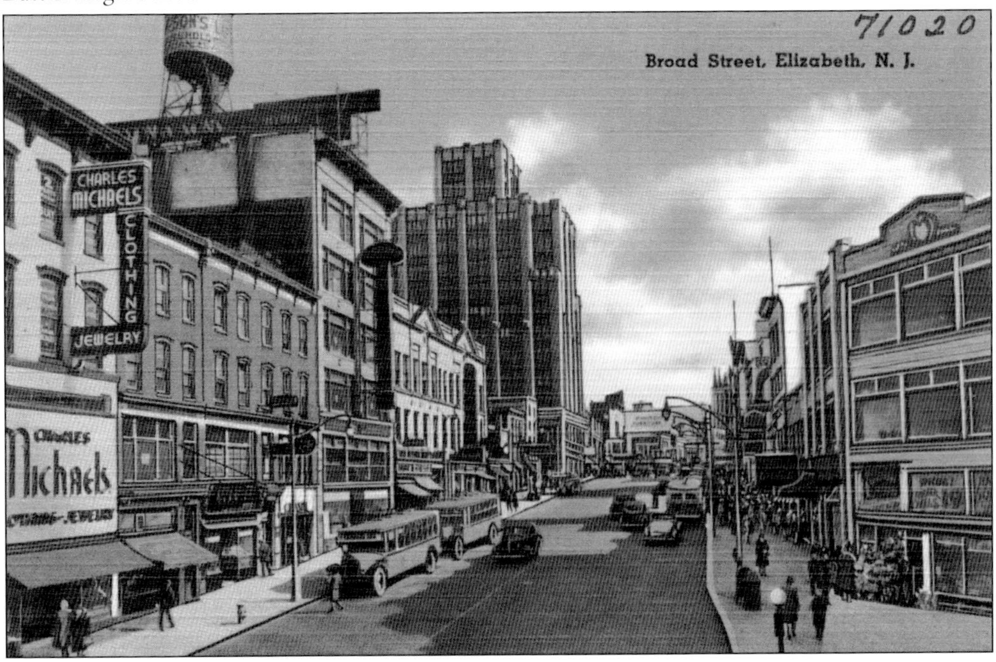

This card, printed by the Tichnor Brothers between 1930 and 1945, shows a bustling section of Broad Street in Elizabeth. As the country attempted to rise out of the Great Depression, capitalism and consumerism played an important, if overstated, role, even as FDR's New Deal brought social progress to the welfare state. In the foreground, one can see Charles Michael's Clothing and Jewelry store, as well as several taxi buses. On the right, if one looks closely, a faint Coca-Cola marquee is visible. (Courtesy of the Boston Public Library Digital Commonwealth.)

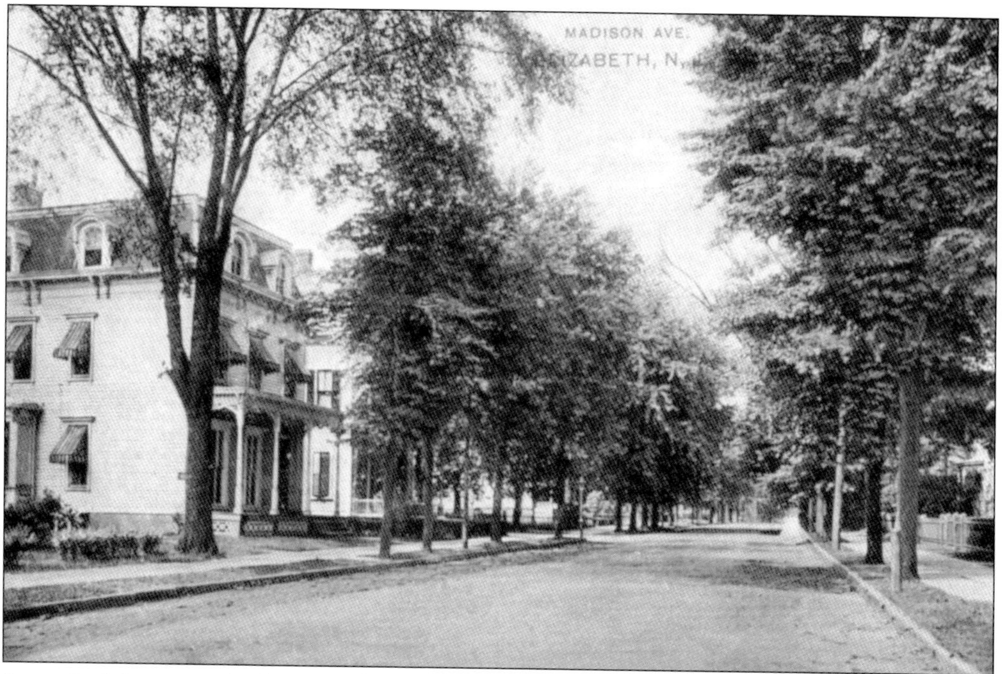

Several of the streets in the city of Elizabeth are named after the first presidents of the United States. This lovely street-view postcard shows a Victorian house–lined street, replete with trees, which is representative of what most residential streets in Elizabeth looked like in its early years. Madison Avenue is a part of a series of streets that contain avenues named after the chronologically ordered presidents: Jefferson, Madison, Monroe, Adams, Jackson, and Van Buren.

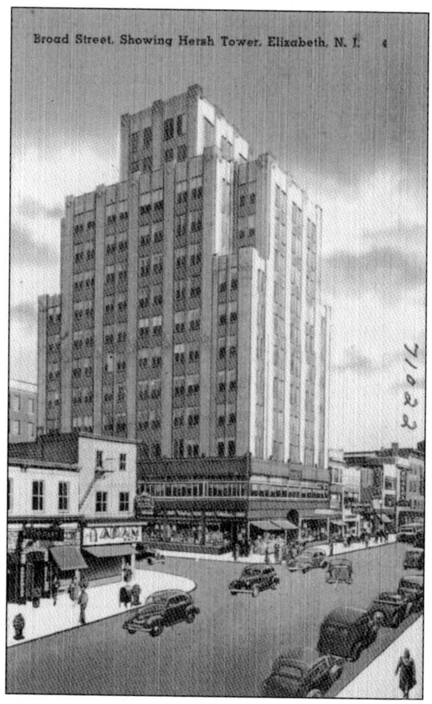

This view of Broad Street in downtown Elizabeth shows the historic Hersch Tower. Constructed in 1931, at the onset of the Great Depression, this brick, marble, and nickel Art Deco–style building is 14 stories and 140 feet tall. Architects Nathan Myles (Newark) and Joseph Shanley (Princeton) were responsible for its design and construction. The building was just the second in the United States to support an internal fire-escape mechanism. Purchased out of foreclosure in 1990 by the Brooklyn-based Wybro brothers, the building is, as of 2018, undergoing conversion and renovation into residential housing. It is listed in the National Register of Historic Places. (Courtesy of the Boston Public Library Digital Commonwealth.)

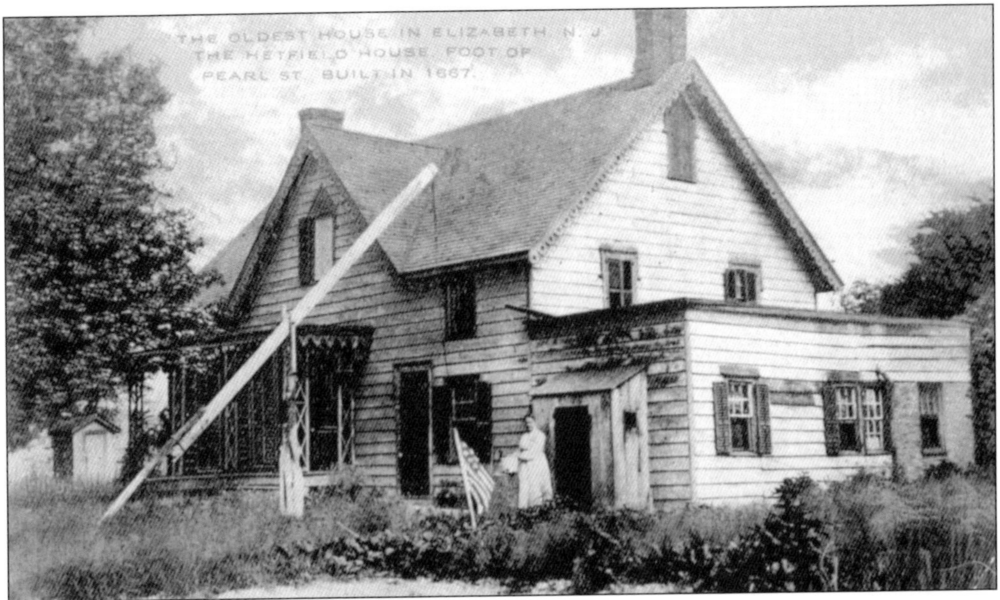

The caption for this postcard reads, "The Oldest House in Elizabeth, N.J.; The Hetfield House. Foot of Pearl Street. Built in 1667." The house was likely named after Andrew Hetfield, a Presbyterian deacon in Westfield. The house was built in a Victorian style and shows a typically dressed lady at the front of the house. Its location, Pearl Street, is a centrally located street and would have been part of the town's center; the house, however, is no longer standing.

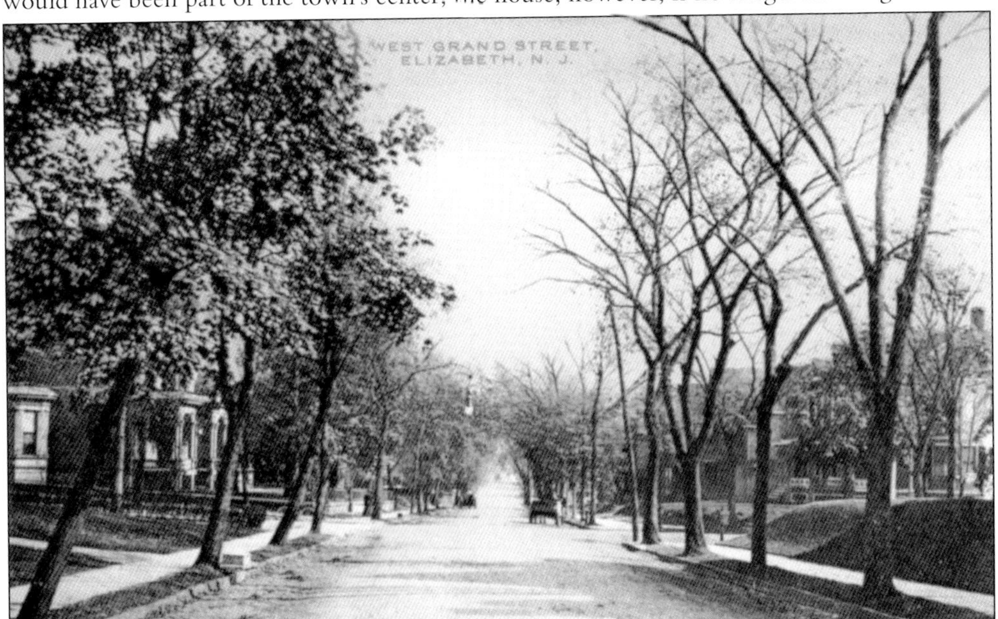

West Grand Street is a broad and long strip that runs from Elmora Avenue up until the end of the city limits and into a neighboring city, Roselle. The view on this postcard shows the large, typical Victorian-style home that Elizabeth was known for in its residential neighborhoods. It is interesting to notice, however, that the streets on this view are not yet paved, and the postcard even shows a couple of carriages in the view: Carriages would have been the most common form of transportation on the streets at this time, since cars were considered more of a luxury.

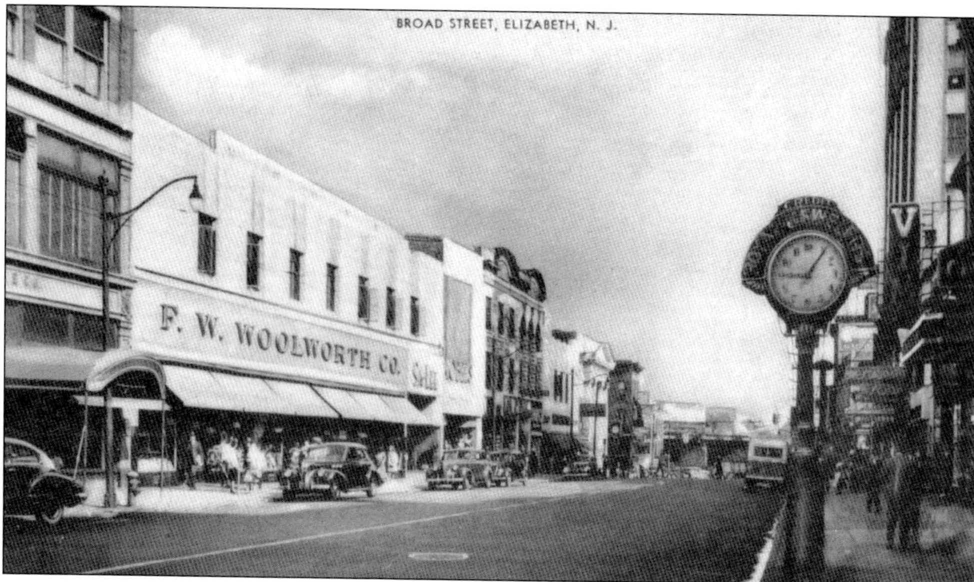

Many of Elizabeth's earlier postcards capture some of the city's most famous and iconic location. For that reason, Broad Street is a common image depicted on these postcards. This particular view of Broad Street shows F.W. Woolworth Co. The store is no longer in Elizabeth, but it has historical significance because F.W. Woolworth Co. was a pioneering chain in the dollar-store business and at the time was one of the biggest and most successful chains for this particular niche of economic variety stores. The fact that this store had a location in Elizabeth shows just how important the city was as a commercial hub in New Jersey.

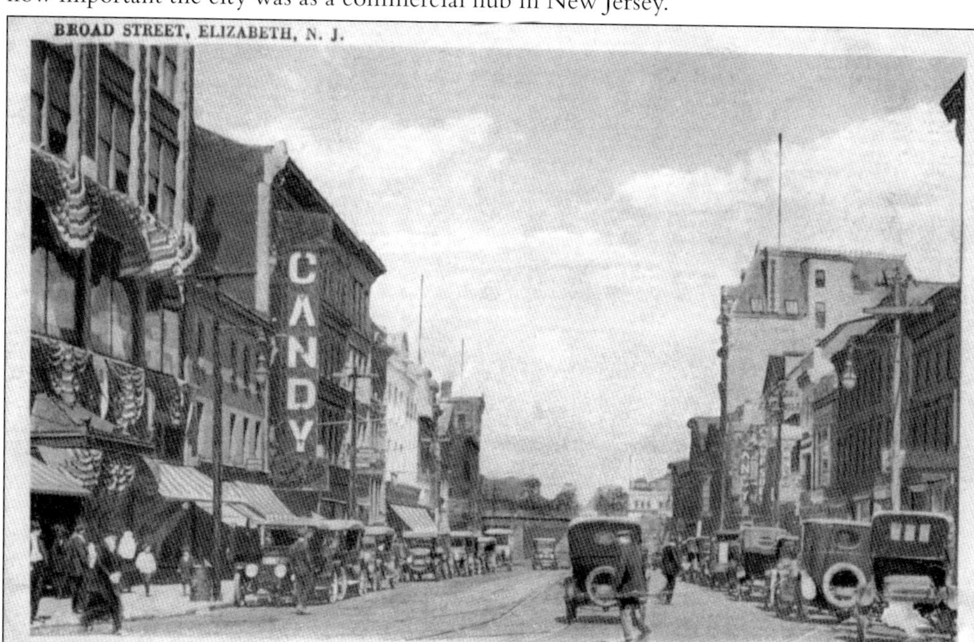

This postcard shows a generic image of Broad Street. It is interesting to notice, however, that this image of Broad Street shows the street when it still had trolley tracks. There is a main sign that reads "Candy" in this street view, and a closer look reveals another smaller sign on the opposite side of the street that reads the same.

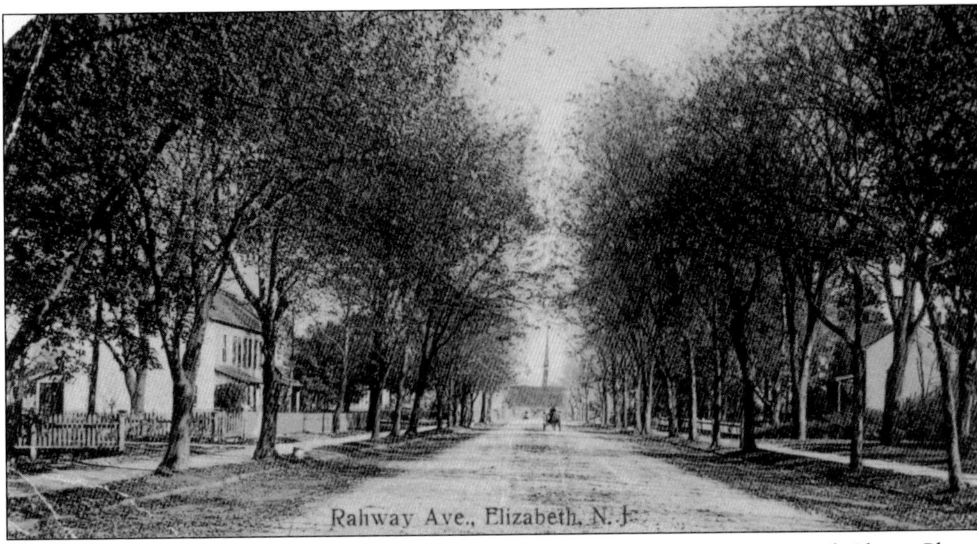

Rahway Avenue starts at Elmore Avenue and intersects Hayes Avenue, Newcomb Place, Clover Street, Dewey Place, Grove Street, DeHart Place, South Street, Clinton Street, Pearl Street, Lyon Place, and Cherry Street before merging into Elizabeth Avenue. Along its route, one can find KFC, Super Value Liquor, Dunkin' Donuts, Papa John's Pizza, Pro Window Tinting, Don Alex's diner, Walgreens, Wendy's, Inklightened Tattoo and Piercing, Wells Fargo Bank, Delta Gas Station, Shell, Super Discount Liquors, Park View Tavern, and Warinanco Park.

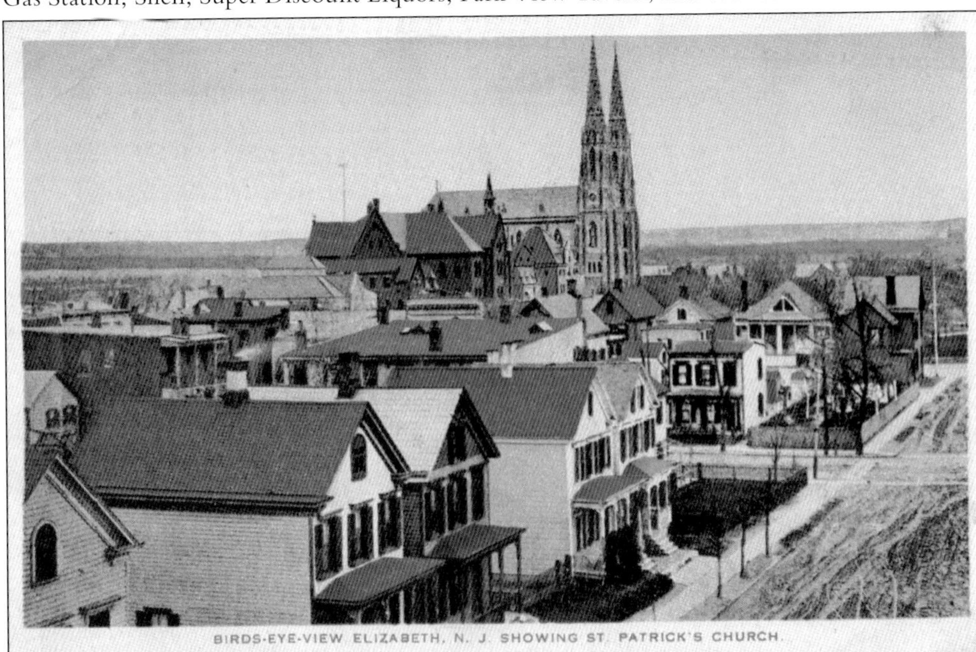

This aerial view of Elizabeth shows St. Patrick's Church, which was built in the Gothic style starting in 1887. The church used to be home to St. Patrick's School, which was a New Jersey basketball powerhouse for decades. Among the school's famous alums is Kyrie Irving, an all-star point guard for the Boston Celtics, who helped lead the Cleveland Cavaliers to the city's first sports championship in 52 years by hitting the deciding basket in Game Seven against the Golden State Warriors, a game the Cavaliers would win 93-89.

This postcard, published on linen and colorized, shows a bright, gay view of Broad Street in downtown Elizabeth, sometime between 1915 and 1930. Visible with its familiar red background and gold lettering is the Woolworth department store. Next to it, with this grey and gold color scheme, is the Canadian department store, another relic of a bygone era. The marquee shows a third department store, Goerke's, which was a local chain that would be bought out by another local chain, Steinbach's, in 1962. (Courtesy of the Boston Public Library Digital Collections.)

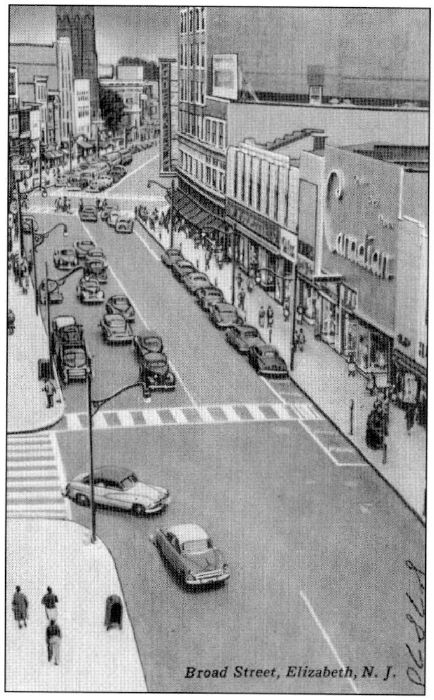

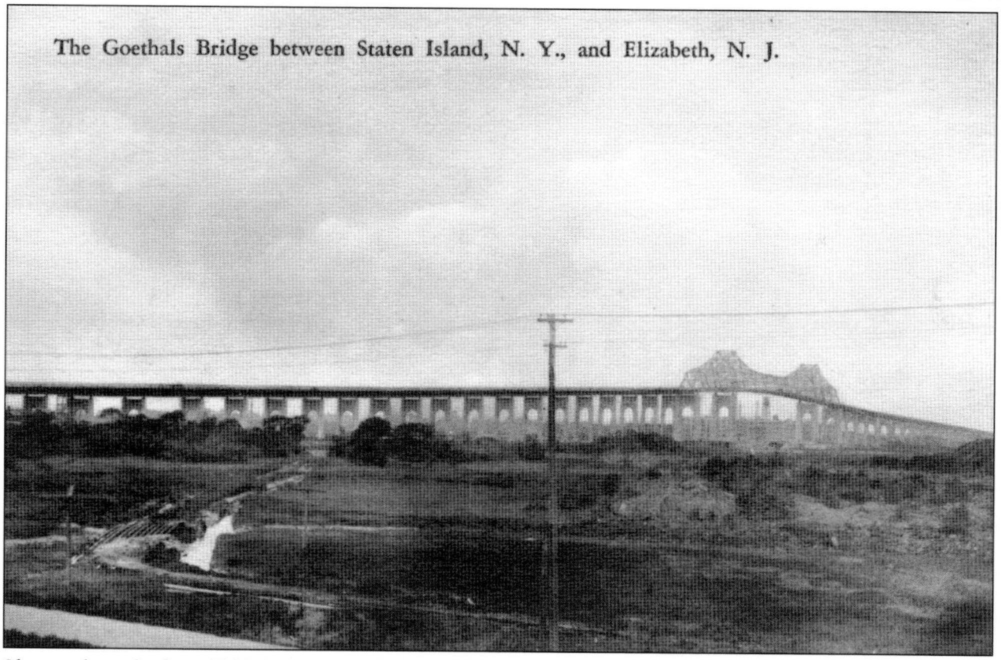

Shown here before 1907 is the Goethals Bridge, which crosses Arthur Kill to connect Elizabeth to Staten Island. The bridge is 7,109 feet long, 62 feet wide, and stands 140 feet above Arthur Kill. Constructed started on September 1, 1925, at an estimated cost of $7.2 million, or almost $95 million in 2018. The bridge was set for a rebuild in 2014, and the spans closed in 2017 so that construction could begin. The bridge reopened in summer 2018 to great fanfare, although the $15 toll to cross into New York was less than welcome. (Courtesy of the New York Public Library.)

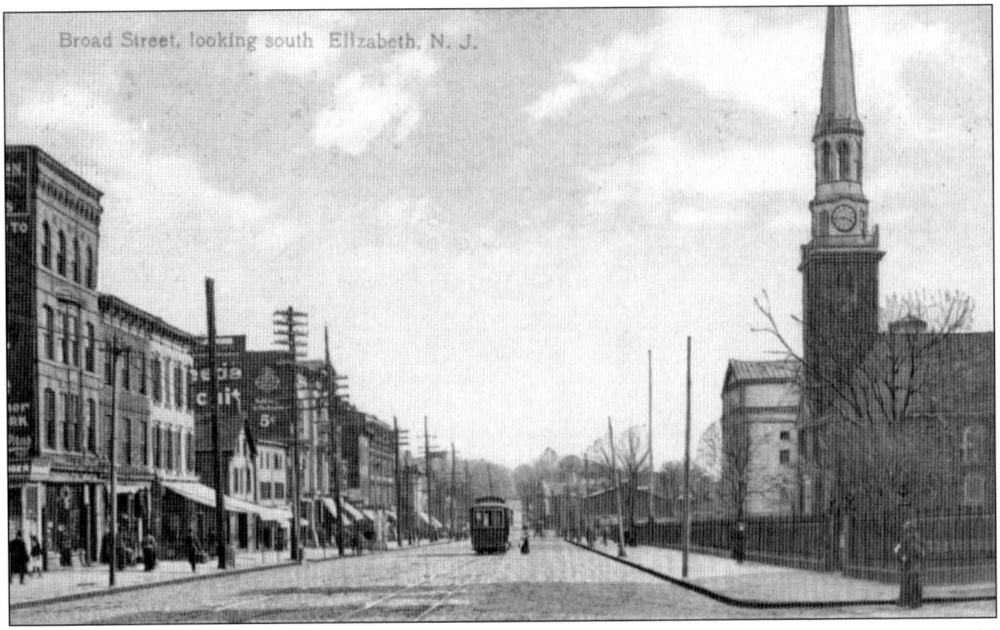

While there are several postcards in this collection that show a view of Broad Street in Elizabeth, each one has a unique element that makes it historically significant for this book in postcard history. This particular street view, looking south, shows Broad Street before any of its iconic buildings were constructed. One can see a trolley in the middle of the street, approximately in front of where the Superior Court of New Jersey building is located today. One can also see the First Presbyterian Church.

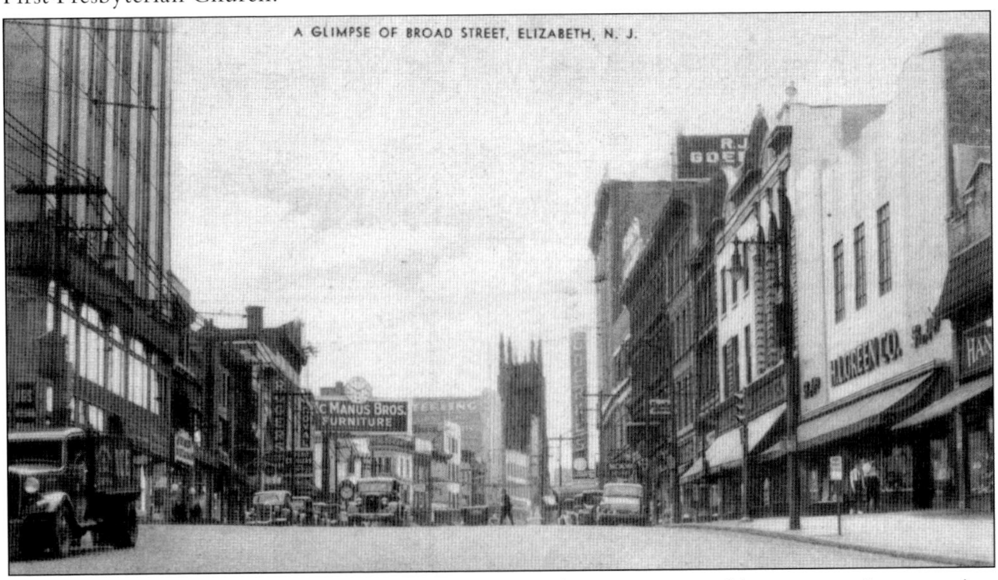

This "glimpse" of Broad Street shows the city once it began to expand in construction, creating what is known today as the commercial strip that is Broad Street. In the distance is a sign for the McManus Bros. Furniture Store, which no longer exists. Most of the buildings on this postcard have either been entirely changed or greatly renovated since the time that this picture was taken, but the distinctive character of Broad Street is still noticeable and traceable, thanks to landmarks such as St. John's Episcopal Church in the center background.

This bird's-eye view of Elizabeth shows the city plans as they looked in 1898. The surrounding border of the postcard displays various buildings throughout the city, with a neat index that explains which building is which. This is likely the type of map that would have hung inside a municipal building as a reference for city planners or city officials.

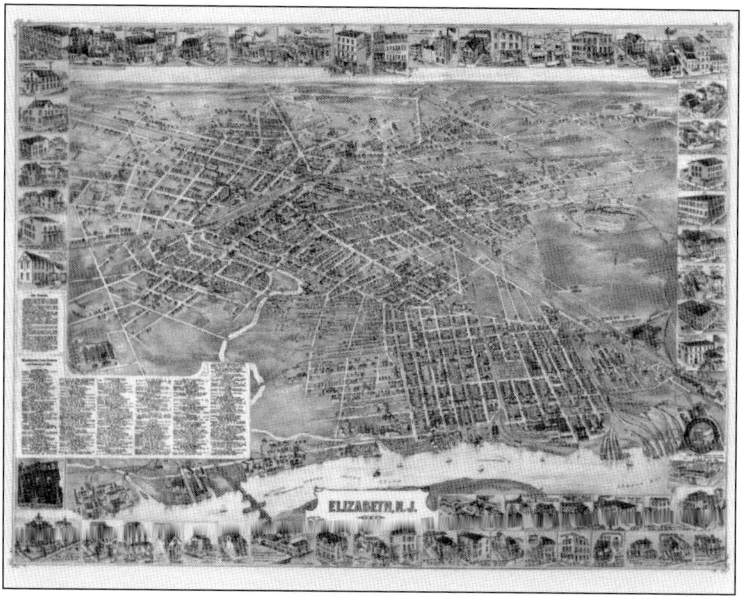

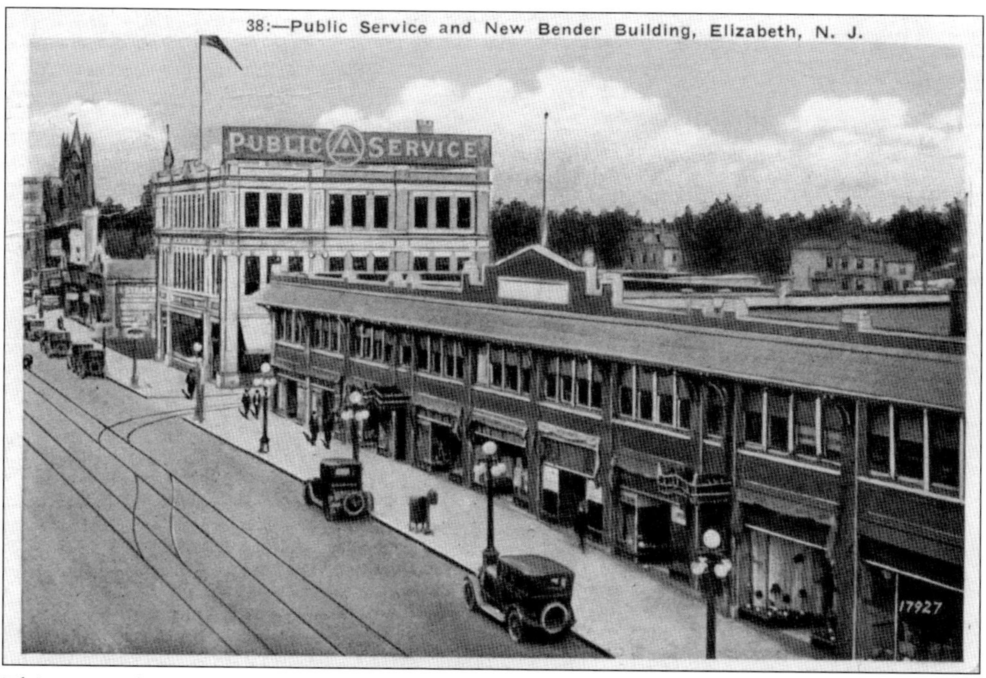

This postcard is numbered 38, likely as part of a series that features key places in Elizabeth. The caption for the card reads, "Public Service and New Bender Building, Elizabeth, N.J." The public service building is clearly labeled in the postcard, but the New Bender building, today known as the Albender Building, is a low-rise, brick building with a white and red facade that was designed in a Neoclassical style. It is a commercial building located on East Jersey Street.

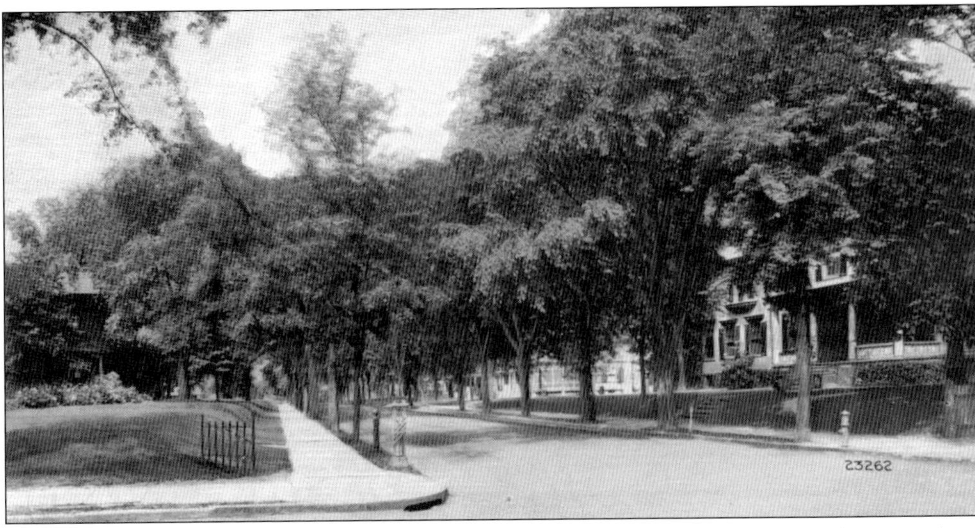

This postcard shows Elizabeth's Westfield Avenue from Cherry Street. Westfield Avenue is an important main avenue in Elizabeth that takes drivers out to neighboring cities. The Victorian-style home on the right hand of the postcard is evocative of the type of homes that could be seen throughout the more suburban neighborhoods in Elizabeth. The long rows of trees were also an important feature of residential areas since they provided much-needed greenery for the city.

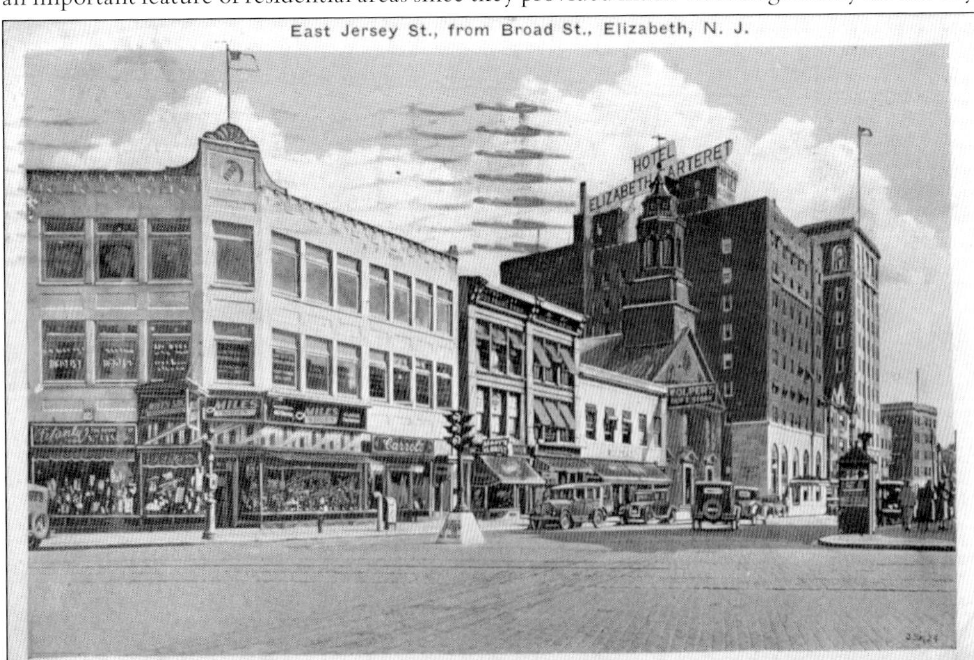

This postcard shows East Jersey Street from Broad Street. The Elizabeth Carteret Hotel is visible from this perspective. Postcards with street views of Elizabeth were popular for both visitors and residents to show their friends or relatives the important commercial streets for which the city was known. Although Broad Street is the main commercial strip in Elizabeth, several of the street's businesses opened on adjacent streets or streets that intersected Broad Street. East Jersey Street was one such street that opened several businesses, including the popular Carteret Hotel, just along Broad Street.

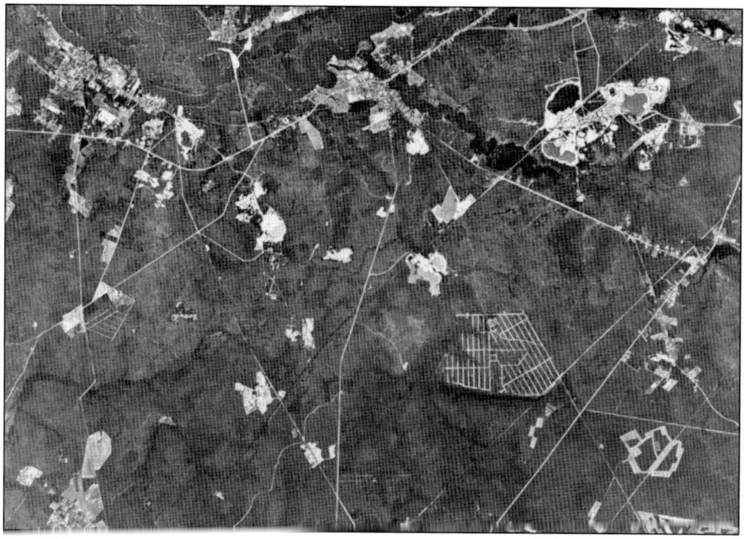

This aerial view of Elizabeth from the 1960s shows the concentration of buildings that made up Elizabethtown in the lower left-hand corner of the image. The map shows the abundance of green space that used to predominate over the landscape. Needless to say, the aerial landscape in Elizabeth has changed very much since then.

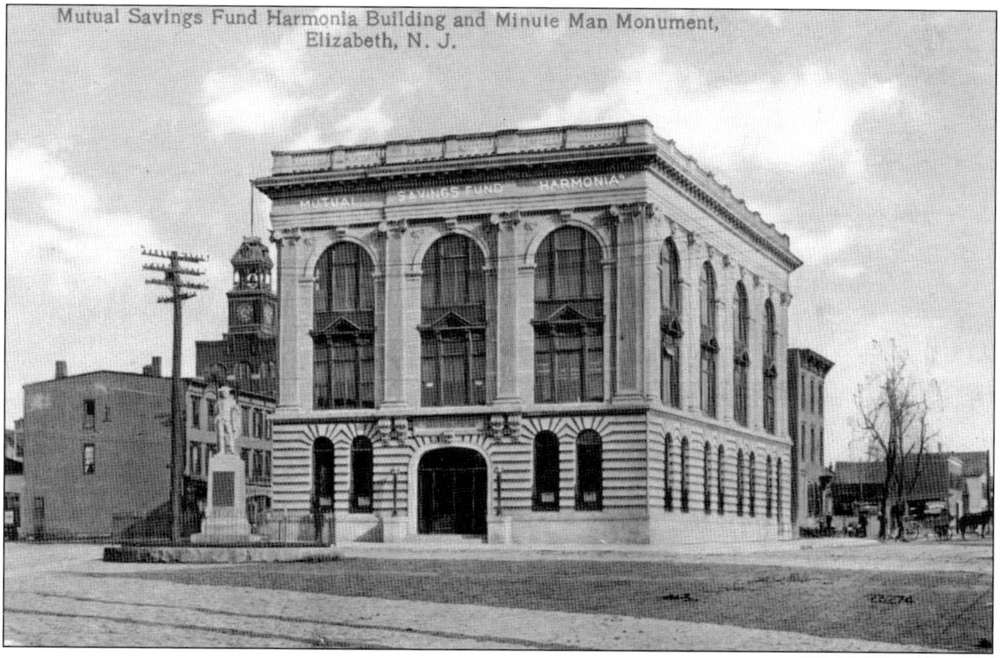

The title on this postcard reads, "Mutual Savings Fund Harmonia Building and Minute Man Monument." Harmonia Bank was chartered in 1851. The original architecture of the bank, shown in this postcard, was renovated and remodeled in the 1960s as the bank become the Sovereign Bank. The clock tower near the left side of the bank, seen in the background, was above the Rising Sun Brewery that was located at Seventh and Marshall Streets. The statue in the front of the building is of a minuteman, which was the name given to a soldier fighting in the Revolutionary War. Elizabeth was an important site for the Revolutionary War. To this day, this tribute to Elizabeth's contribution to the Revolutionary War continues: the Elizabeth football team is called the Elizabeth Minutemen.

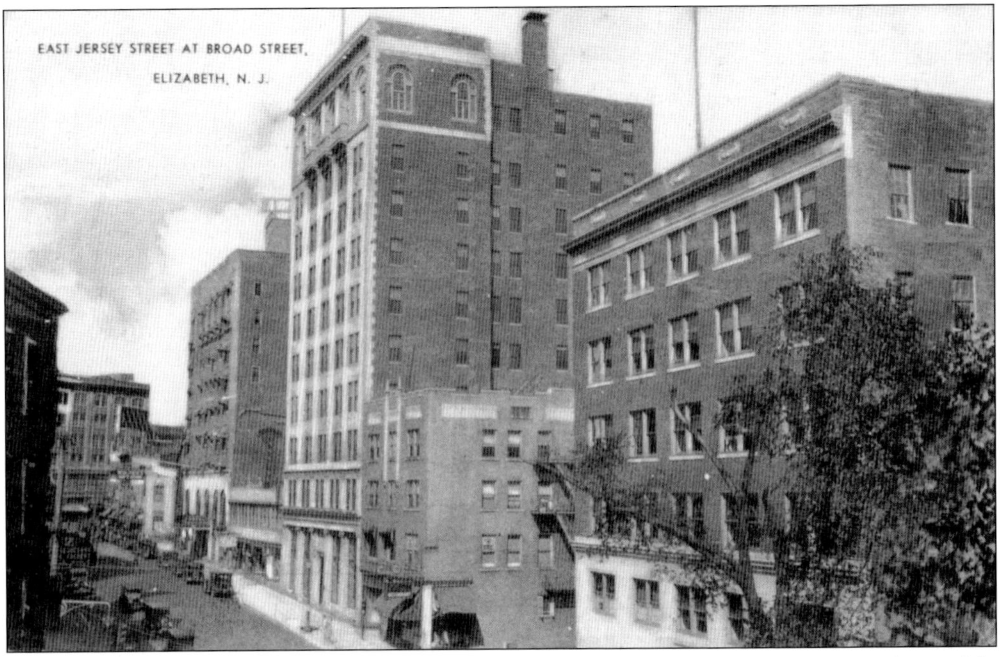

This postcard shows East Jersey Street at Broad Street. The Elizabeth Carteret Hotel is visible at a distance. Notice the cars that appear to be lined up in front of the hotel. East Jersey Street was a popular location from which visitors and residents could visit the bustling streets of Elizabeth's commercial center. Several residential buildings and hotels, such as the ones shown on this postcard, were built to accommodate the high concentration of residents and visitors in Elizabeth. Elizabeth continues to be one of the most highly populated cities in New Jersey.

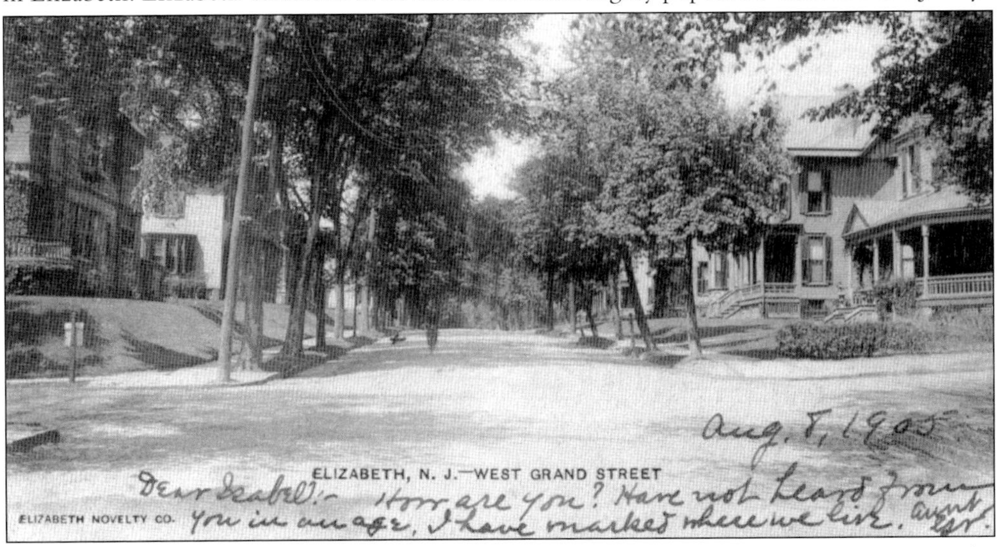

The image on this postcard is of a residential street in Elizabeth called West Grand Street. The postcard is dated August 8, 1905; the text on the postcard reads, "How are you? Have not heard from you in ages. I have marked where we live." The author of this postcard placed a tiny "x" on the street to mark their home. Many of these postcards that showed street views or other obscure locations that would not be familiar to a wide audience were meant for more personal use, for residents or visitors of the city to mark places that were meaningful to them.

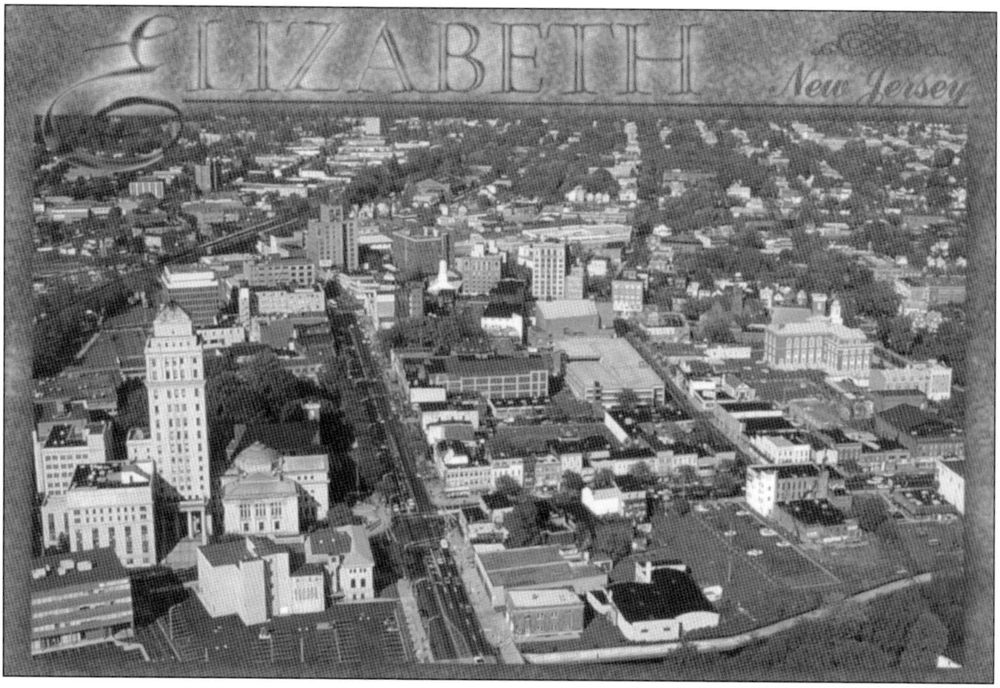

This postcard shows a modern, overhead view of Elizabeth's main commercial street, Broad Street. A more recent snapshot, this postcard demonstrates Elizabeth's popularity as a tourist location or at least as a famous and iconic part of New Jersey. From above, one can see the Union County Courthouse, the Hersh Tower, the Elizabeth Public Library, and the back of city hall.

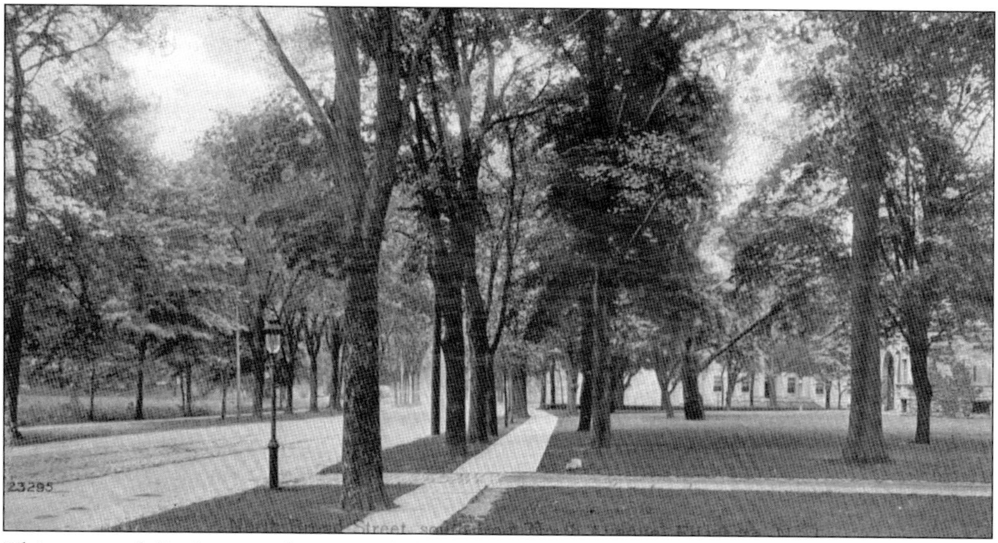

This postcard displays another one of Elizabeth's iconic residential streets, lined with tall, large trees. The bottom of the postcard reveals the street view to be a south view of North Broad Street, viewed from North Avenue. While the postcard image shows mostly trees, thus hiding the view of North Broad Street, it is worth bearing in mind that a recipient of this lovely postcard would have been pleasantly surprised by the greenery of Elizabeth, since it was known mainly as a major city in the state of New Jersey.

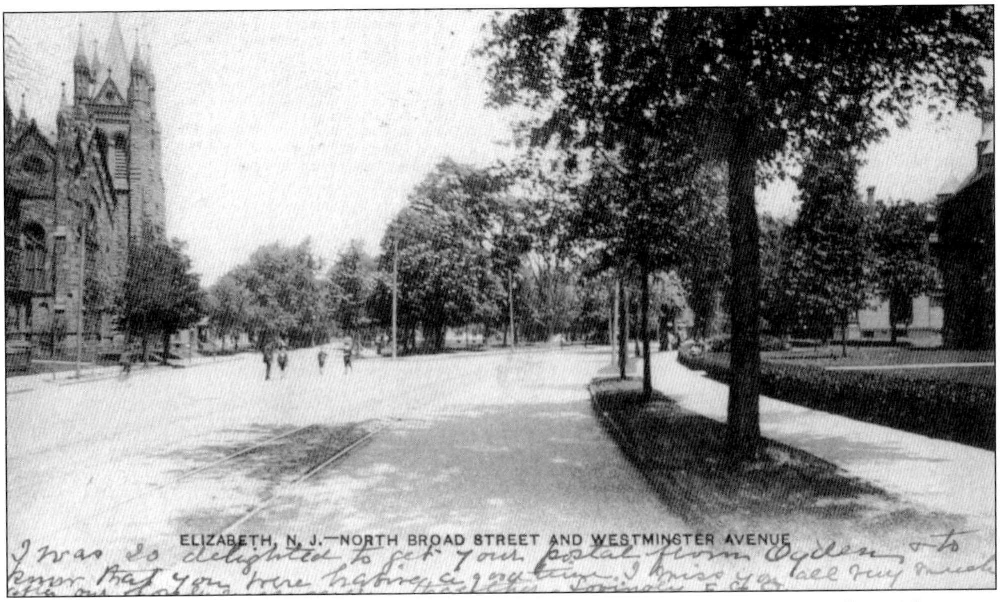

This wonderful view of North Broad Street and Westminster Avenue shows the wide street with trolley tracks, a church on the left and residential houses on the right. The church is the Westminster Presbyterian Church, erected in 1866–1867 at the corner of Westminster Avenue and Prince Street. The church was constructed to resemble a Norman style of architecture, known for its intricate stone layering. The church was destroyed in 1944 due to a fire, and it has been reconstructed twice.

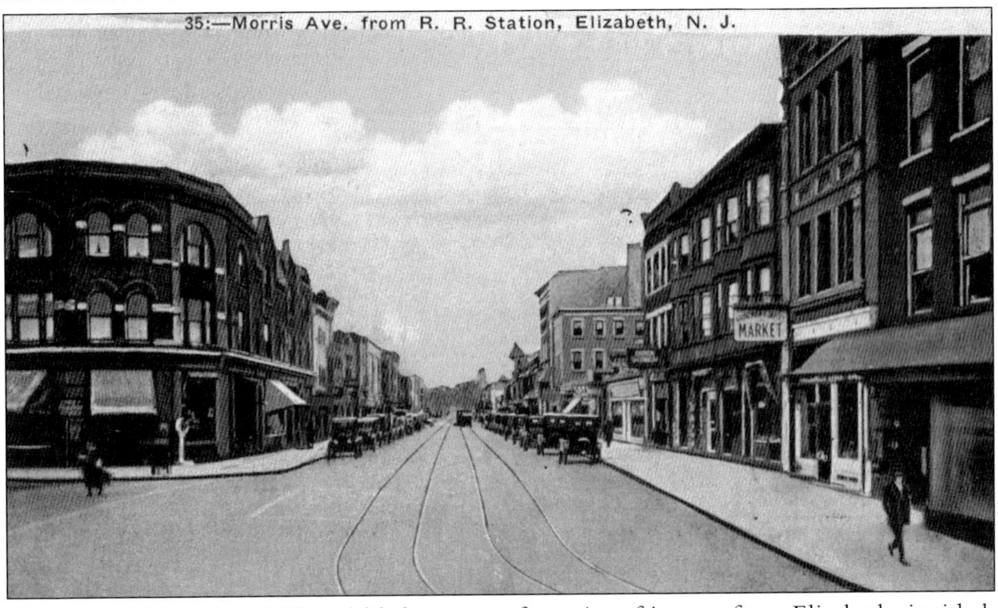

This postcard, numbered 35 and likely a part of a series of images from Elizabeth, is titled, "Morris Avenue from R. R. Station in Elizabeth." To a contemporary resident of Elizabeth, or to anyone who has visited the city recently, seeing trolley tracks on the street might seem bizarre. It might surprise people to know that Elizabeth, in fact, had an extensive trolley service in the early 1900s. Many of the trolleys were replaced by buses around the 1940s, and the tracks that were removed, made from steel, were used for World War II production.

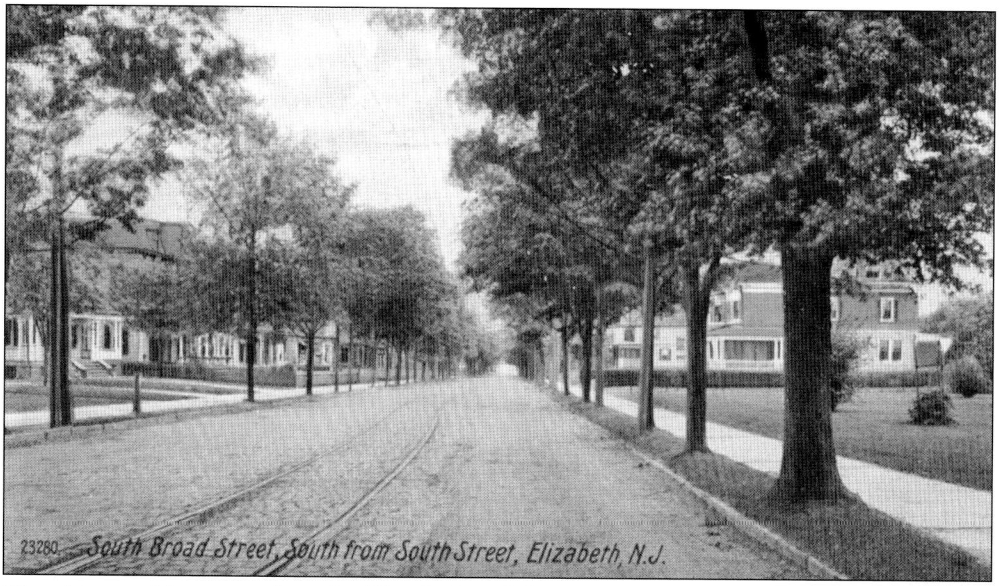

The title on this postcard reads, "South Broad Street, South from South Street, Elizabeth, N.J." This view of South Broad Street shows the trolley tracks that once ran through many of Elizabeth's residential and commercial streets, mainly during the 1930s before bus services were implemented in the 1940s. This street view also shows the popular residential streets of residential neighborhoods in the city, with large streets and Victorian-style houses lined by large trees.

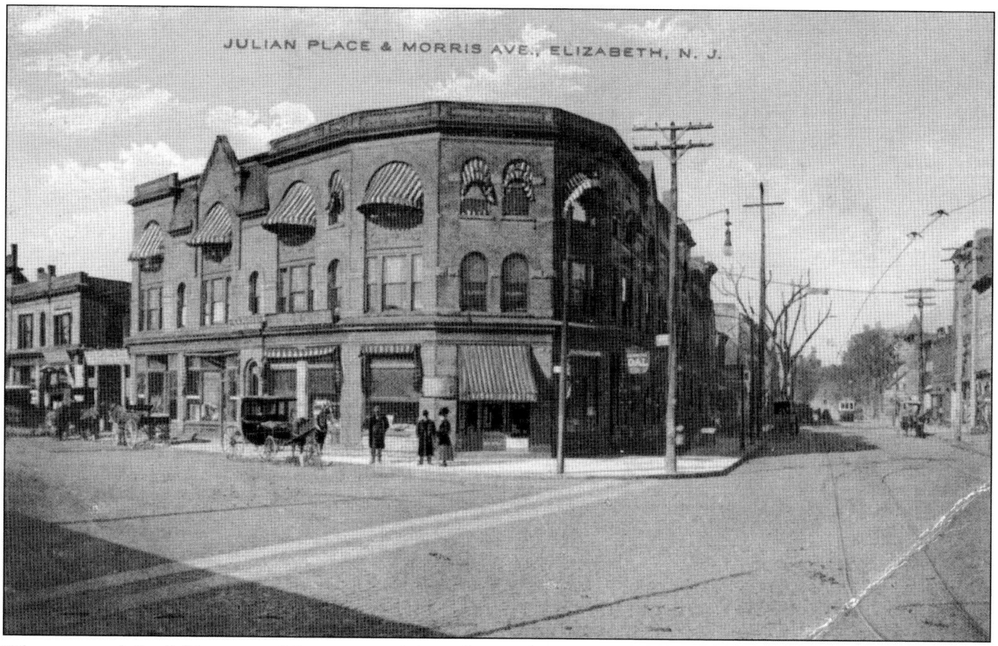

The central building on this postcard is Julian Place, which was a 19th-century three-story brick building on Morris Avenue. The building was used for commercial purposes at street level, while the higher levels were used mainly as professional offices. Two famous Elizabeth architects, C. Godfrey Poggi and Clinton Mackenzie, had their offices in this building in the early 1900s.

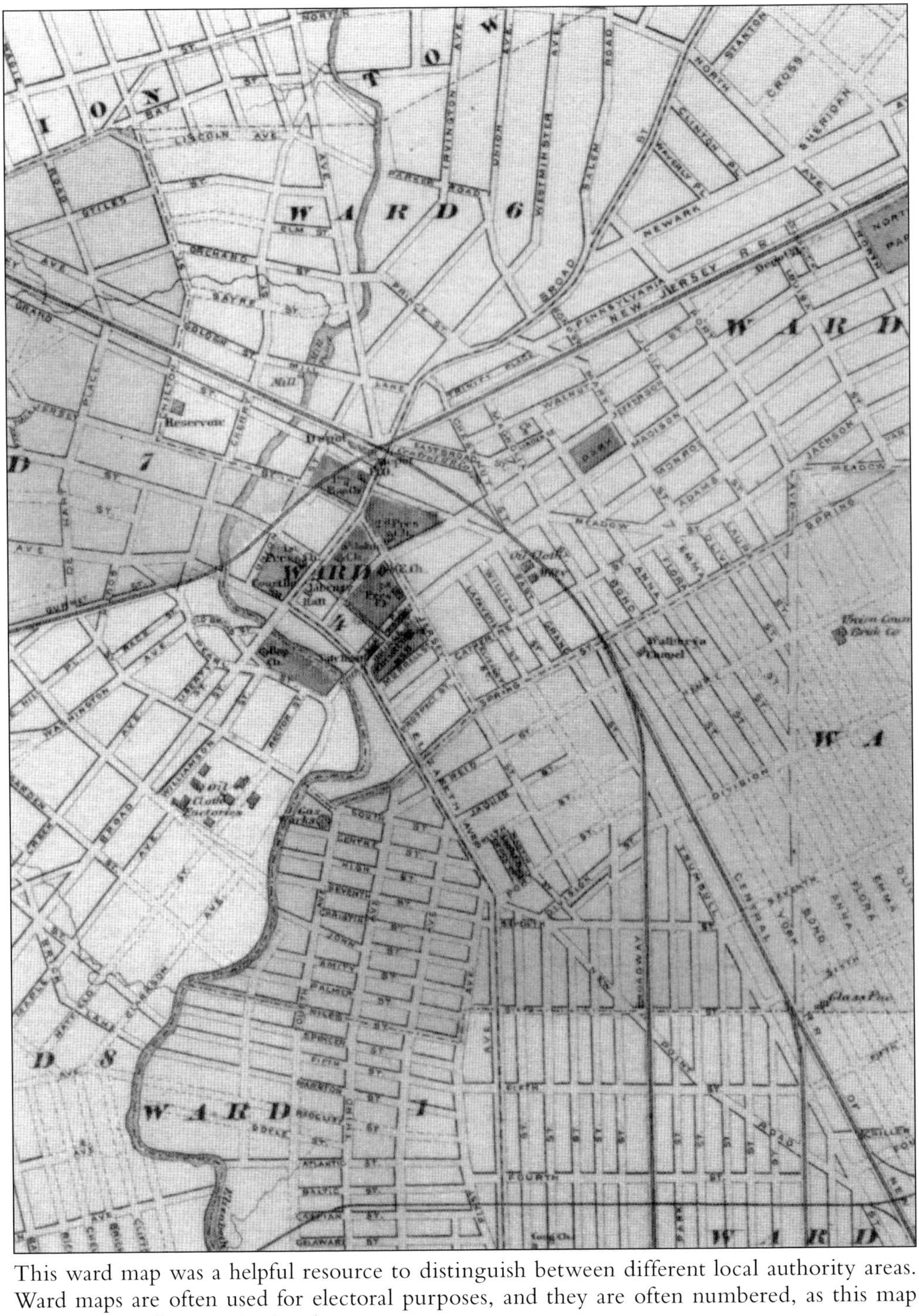

This ward map was a helpful resource to distinguish between different local authority areas. Ward maps are often used for electoral purposes, and they are often numbered, as this map demonstrates, for organizational purposes.

Six

The Red Strokes
The Art and Arts of Elizabeth

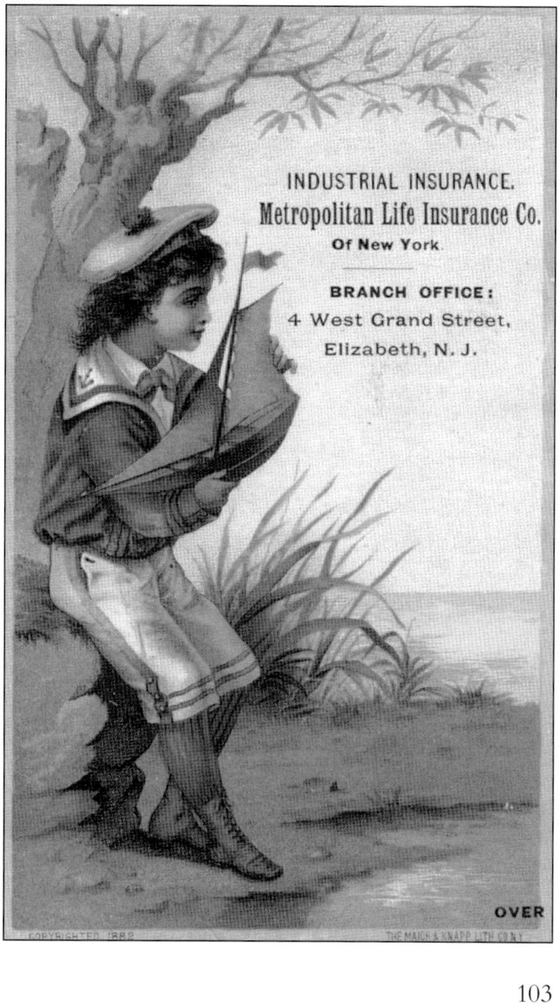

This trade card, with an idyllic view of a young child with a sailboat, was published in 1882 for Metropolitan Life Insurance Co., or what is known today as MetLife. The back of the card lists all of the company's many officers, as well as details on its holdings, liquidity, and available policies "to persons of moderate means." Today, MetLife is one of the largest global providers of insurance, annuities, and employee benefits, with offices in over 60 countries, and the naming rights to the home of the New York Giants and New York Jets. The Elizabeth address listed at 4 Grand Street is now the home of Garden State Community Bank.

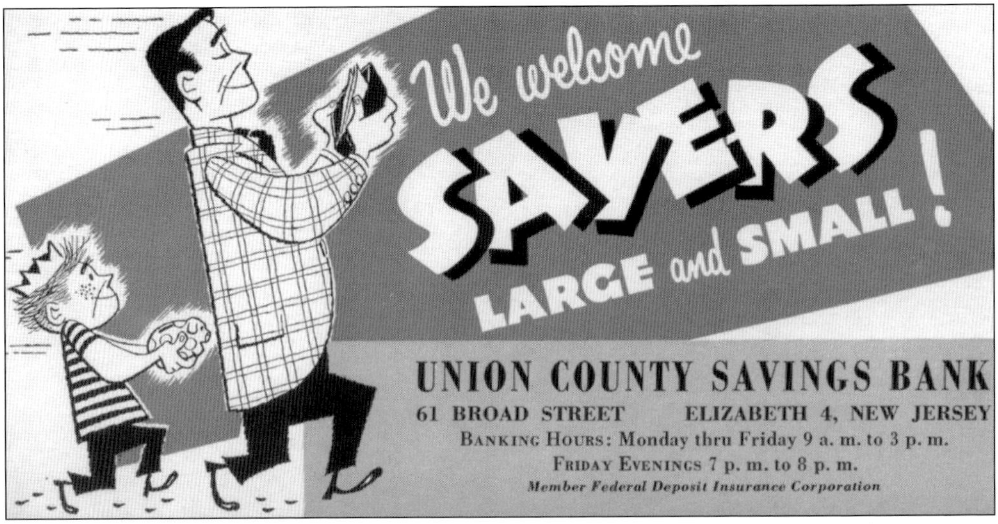

Something funny and peculiar about this little postcard is the fact that it is also an advertisement for the Union County Savings Bank, which was once located on Elizabeth's main commercial street: Broad Street. Elizabeth was one of the largest and most important cities in Union County for commerce and banking, and it still continues to play this role today. This particular bank, however, is no longer active. The image on the postcard is a visual representation of the slogan on the postcard, "We welcome savers large and small!" by showing a grown adult on his way to the bank with his wallet, accompanied by a young boy carrying a piggy bank.

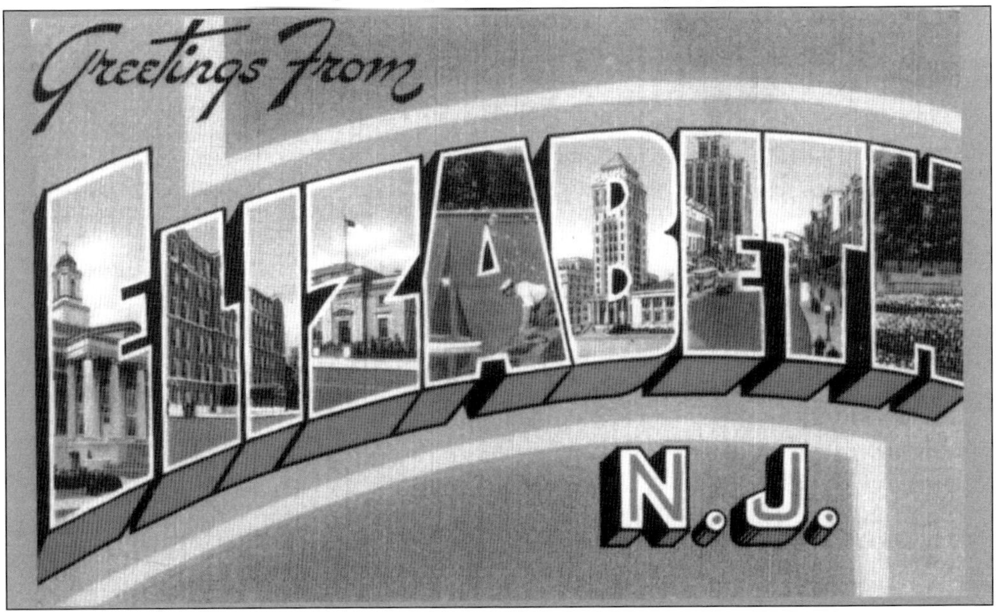

This lively animated postcard reads, "Greetings from Elizabeth N.J." The largely printed letters that read "Elizabeth" display an interesting feature: Each letter shows a specific and important part of Elizabeth. The letter "E" shows town hall; the letters "L" and "I" show an unidentified building; the letter "Z" shows the public library; the letter "A" shows a pond in Warinanco park; "B" shows the municipal courthouse; the letters "E" and "T" show a view of Broad Street; and the letter "H" shows a garden in Warinanco Park. It is likely that all of these images are themselves taken from other postcards of Elizabeth (which have been highlighted in this book).

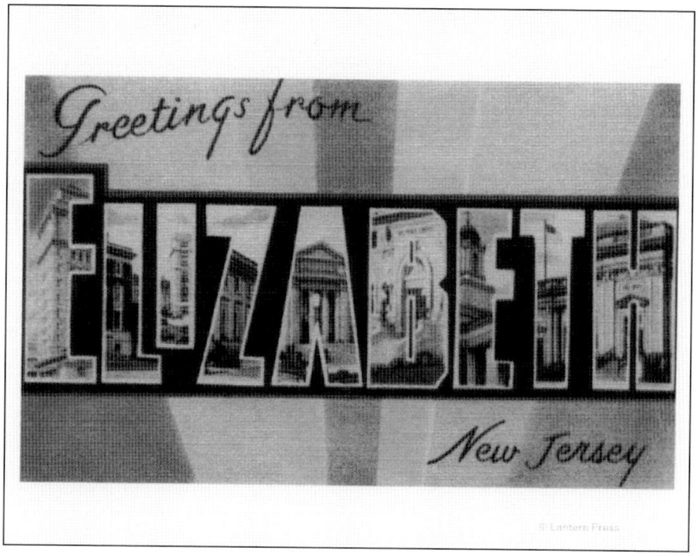

This postcard is another graphic display that reads, "Greetings from Elizabeth N.J." The letters in this graphic also display important buildings throughout the city of Elizabeth, consisting mainly of the municipal buildings that contribute to the Elizabeth city skyline. The postcard resembles the black and white version of "Greetings from Elizabeth N.J.," and it maintained several of the same elements.

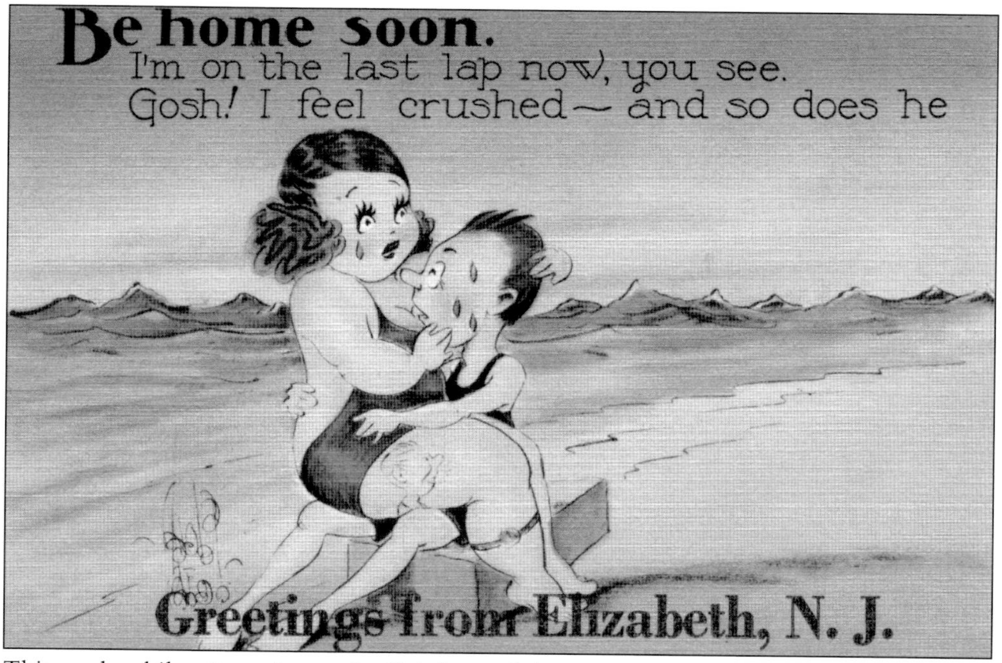

This card, while attempting to be lighthearted (as were many cards in the post-1940 war years), speaks to a serious issue in America: obesity. The current adult obesity rate in Elizabeth, according to the State of Obesity, is a whopping 27.4 percent. For the 10-to-17-year-old demographic, that number shoots up to a whopping 31.4 percent, or nearly a third of New Jersey children in that demographic. Approximately 9.2 percent of adults suffer from some form of diabetes, and 30.9 percent suffer from hypertension. New Jersey does get credit for having some of the best laws to combat this epidemic.

This card features a scenic view of what is said to be Elizabeth, with a pennant declaring the loneliness one suffers while in Elizabeth and away from their beloved. Love is still alive and well in Elizabeth, with, according to 2010 census records, 39.2 percent of homes consisting of married couples. On top of that, 29.5 percent of homes consisted of couples living outside the bonds of matrimony. This card was sent to a Howard Atwood of New York City by a woman named Fillie and seems to be one of several exchanged cards.

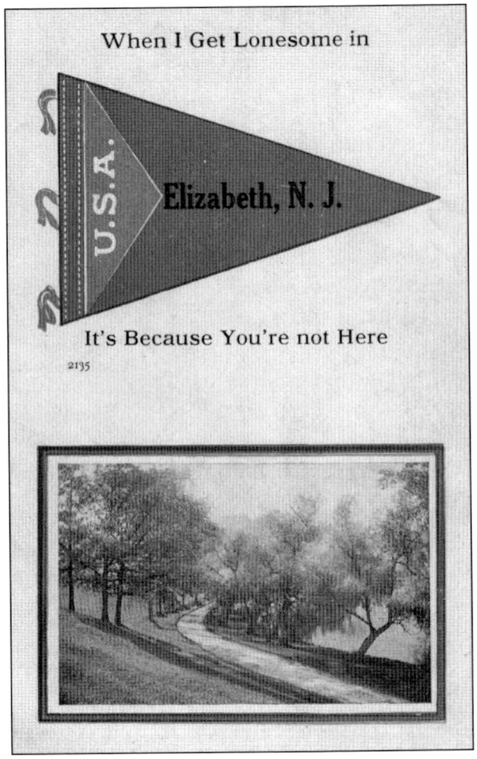

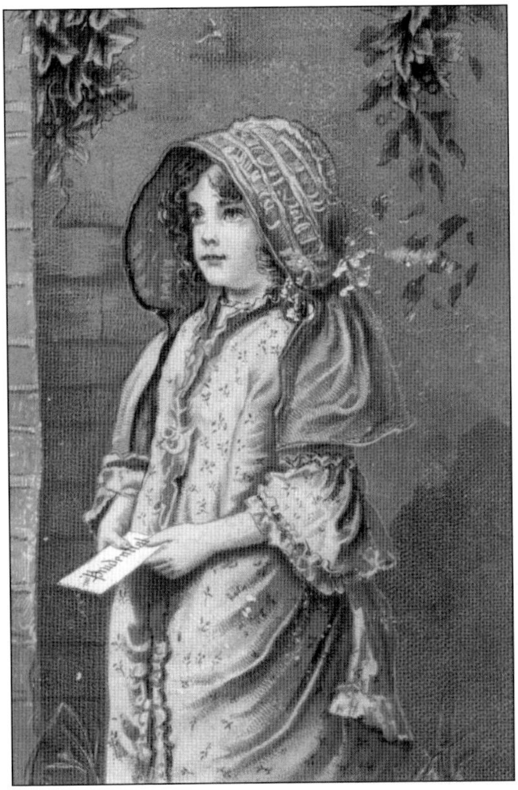

This trade card was provided by the Elizabeth office of the Prudential Insurance Company, which, at the time, was located at 233 Broad Street in Elizabeth. The branch was run by Henry "H.J." Stratemeyer Jr., who was recorded as having four children in the 1885 New Jersey census. As for Prudential, it is still headquartered in nearby Newark, New Jersey. The company boasts nearly 50,000 employees, nearly three-quarters of a trillion dollars in assets, and a place on the prestigious Fortune 500. It has been named, for 20 years running, one of the top places to work for mothers.

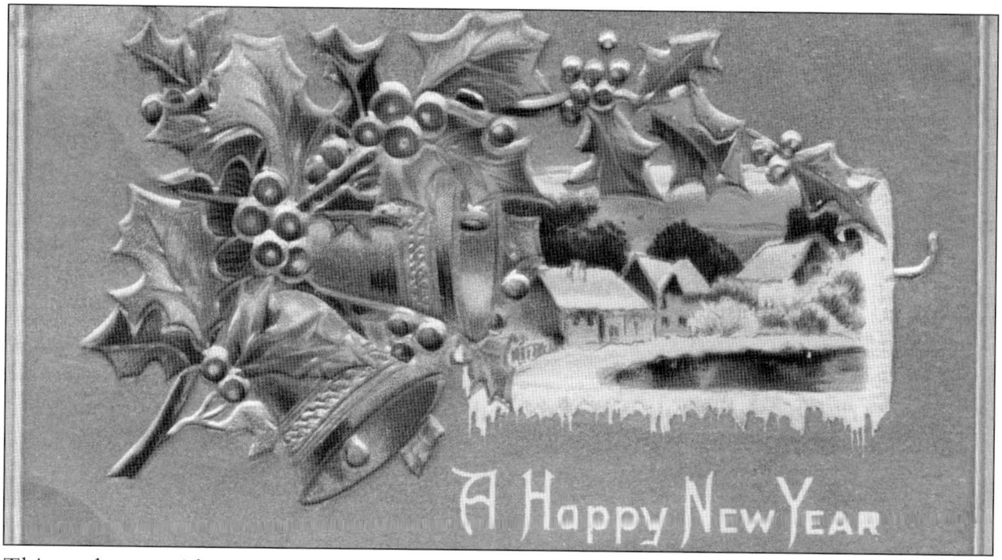

This card, sent with New Year's wishes, was mailed from Rochester, New York, on New Year's Eve in 1910. The message to C.J. Schone reads, "Am patiently waiting for my letter. I have such a cold I can hardly see. We are snowed in here. If it storms don't look for me as she can't let me out of here if she wants. Sincerely G. Bls." The winter storm is not an odd one for the city of Elizabeth, as winter has been known to pound the area with subzero temperatures and inches of snow.

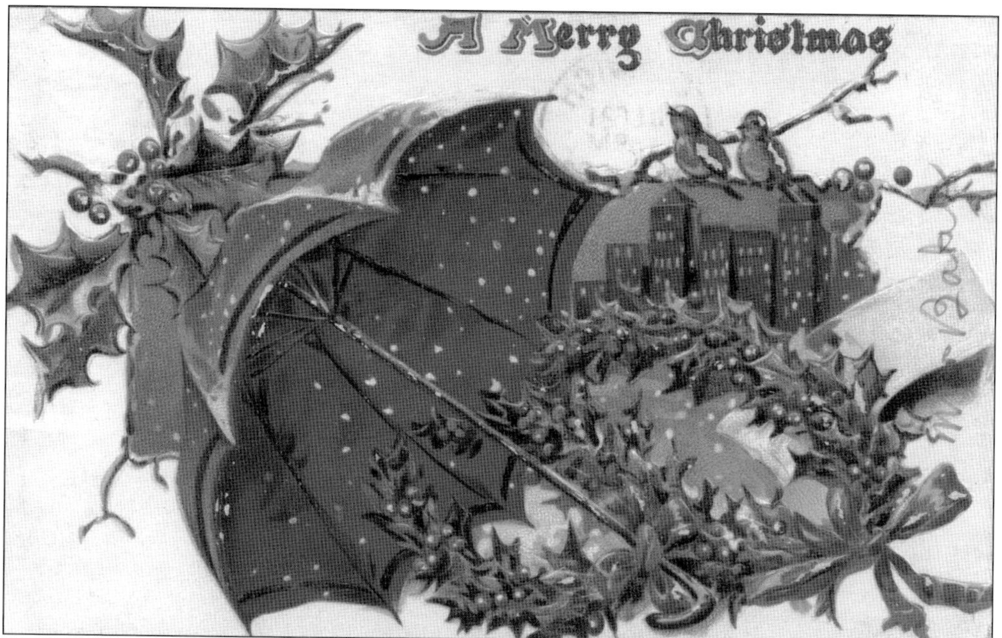

This card, sent from Norwich, Connecticut, on December 21, 1908, sends Christmas wishes to a Mrs. Love at Elizabeth Hospital. Christmas is a fun time in Elizabeth, with one of the draws being the Dr. Rose Marie Battaglia Christmas Basketball Tournament, hosted by Benedictine Academy, a girl's 9-12 preparatory school located at 840 North Broad Street in Elizabeth. The town also takes part in the Salvation Army's "angel" program, where families can "adopt" a child by providing them with gifts for the Christmas season.

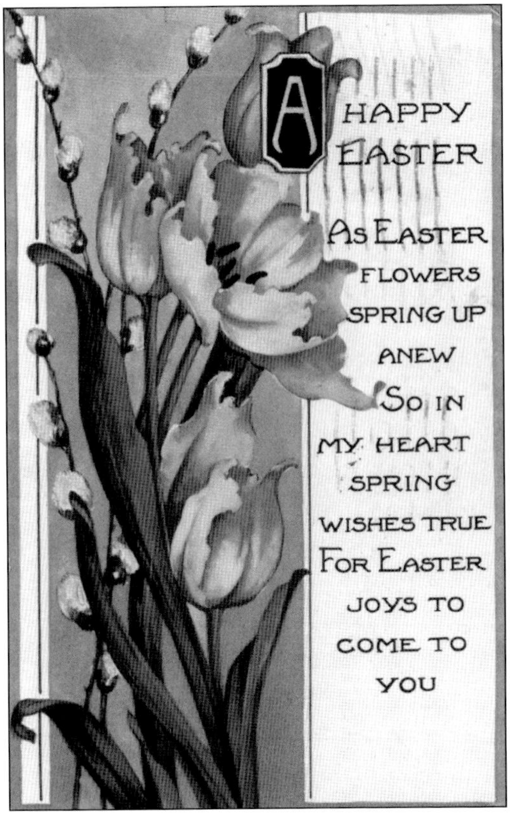

The Easter holiday has a mixed history in Elizabeth. Each year, the city hosts two Easter egg hunts, both in different parts of town (one at Kellogg Park and one at Carteret Park) so that the children of the area have ample opportunity to hunt eggs. However, Easter has had its dark moments, such as the 2018 strip club shootout at Exotics Gentlemen's Club, which led to the death of one Daniel Louis, an unarmed victim. Four men were charged in the shooting.

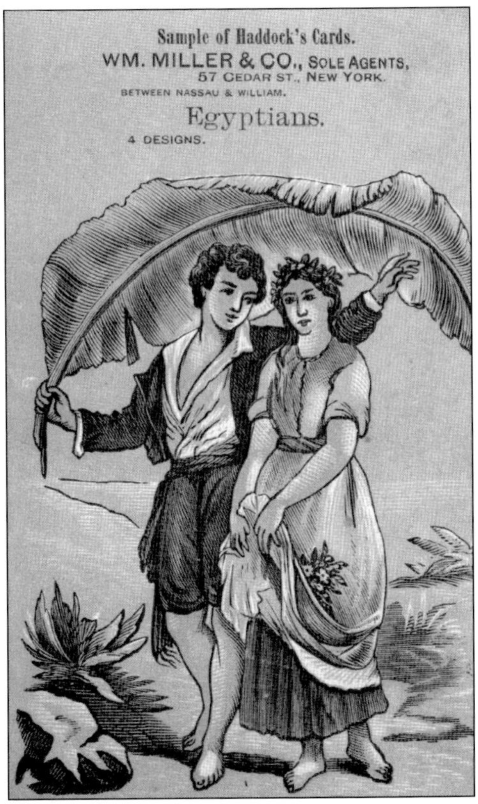

This card, printed before 1900, is a trade card showing both the card stock and the printing prowess of Haddock's Cards, which were sold by Wm. Miller and Company of New York to merchants along the East Coast. This particular sample was provided to the Arcade Grocery Store, located at 136 Broad Street in Elizabeth. The store, undoubtedly like many of its kind, was gobbled up by the bigger chains, who moved away from the downtown core. Now in the location is a Subway restaurant.

Crown dressing was an important fashion necessity for the shoes of any well-to-do lady in the Victorian era, and, based on the ample cards, bottle, and polish tins that survive, Frank Miller's was one of the best, or at least most-used, brands on the market. This particular card was provided by J.N. Burger and Son, wholesale agents of the good who operated at 1172 Elizabeth Avenue. Today, the space where this business used to reside is shared by 3 Guys Clothing Store and Yoly's Cuban Cafe.

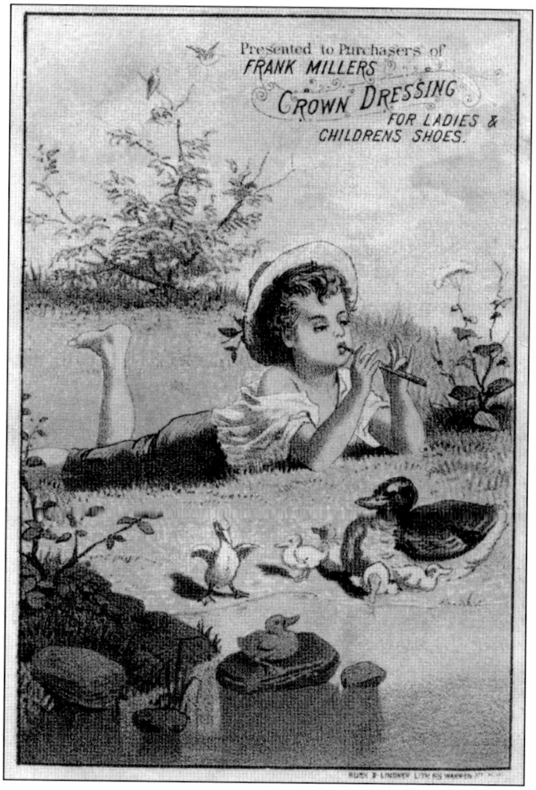

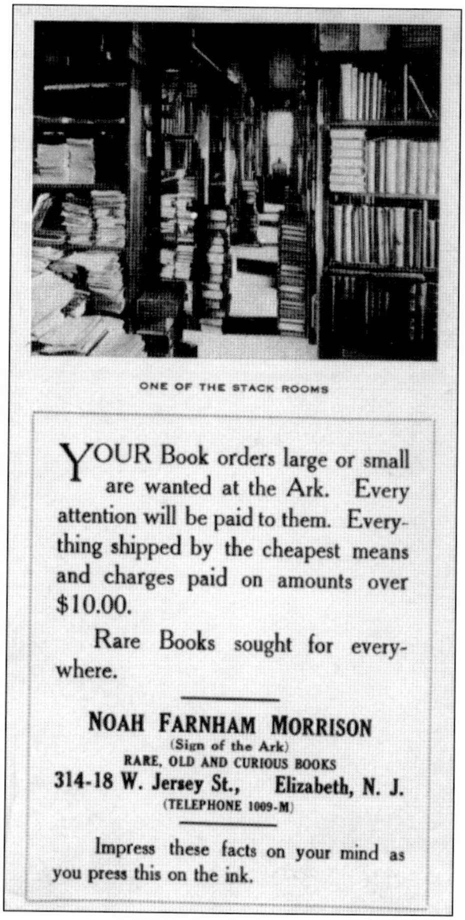

Noah's Farnham Morrison was a rare book and manuscript seller in Elizabeth in the early part of the 20th century. His shop of books, which was massive, given the volume of his collection, took up the entirety of the building at 314-318 West Jersey Street in Elizabeth. Today, the building still stands, albeit repurposed for apartments. The authors of this volume have a connection to Morrison's trade, as they met while working for the Kislak Center for Special Collections, Rare Books, and Manuscripts at the Van Pelt Library of the University of Pennsylvania.

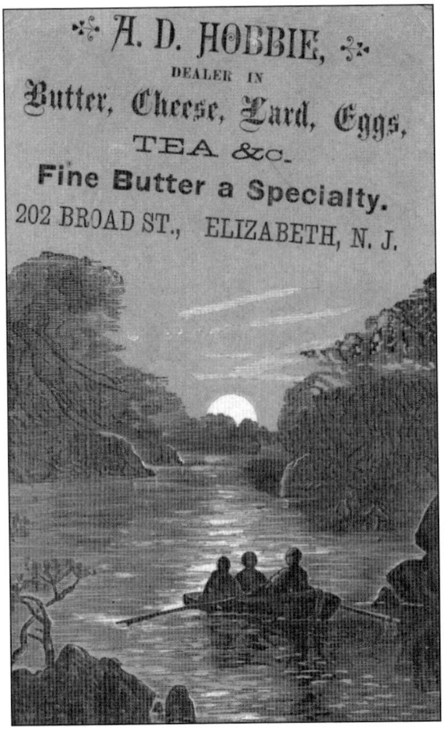

Unlike today's retail environment, where most stores are specialized to the point of annoyance, stores during the beginning of the 20th century had a more generalized feel to them. One such store was run by an A.D. Hobbie, who, through his trade card, proclaimed himself a "dealer in Butter, Cheese, Lard, Eggs, Tea, and etcetera." "Fine" butter was apparently "a specialty" in Hobbie's store. The store was located at 202 Broad Street, which would have put him in the heart of the downtown core. The location is currently occupied by a Cricket Wireless store.

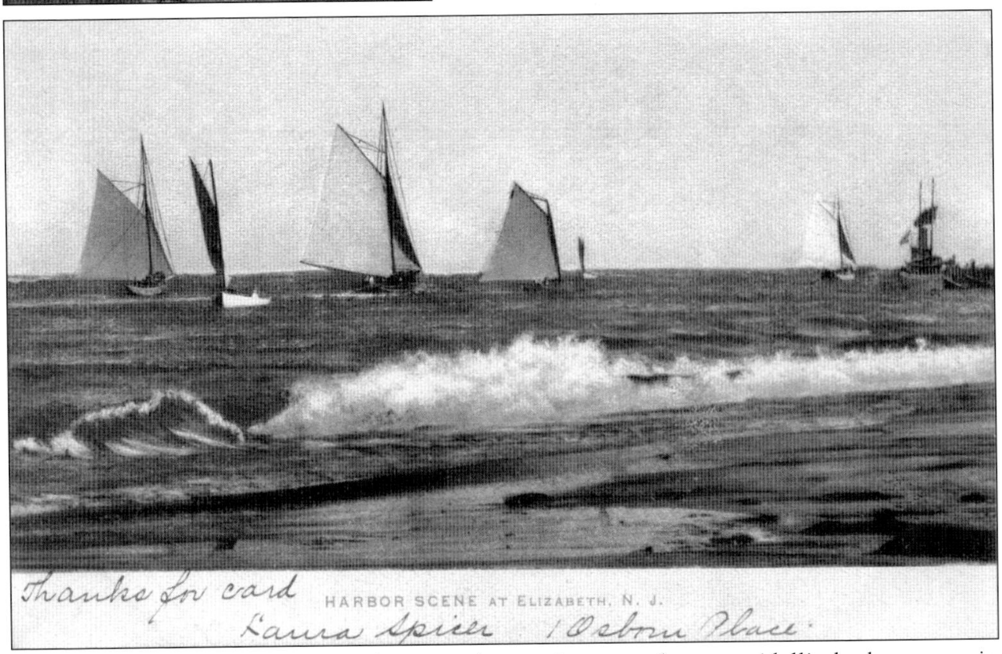

This card, no doubt designed to draw tourists to the area, shows an idyllic harbor scene in Elizabeth, New Jersey. In truth, the ports at Newark and Elizabeth are run jointly by the Port Authority of New York and New Jersey and serve as commercial hubs for goods coming in and out of the country. Built mainly by soldier labor during World War I, the shipyard saw an increase in activity during World War II. This particular card predates event that; it was sent on March 13, 1906, to Addie F. Snyder, of 1282 Globe Street, in Fall River, Massachusetts.

This card is the second in a series of trade cards put out by H.J. Stratemeyer Jr.'s office at 233 Broad Street in Elizabeth that sought to sell the fine insurance products of Prudential Life Insurance, which has its global headquarters in nearby Newark, New Jersey. Prudential, despite its status as an industry leader, is not without controversy. In 1997, the company was forced to settle a class-action lawsuit to settle claims that their sales agents had misrepresented life insurance policies. In 2010, the company was accused of manipulating the payouts of service members who had died in action.

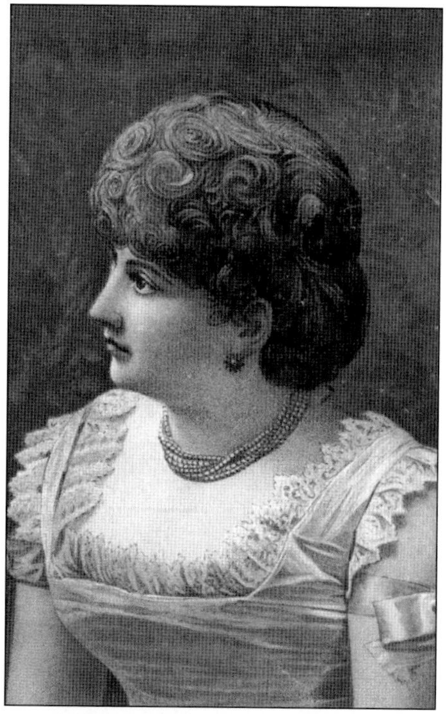

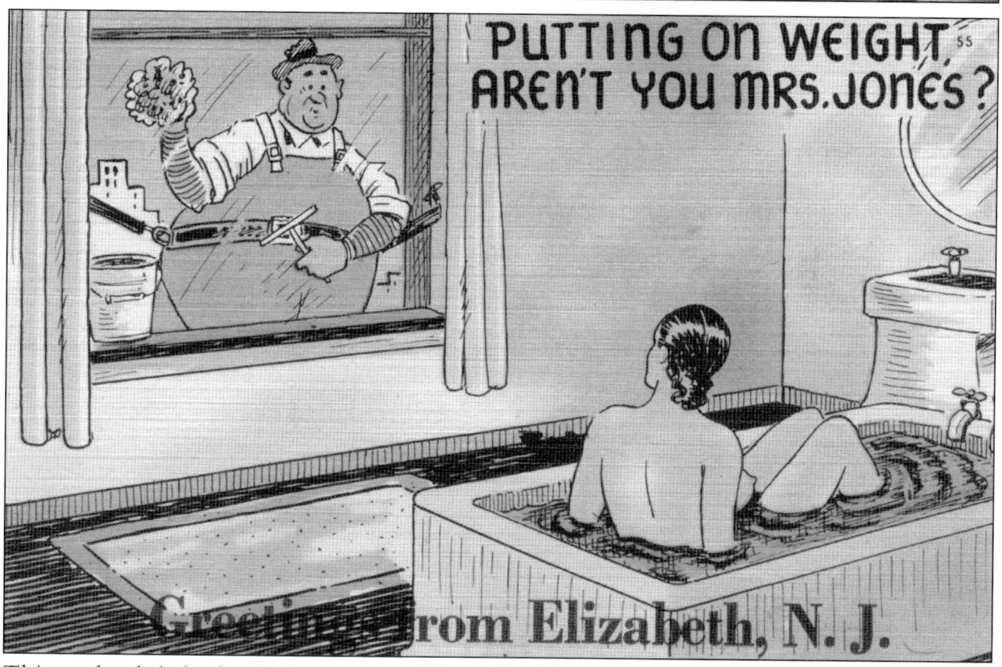

This card, while both mildly pornographic and lighthearted, gives a nod to Elizabeth's strange relationship with being in the buff. Elizabeth, for example, is a hotspot for "gentlemen's clubs," with locations with names such as Jersey Girls, Angels, Lookers, Copa Cabana, Nardone's, XO, and others. However, Elizabeth, like most places in New Jersey, suffered when nude beaches were shut down. The area still hosts nude events with some art attachment, such as the 2018 Grown and Sexy Nude Model Paint Night.

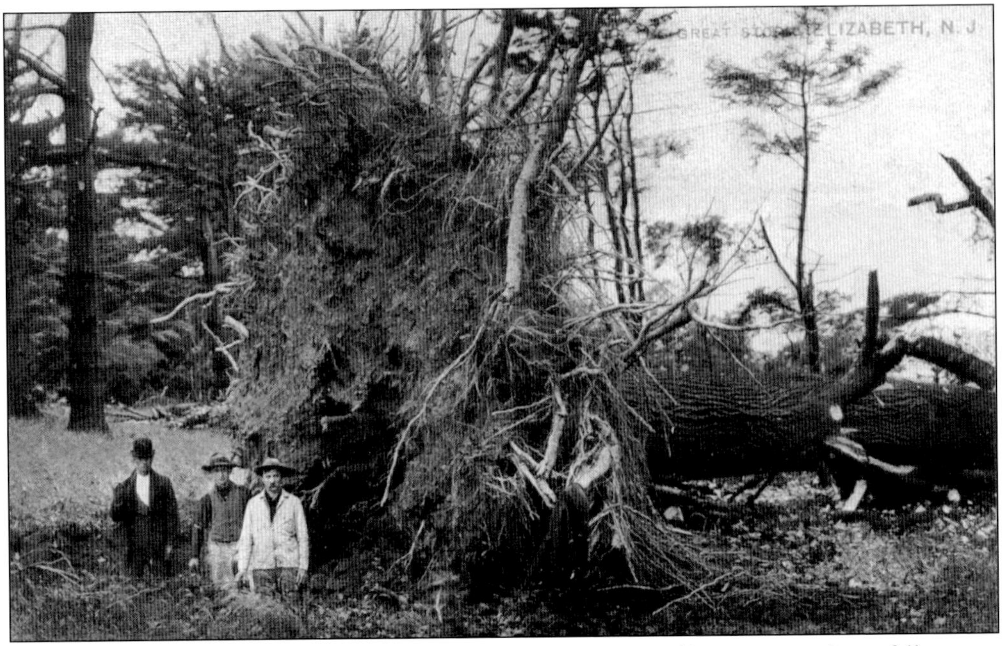

This postcard, titled "The Great Storm," shows three men standing next to a large fallen tree. The postcard is likely meant to showcase the gravity of this "great" storm by depicting the immense tree that managed to topple over, roots and all, as a result of the high winds. The location of where this postcard image in Elizabeth was taken is uncertain, though the city is no stranger to storms, and it has seen many storms since this one because of the proximity to the coast, making it a city susceptible to hurricanes whenever they come near the area.

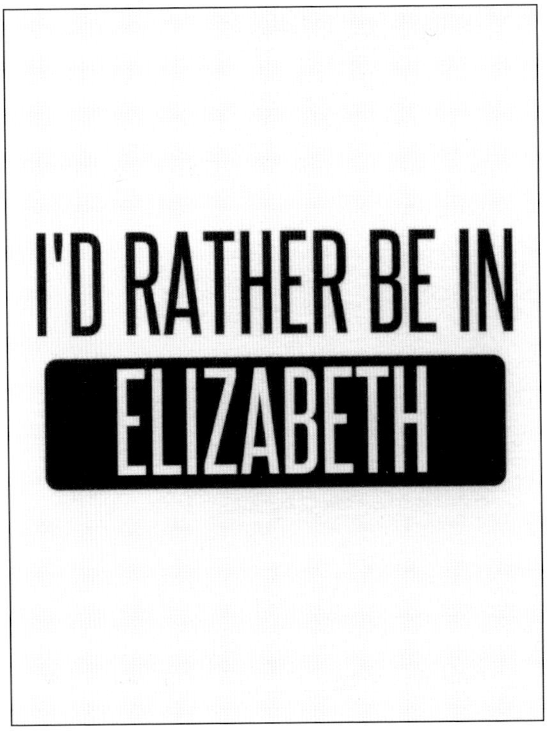

"I'd Rather Be in Elizabeth" is another, modern attempt to promote the city of Elizabeth and to revitalize its tourism in the state of New Jersey. Since the city of Elizabeth is well known throughout the state, this postcard plays on that familiarity by simply mentioning the name of the city without the need for a picture. This form of postcard art, which leans more toward pop art and graphics, demonstrates the contemporary bend of Elizabeth postcards.

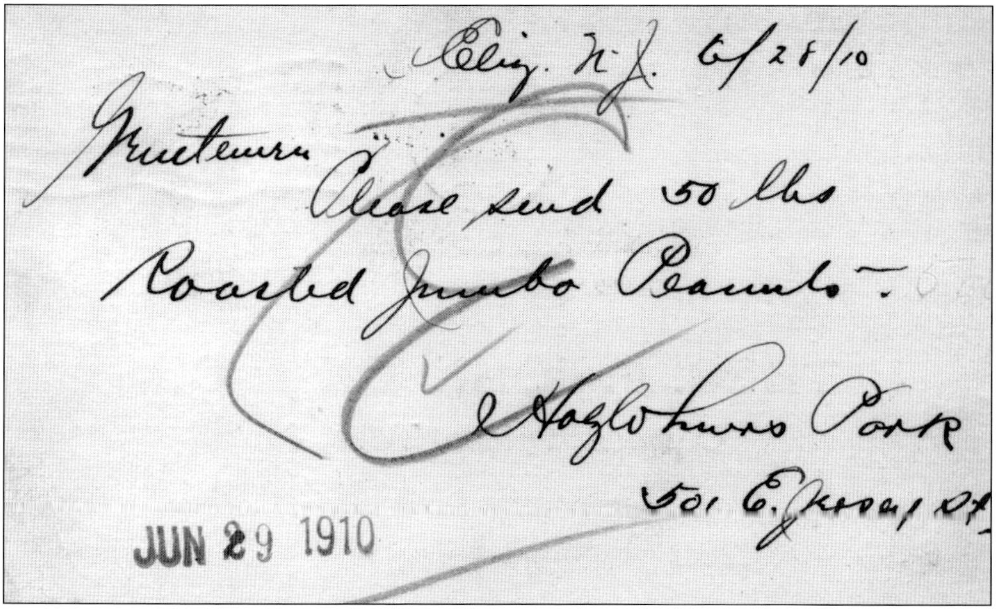

Dated June 29, 1910, this card was written from Elizabeth. It is an amusing card because of the note that is written inside it: "Please send 50 lbs Roasted Jumbo Peanuts." There is a rich history of letters written in Elizabeth, many of which were sent to various parts of the country, due to its opportune location on the East Coast and its proximity both to New York City and to the Elizabeth port.

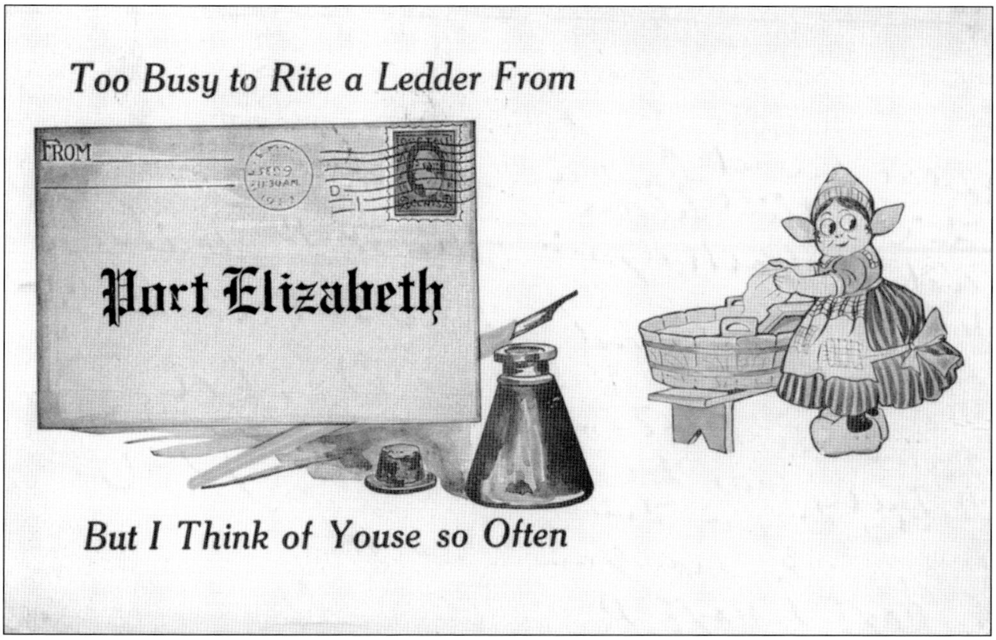

The funny and colloquial text on this postcard is meant to mimic the accent of a New Jersey native. The postcard would have been sent from Port Elizabeth, and it shows an elf-like creature washing clothes on the right-hand side of the card. The important words from the text that best convey the North Jersey accent are the words "ledder," instead of "letter," and "youse," which is a colloquial way of saying "you."

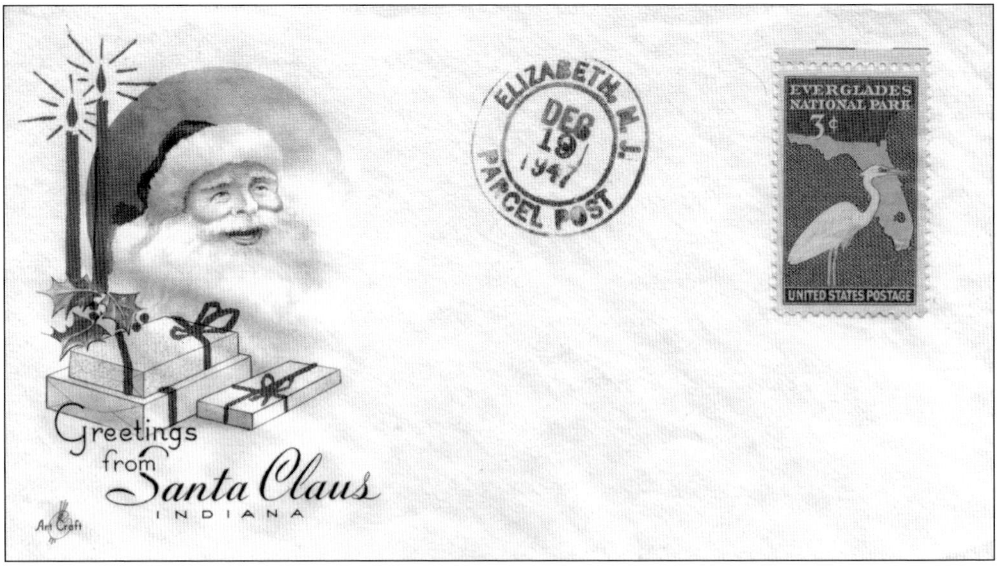

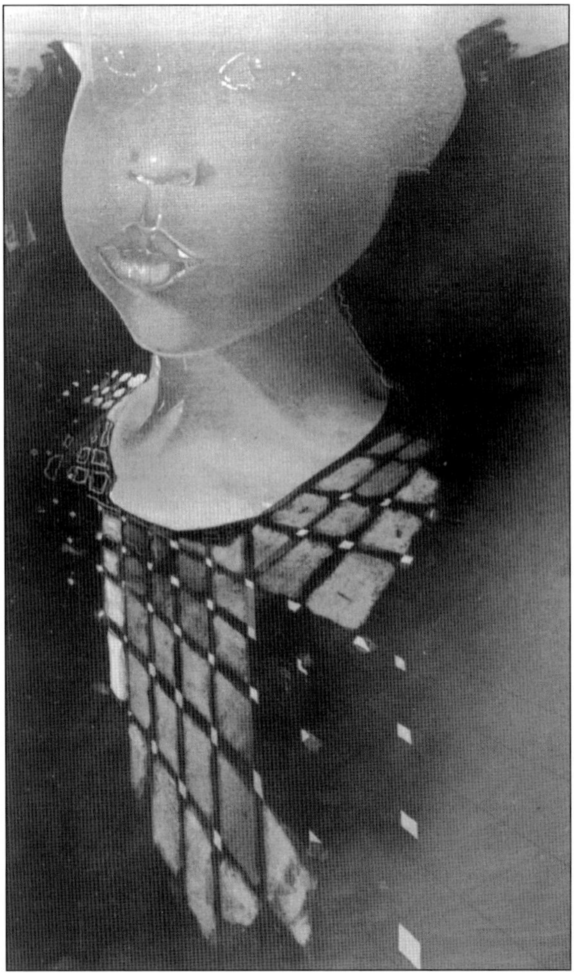

This postcard is stamped by the Parcel Post of Elizabeth, and it is dated December 19, 1947—just before the holidays. The card, itself likely a holiday greeting, shows a picture of Santa Claus, who shares his name with a holiday town in Indiana.

The back of this image shows an address belonging to John N. Rowe. The image is an example of the artwork by Rowe, a contemporary artist specializing in fine art and illustration. The topics of his artwork vary: portraiture, landscape, still life, and figurative subjects. This image appears to be a combination between a portrait and a figurative subject, and it demonstrates Rowe's unique artistic style that blends realistic elements with abstract patterns. It is likely that he was based in Elizabeth for some time before moving out to the West Coast.

Captioned as "Peaches that grow in Elizabeth, N.J.," this image shows a young girl sitting at the center of the room, smiling. These types of postcards were amusing caricatures that could be sent to friends and family alike as a simple way of keeping in touch without necessarily always including important historical sites in Elizabeth.

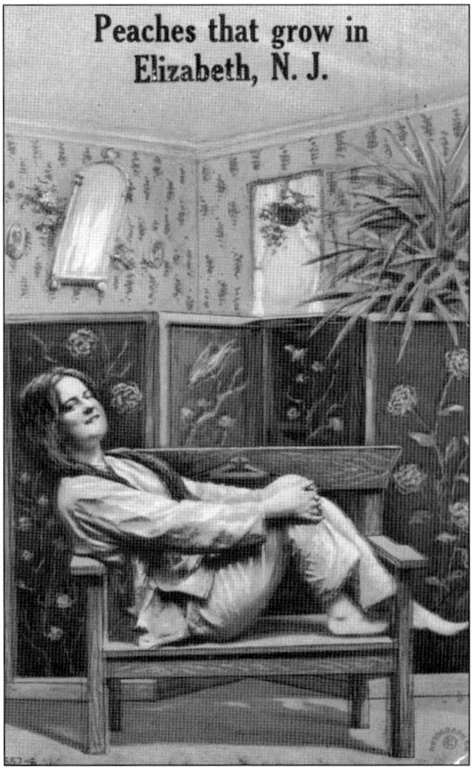

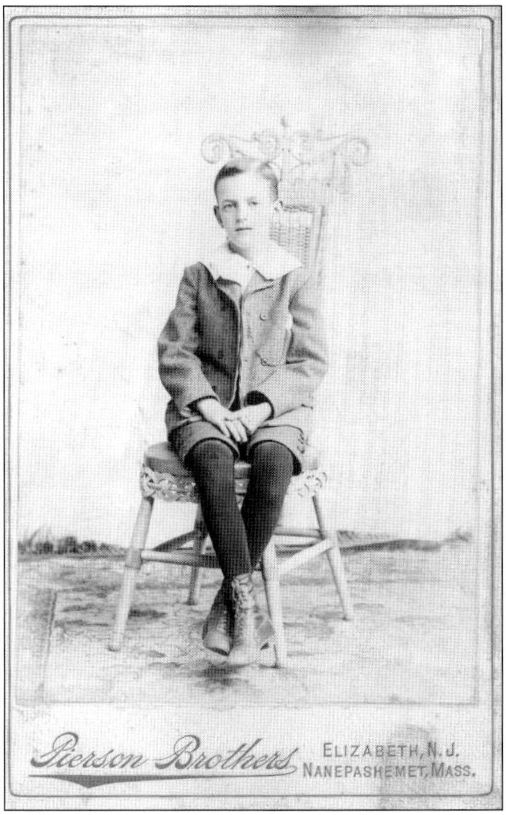

This postcard shows a young boy sitting on a chair. The bottom of the image reads, "Pierson Brothers," and highlights two locations: Elizabeth, New Jersey, and Nanepashemet, Massachusetts. The Pierson Brothers were a local business on Broad Street, known as frame makers and art dealers. The business also featured the photographic and freehand portraits by Fred H. Pierson. This image of the well-dressed young boy is very likely an example of Pierson's photographic portraits, and the bottom inscription the business's logo and promotional mark.

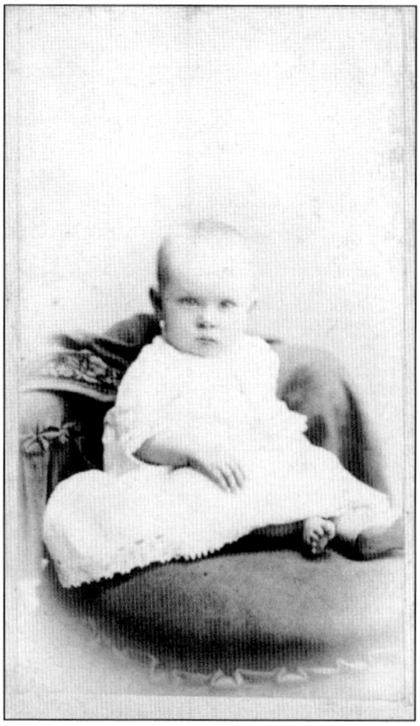

This image, showing a young baby girl sitting on an elegant chair, is likely a photographic portrait. The back of the image features a last name, "Hill," and is marked "Elizabeth, New Jersey." The photographer of this image is likely to be Mr. or Mrs. Hill, and the location hints that this photographer likely kept their studio or business in the city of Elizabeth.

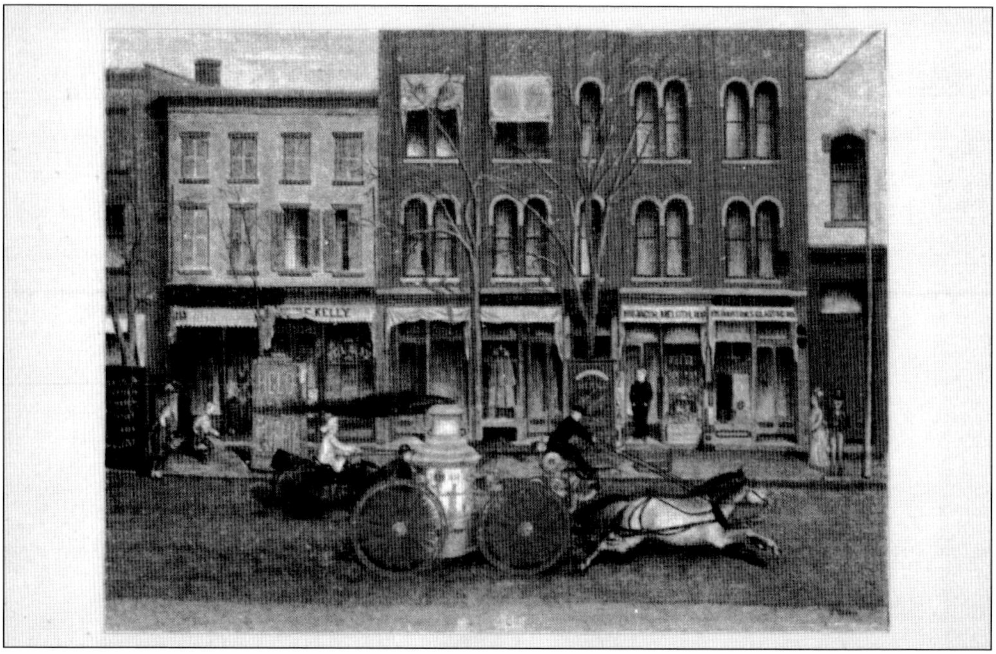

The image on this postcard shows an Ernest Opper oil painting titled, "Fire Engine, Main Street, Elizabeth, New Jersey." The painting is a part of the Rhode Island School of Design's Museum of Art collection in Providence, Rhode Island. The painting was made around the 1880s, and it features a fire engine in front of the Cory Building on Broad Street. The painting is famous for its depiction of a steam Amoskeag horse-drawn fire engine with a fire chief racing to put out a fire. Bystanders look on at the action, with some excited and some worried. The colorful and lively painting is a historical example of an artist making Elizabeth the setting of his artwork.

This image of an infant sitting on an elegant chair is similar to other pictures highlighted in this section that depict portrait-style poses of young children; these were typical setups for photographers of the day when they were arranging the pictures of toddlers. The back of this image, in fact, features the name "H. Schaefer," and it mentions his profession—photographer—as well his business address, which was once at 96 Broad Street in Elizabeth. Many photographers had their business on Broad Street, and one of the most popular forms of photography was baby portraits. The baby in this picture is not named.

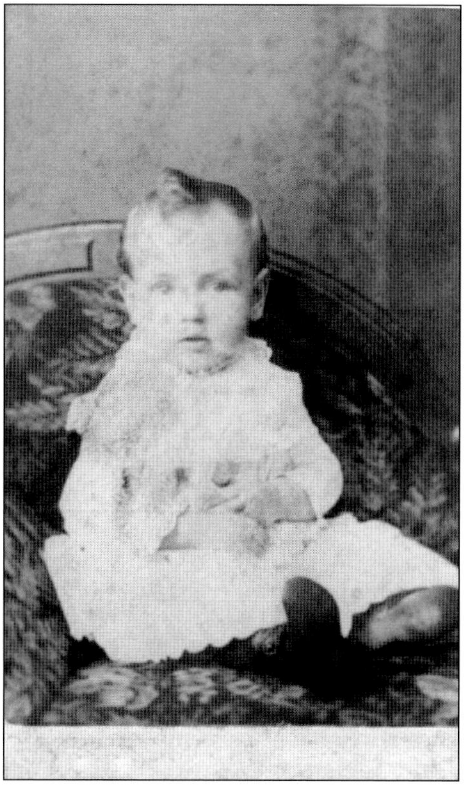

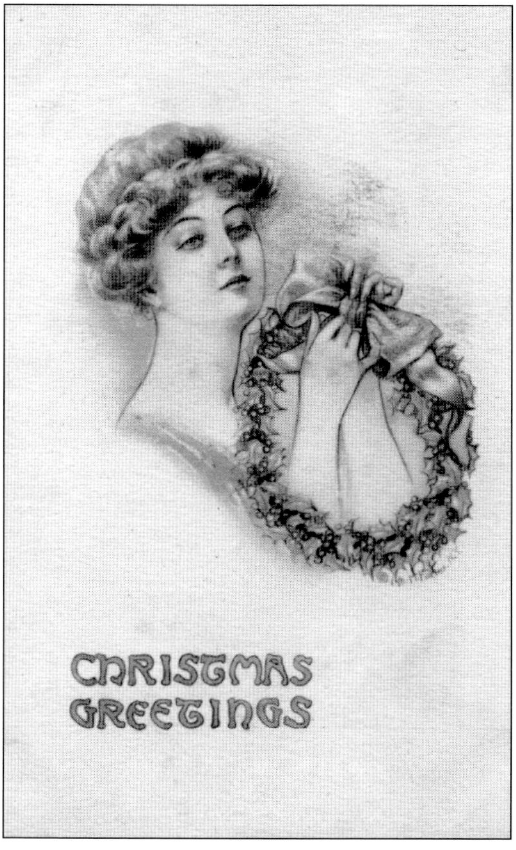

This Christmas greeting card features a delicate sketch of a woman holding a Christmas wreath adorned with a large bow. This is an example of a type of Christmas card that would be sent during the holidays to friends and family members. Many of Elizabeth's residents during the city's earlier years had familial ties throughout the country, and so it is common today to find several greeting cards and postcards that were sent from Elizabeth.

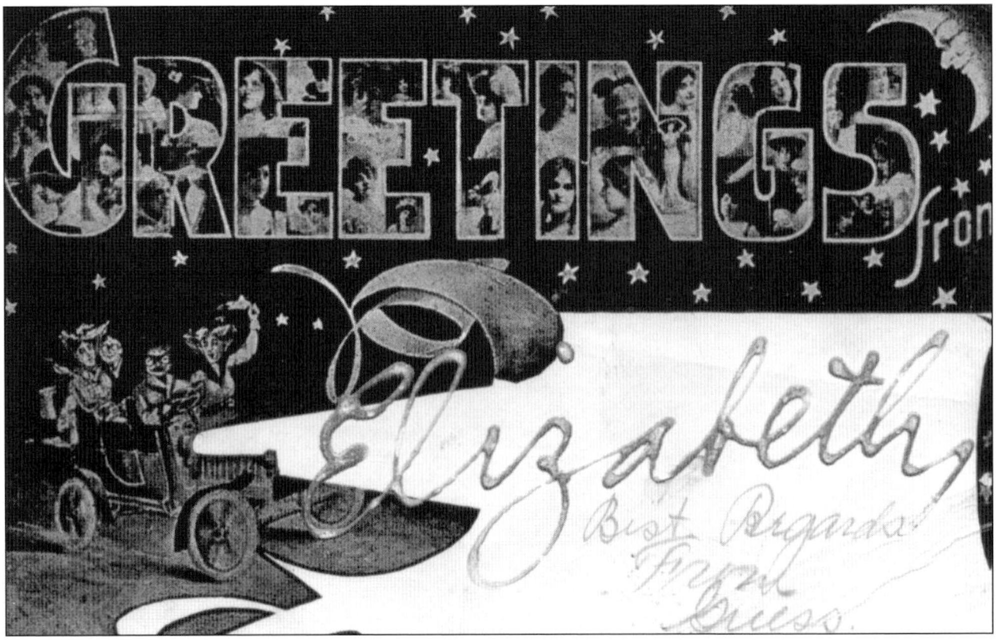

This postcard reads "Greetings from Elizabeth," and it is signed at the bottom-right corner from its sender. Postcards from Elizabeth were popular because the city was well known not just in the state of New Jersey, but in other states as well. Some postcards like this one did not need to feature a picture from the city but, instead, simply relayed a message from the sender to the receiver. In this case, it was possible to write in the name of the city, state, or country from which the sender wanted to send his/her greetings—and they were writing from Elizabeth.

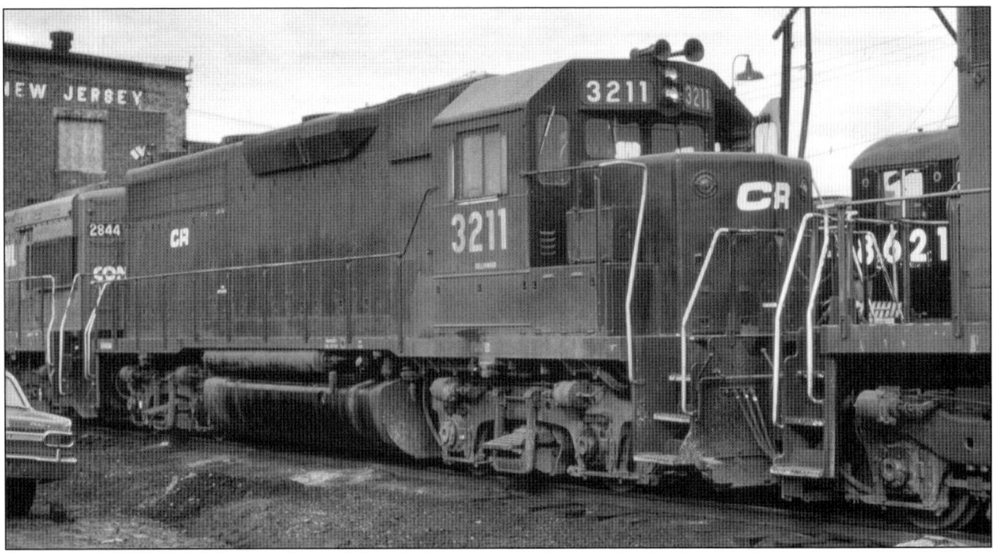

This photograph shows engine No. 3211, operated by Conrail, a freight carrier based out of Philadelphia from 1976 to 1999. It is an EMD GP40 model, later converted from a steam engine to diesel. Conrail was formed by the US government to take over several bankrupt, yet profitable, routes from the Midwest to New England after several small lines were forced to cease operations. The diesel replacement engines are able to produce 3,000 horsepower, which seems obscene until one takes into account the weight of a row of train cars.

Seven

Ramblin' Man: Transportation in Elizabeth

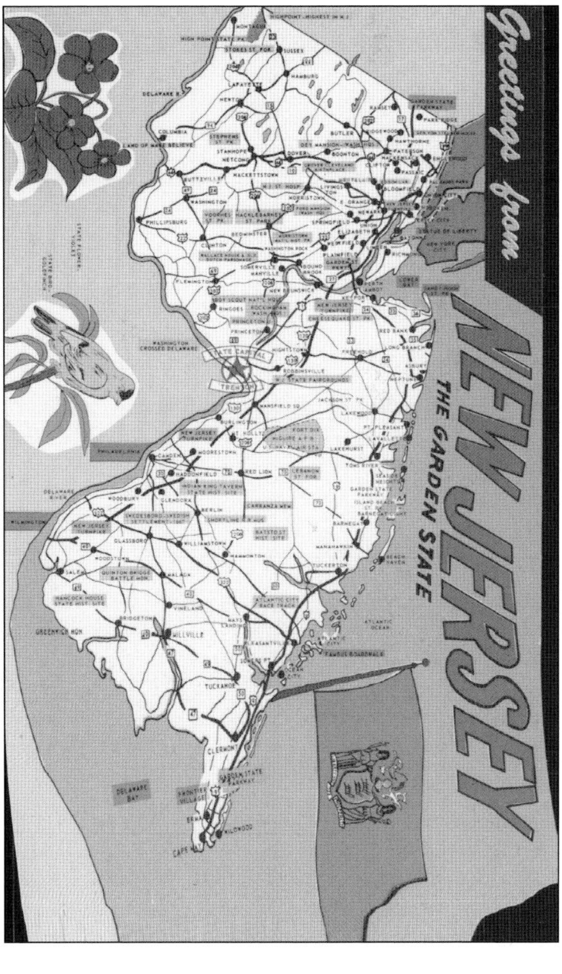

This 1972 postcard shows Elizabeth, along with close to a hundred other New Jersey cities, on a map. The back of the card reads, "The State of New Jersey. The Garden State. Capital: Trenton. Population: 7,091,995 (1970 U.S. Census). Area: 8,204.37 sq. mi. State Flower: Purple Violet. Bird: Eastern Goldfinch. Tree: Red Oak. Motto: 'Liberty and Prosperity.' Third of the original 13 states." This card was published by the New Jersey State Museum in Trenton.

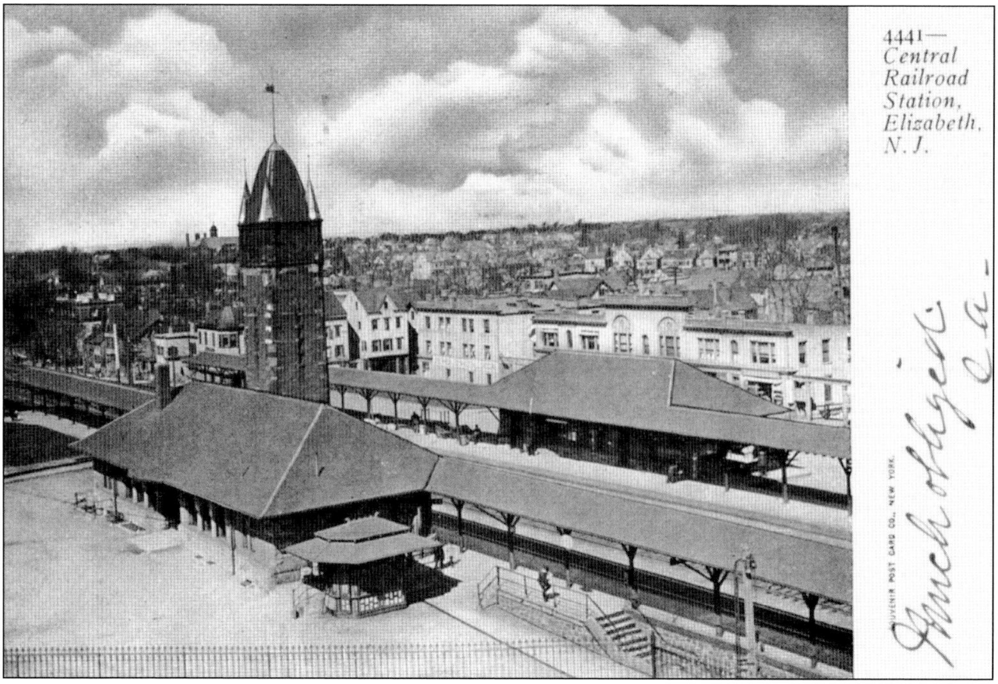

The Central Railroad Station in Elizabeth, New Jersey, was built in 1893 to be in close proximity to the city's major commercial streets: Morris Avenue and Broad Street. The station building itself was designed to be in a Victorian Romanesque style. The tracks visible in this picture have been removed since then, making it a disused train station. Today, the station is often renovated and used for different commercial purposes such as restaurants or clubs, and the space that the tracks once occupied is now a parking lot that is in close proximity to the active Elizabeth Station, which replaced the Central Railroad Station.

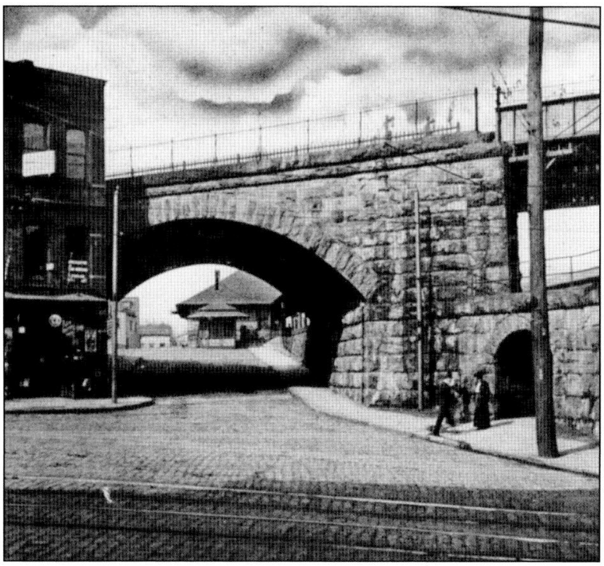

This postcard shows the Pennsylvania Railroad Crossing in Elizabeth. The tracks above, on the stone bridge, are what today belongs to the functioning Elizabeth Station that replaced the old Central Railroad Station. The Pennsylvania Railroad Crossing was built by Pennsylvania Railroad, and when both stations operated independently, it was possible for passengers to transfer between the two stations since they were built adjacent to one another. This image also shows the old trolley tracks that once ran down Broad Street, back when it used trolleys as a mode of transportation for citizens.

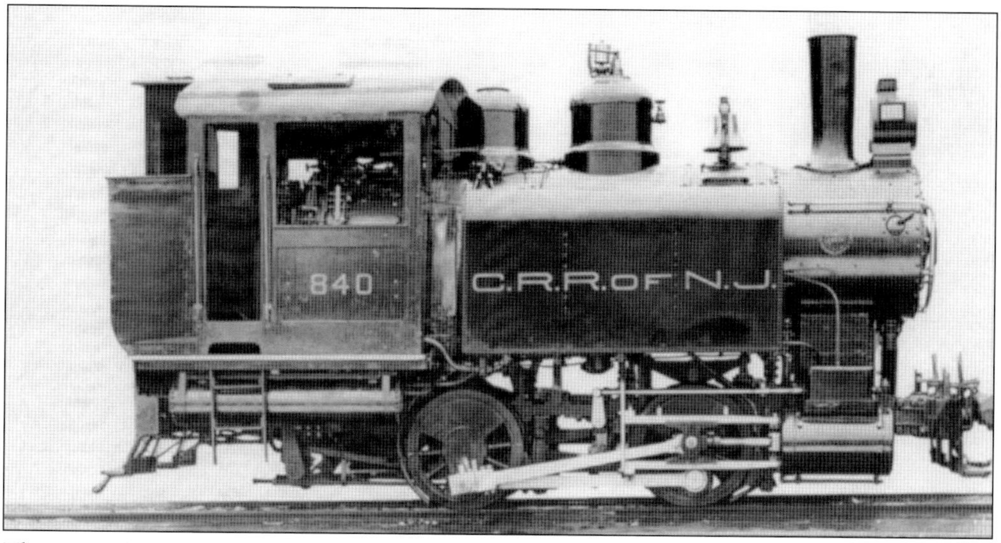

The Central Railroad of New Jersey is synonymous with the Jersey Central Lines that converge at the Central Railroad of New Jersey Terminal in Liberty State Park in Jersey City. This locomotive, showing the initials of the Central Railroad, would have been one of many engines running along the state of New Jersey used for commercial purposes. The locomotive was likely built by Baldwin Locomotive Works, which provided many of the trains used throughout the state.

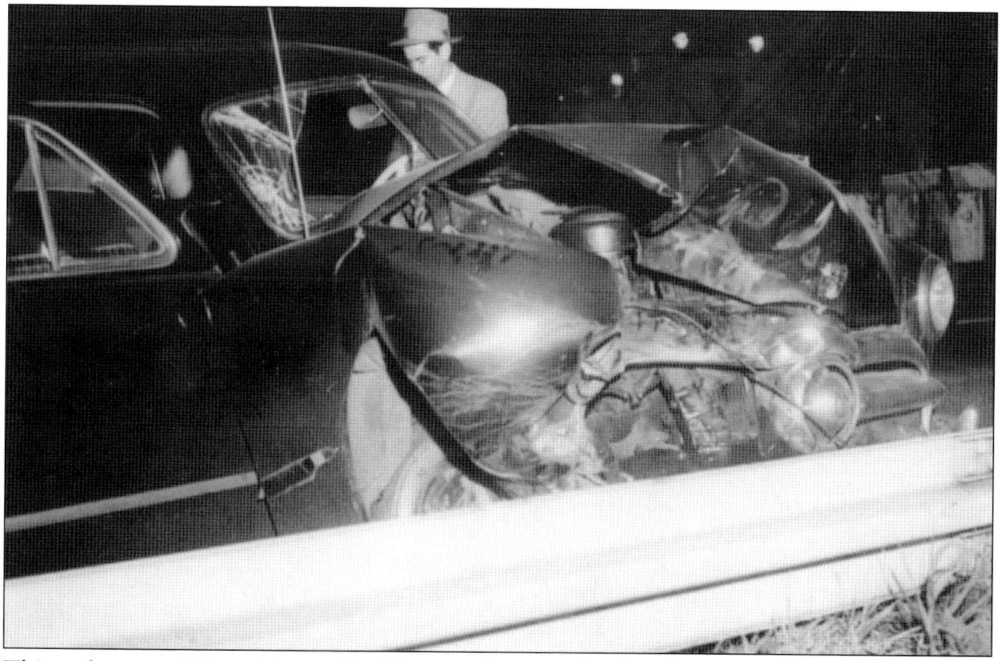

This rather morbid card began its life as a photograph taken by United Press in 1952. The text on the original reads, "Newark N.J. Driver and three passengers of this car were taken to the Elizabeth General Hospital after a three-car crash on the northbound lane of the Jersey Turnpike, today UP Telephoto." The consequences of such accidents were often compounded by a lack of safety features on the early automobiles, so, needless to say, Elizabeth General Hospital surely saw its share of accident victims in the 1950s.

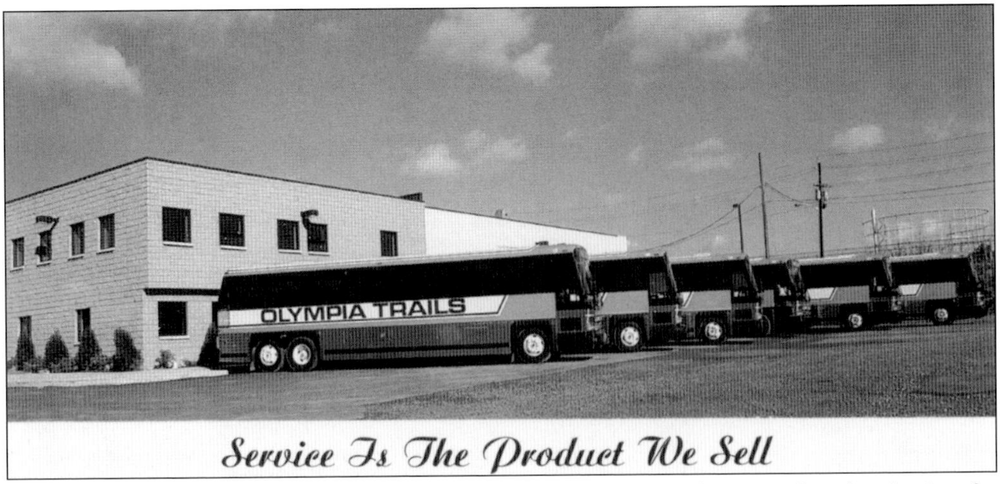

"Service is the product we sell"—Well, that, and transportation, if one needs to book a bus for a tour or a trip. Olympia Trails is still in business as one of the largest regional bus operators in the Mid-Atlantic. They currently operate MegaBus, a regional discount carrier that services Boston; New York; Philadelphia; Washington, DC; Baltimore; Syracuse; Rochester; Buffalo; Albany; and Toronto. They also operate shuttles from the Newark International Airport and regional service in Essex and Union Counties. They were also formerly responsible for the Red and Tan local service in Hudson County.

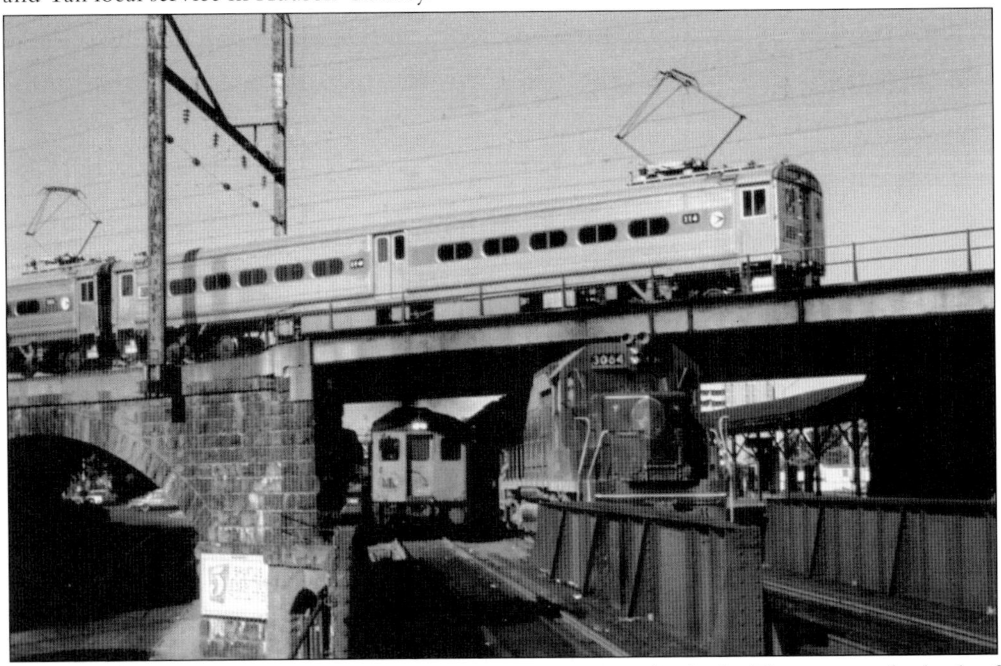

This card shows three trains converging at the same spot in Elizabeth. The text on the back of the card describes the scene: "Rail activity abounds at Elizabeth, NJ as CNJ [Central Railroad of New Jersey] RDE, 551 enroute to Cranford, NJ from Bayonne, NJ, overtakes a B&O [Baltimore & Ohio] Freight, while a Penn Central, New Brunswick, NJ local passes overhead on the electric New York to Philadelphia mainline, on September 3, 1969. Today, Amtrak and New Jersey Transit trains still pass overhead, but only one track remains below, of what once was the CNJ mainline to Jersey City."

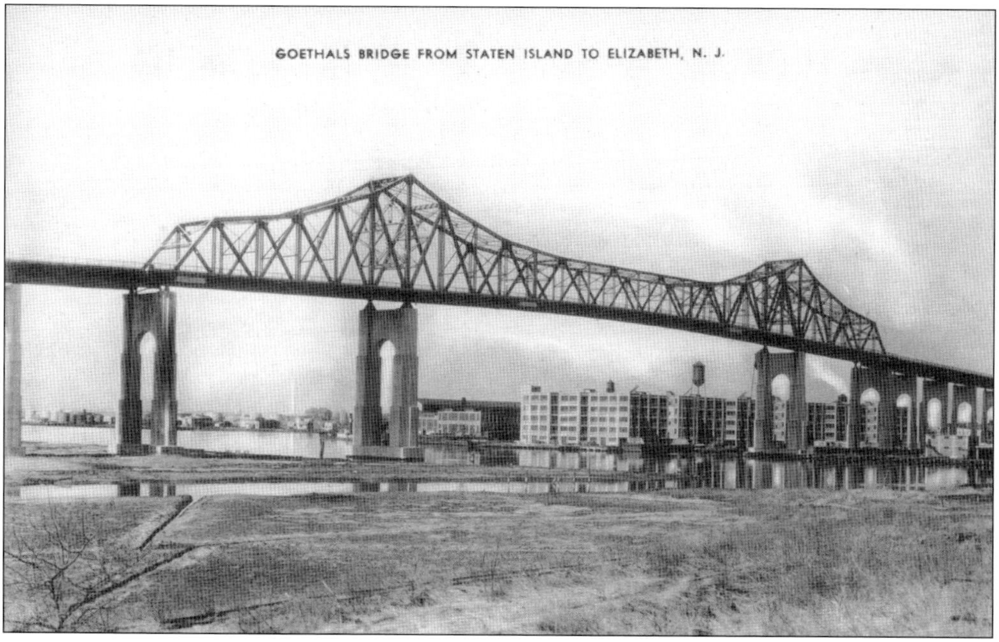

The Goethals Bridge connects Elizabeth with Staten Island, and it is one of the city's most important bridges since it serves as a commercial gateway between the Elizabeth Port and New York. The view from this postcard shows a wide view of the Goethals Bridge from Staten Island, meaning that it is also providing a view of Elizabeth. A little-known fact about the bridge is that it is named after the civil engineer George Washington Goethals, who played an important role in the history of the state and served as the state engineer of New Jersey. Since the summer of 2006, plans began to propose demolishing the bridge and replacing it with a more modern design.

This train cart shows the Central Railroad of New Jersey's first rebuilt RDC, which stands for Budd Rail Diesel Cart or Buddliner. This type of cart is self-propelled, and most of them were built by the Budd Company of Philadelphia, Pennsylvania. The RDC was used primarily for passenger service, and they were cheaper than a diesel locomotive-drawn train with coach carts. Between the years of 1949 and 1962, Budd built a total of 398 RDC's, 7 of which went to the Central Railroad of New Jersey. This train cart is probably one of these original seven.

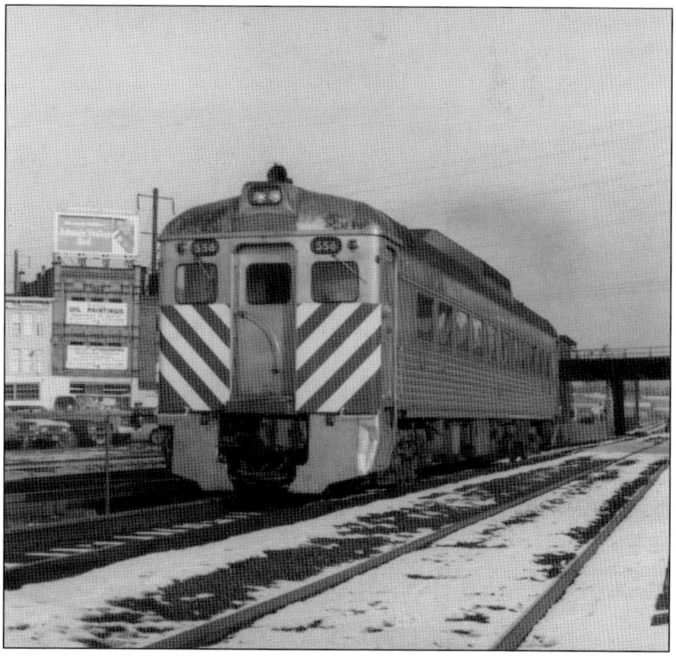

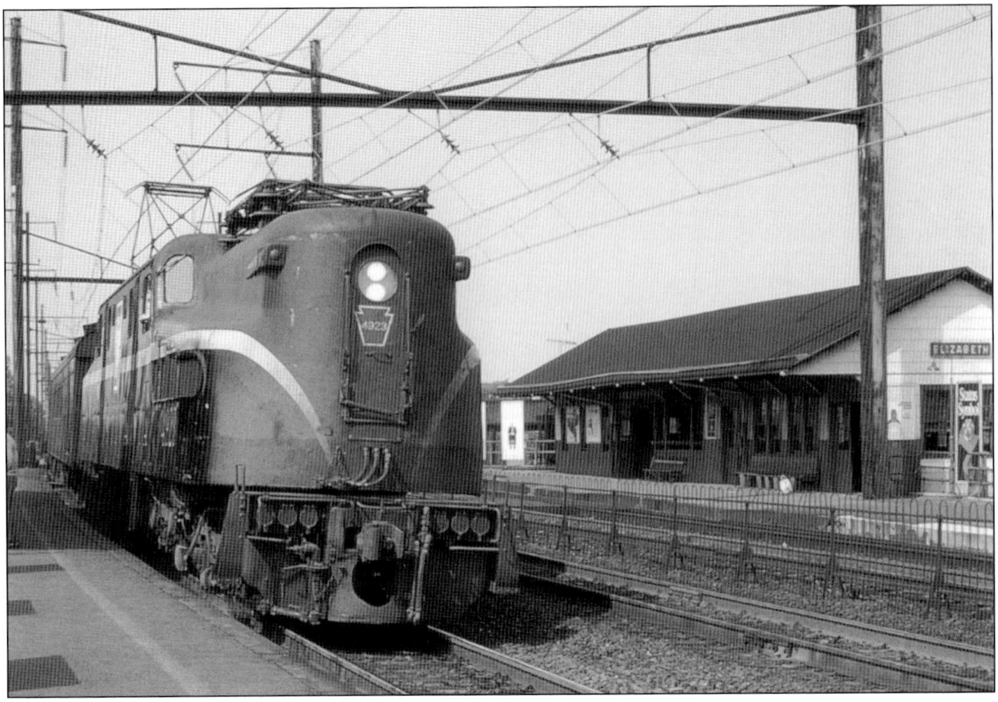

The train in this postcard, No. 4293, provides a view of the Elizabeth Train Station, located on a platform above Broad Street. This postcard is a part of the TRP Large Transportation Series: the back of the postcard reads, "In the summer of 1968, Pennsylvania Railroad GG1 P, No. 4923 glides to a stop with an old train set at Elizabeth, New Jersey, under the energized catenary of the Northeast Corridor." The photograph of the train was taken by Bill Myers.

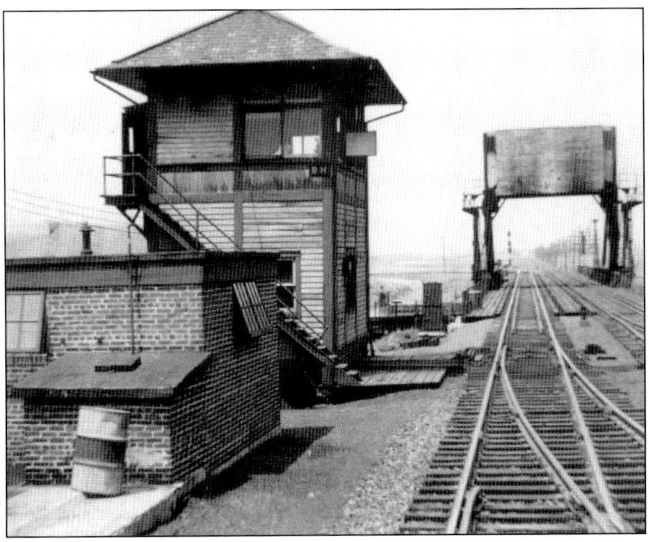

The buildings in this postcard form a train signal tower, used primarily to navigate railroad traffic throughout the state of New Jersey. From the black and white depiction of the signal tower, it is difficult to infer where this tower would have stood in the 1950s. For railway signaling, this type of tower would have been common at an interlocking junction in order to prevent any traffic problems. This signaling tower combined with tracks would often be called an "interlocking plant."

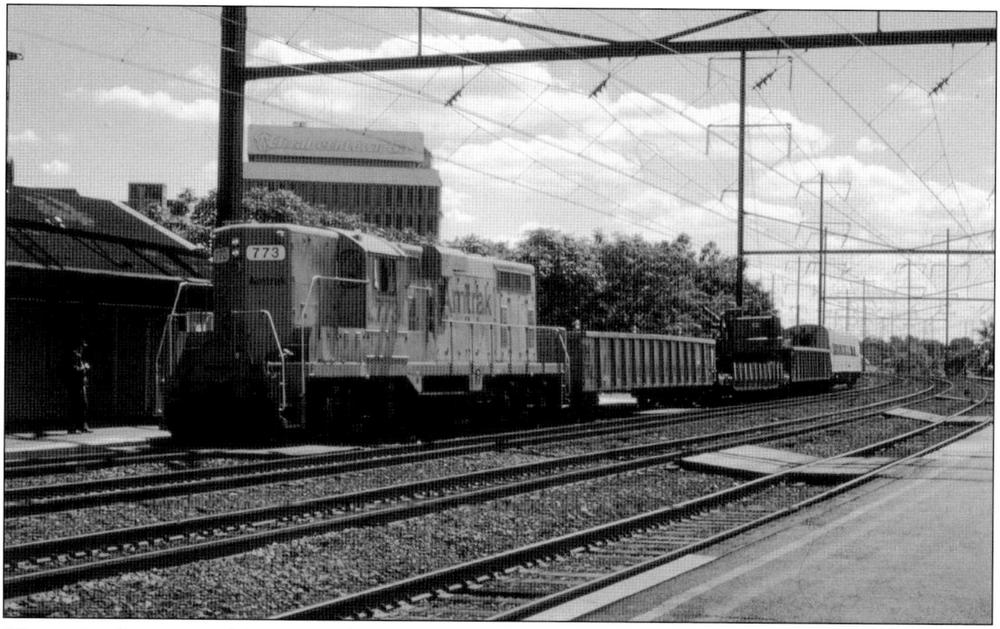

The train shown on this postcard is an Amtrak 773 GP7, and it is stationed and stopped at the Elizabeth terminal or the northeast corridor. This specific model of the train is a non-passenger unit, meant mainly to power the work trains that help maintain rail infrastructure. The stop in Elizabeth served more purposes than to host passenger trains for traveling residents; it was also used as a maintenance site for other trains in emergency situations. Because the Elizabeth station is one of the last stops before reaching New York City's Penn Station, it is important to fix any trains before they arrive at such a busy terminal.

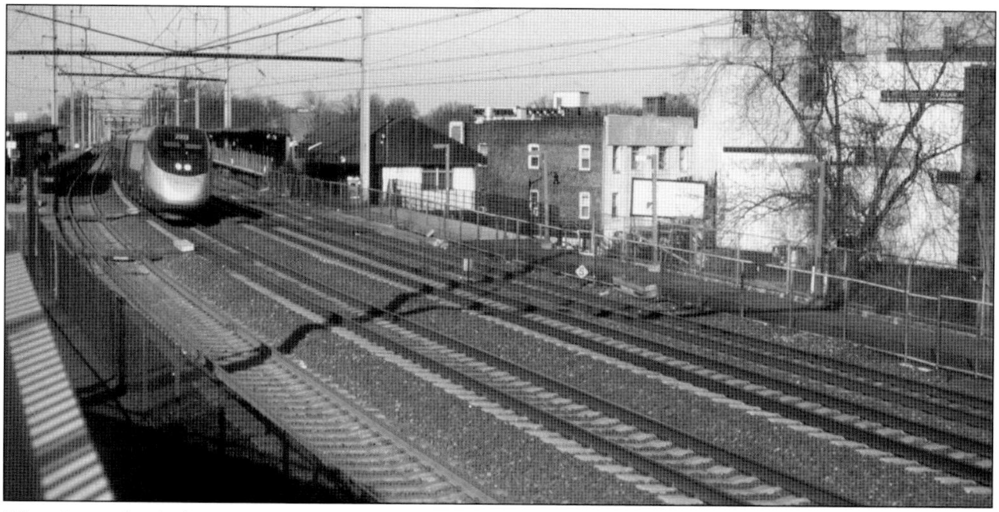

The Amtrak *Acela Express* pictured here is a more contemporary train. The main cities that this express train visits are Boston, New Haven, New York, Philadelphia, Baltimore, and Washington, DC. This train service passes the Elizabeth station often, and it boasts "superior comfort, upscale amenities and polished professional services at speeds up to 150 mph." The *Acela Express* is one of the trains that are most likely to be seen servicing the Elizabeth Station, and many people take it when they want to travel long distances quickly, without stopping at smaller-city train stations.

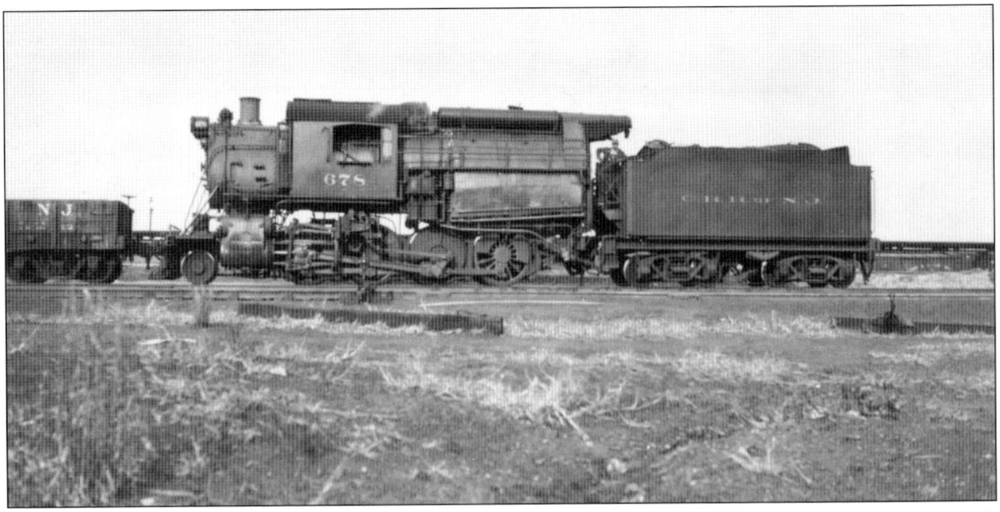

It is not common to see a train engine like the one shown in this picture, but this photograph displays a Central Railroad of New Jersey Railroad engine, with the number 678 on its side, type 2-8-0. This type of train engine was common on the Northeast rails. The 2-8-0 evolved from the Mogul, known as a 2-6-0. The 2-8-0 was a more powerful freight locomotive because it added another pair of driving wheels to the Mogul. The new locomotive was called the Consolidation 2-8-0. As the picture shows, these engines were meant to facilitate heavy hauling, and they were used throughout New Jersey for many years.

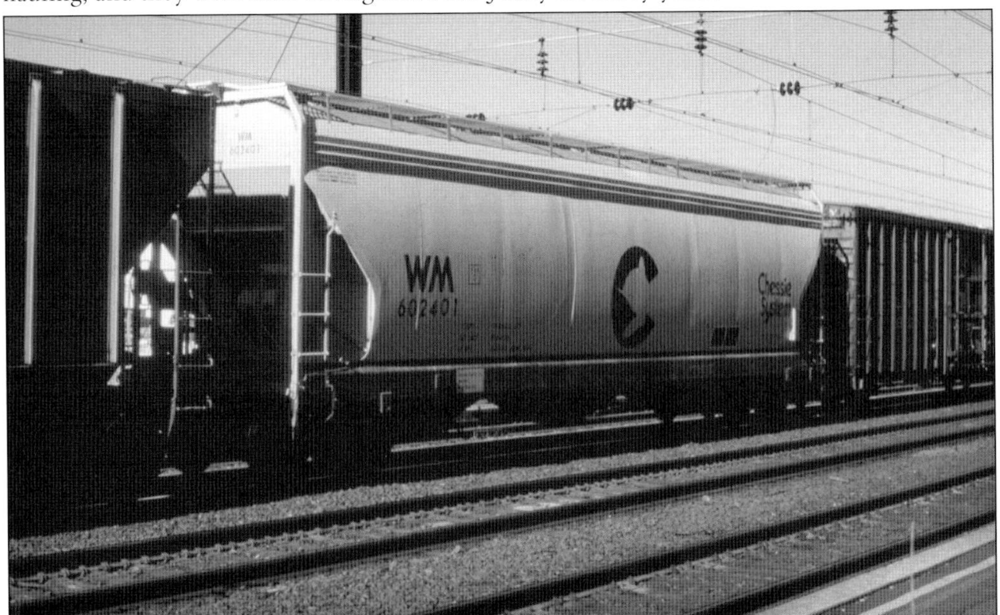

This image of a Chessie Western Maryland 50-foot hopper displays a lesser-known train model. A hopper car, as it is known in the United States is a form of railroad freight cars that are used to transport loose commodities in bulk. Examples of this type of objects would be coal, grain, track ballast, or sand, to name a few. There are covered hopper cars or open hopper cars; this picture shows an example of a covered car. Covered hoppers can carry other forms of bulk cargo that require more protection from outside elements. They can carry salt, fertilizer, or grain, for example.

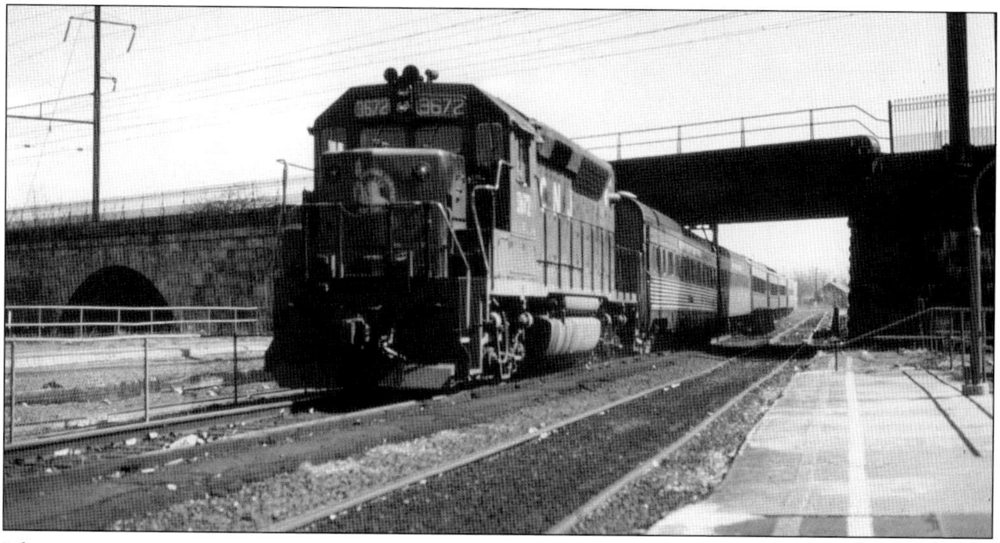

This train is Central New Jersey 3672, approaching the Elizabeth Station. This particular train is a General Motors EMD GP40 model, which is a diesel-electric hood unit, constructed primarily for pulling passenger cars. Quite a few of this model started life as a freight locomotive, only to be converted to passenger work by adding wiring for electric and plumbing fixtures. Thirteen of this particular model were ordered by the CNJ railroad in 1968. The models would be rebuilt in 1982 and again in 1992.

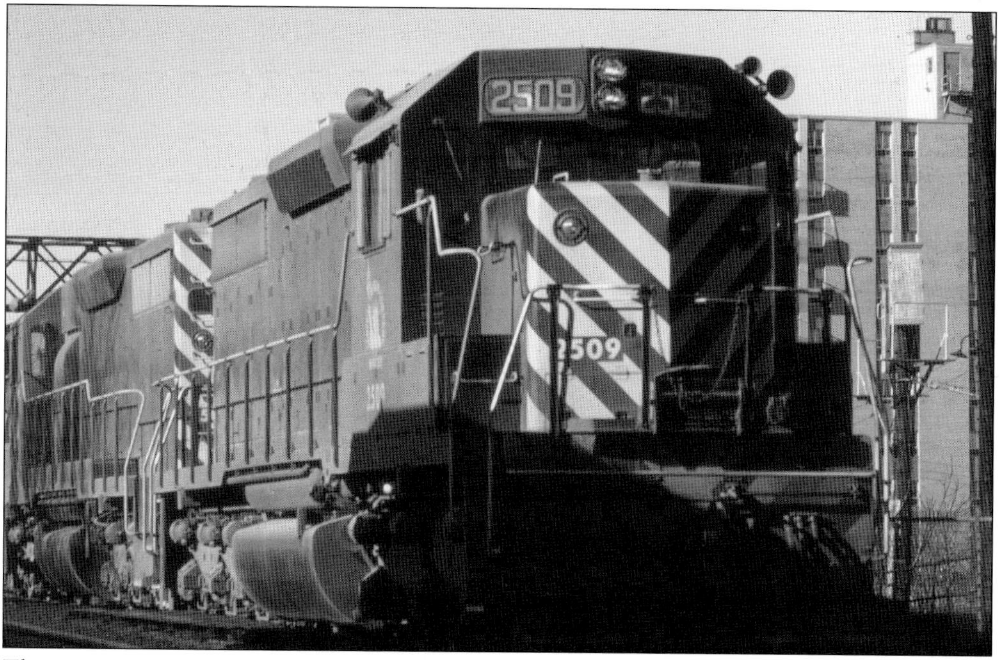

The train in this photograph is an EMD SD35, a six-axle, diesel-electric locomotive. These train models were built by General Motors between 1964 and 1966 in their electro-motive division. Only 360 examples of this train model were built for American railroads, which is why it is a unique opportunity to see it on the CNJ railroads. Certainly, this type of train would have been seen riding past the Elizabeth station, but the location of where this photograph was taken is not known.